Administrative Culture in Developing and Transitional Countries

This book explores theoretical, methodological, and empirical underpinnings of administrative culture as well as prospects and challenges associated with it in the context of and across developing and transitional countries. Referring to dominant norms and values in public organizations, administrative culture is about the attitudes and perceptions of public officials. In many countries civil servants are criticised for being corrupt, incompetent, unreliable and self-centred. Their attitudes, norms and values and the way they act are in constant conflict with rule of law. Recently the virtues of the Weberian model of bureaucracy have been reclaimed as an alternative to New Public Management (NPM): i.e. as a model which emphasizes impartiality, rule-following, expertise, and hierarchy rather than manipulation of incentive structures and market competition. In particular it has been argued that a system of meritocratic recruitment and predictable, long-term careers increases the professional competence of the bureaucrats and fosters a culture of professionalism among them. Still it is unclear how and under what conditions such a model can be adopted. Among main hindrances seems to be established power structures and the existing political and societal culture which undermine the effective implementation of the Weberian model.

This book was published as a special issue of the *International Journal of Public Administration*.

Ishtiaq Jamil and **Steinar Askvik** are at the Department of Administration and Organization Theory, University of Bergen, Norway where they co-direct the MPhil Program in Public Administration.

Farhad Hossain is a Senior Lecturer at the Institute for Development Policy and Management, University of Manchester, UK, where he directs the Postgraduate Programme in Human Resource Management (International Development).

Administrative Culture in Developing and Transitional Countries

Edited by
**Ishtiaq Jamil, Steinar Askvik and
Farhad Hossain**

Routledge
Taylor & Francis Group

LONDON AND NEW YORK

First published 2015 by Routledge

2 Park Square, Milton Park, Abingdon, Oxfordshire OX14 4RN
711 Third Avenue, New York, NY 10017

Routledge is an imprint of the Taylor & Francis Group, an informa business

First issued in paperback 2018

British Library Cataloguing in Publication Data
A catalogue record for this book is available from the British Library

ISBN 13: 978-1-138-81639-8 (hbk)
ISBN 13: 978-1-138-37949-7 (pbk)

Typeset in Times New Roman
by RefineCatch Limited, Bungay, Suffolk

Publisher's Note
The publisher accepts responsibility for any inconsistencies that may have
arisen during the conversion of this book from journal articles to book chapters,
namely the possible inclusion of journal terminology.

Disclaimer
Every effort has been made to contact copyright holders for their permission to
reprint material in this book. The publishers would be grateful to hear from any
copyright holder who is not here acknowledged and will undertake to rectify any
errors or omissions in future editions of this book.

Contents

Citation Information

The chapters in this book were originally published in the *International Journal of Public Administration*, volume 36, issue 13 (October 2013). When citing this material, please use the original page numbering for each article, as follows:

Chapter 9

Implementation of Strategic Organizational Change: The Case of King Abdul Aziz University in Saudi Arabia
Abdulrahaman Ali Alhazemi, Christopher Rees, and Farhad Hossain
International Journal of Public Administration, volume 36, issue 13 (October 2013) pp. 972–981

Chapter 10

Public Sector Reforms in Fiji: Examining Policy Implementation Setting and Administrative Culture
Mohammad Habibur Rahman, Rafia Naz, and Alka Nand
International Journal of Public Administration, volume 36, issue 13 (October 2013) pp. 982–995

Chapter 11

Administrative Culture and Incidence of Corruption in Bangladesh: A Search for the Potential Linkage
Sk. Tawfique M. Haque and Sheikh Noor Mohammad
International Journal of Public Administration, volume 36, issue 13 (October 2013) pp. 996–1006

Please direct any queries you may have about the citations to
clsuk.permissions@cengage.com

Introduction to the Special Issue on Administrative Culture in Developing and Transitional Countries

Ishtiaq Jamil and Steinar Askvik

Department of Administration and Organization Theory, University of Bergen, Bergen, Norway

Farhad Hossain

Institute for Development Policy and Management, School of Environment and Development, University of Manchester, Manchester, United Kingdom

This special issue on administrative culture explores and charts administrative culture in developing and transitional countries. The articles published in this special issue are genuinely international in scope. They include a myriad of perspectives for exploring aspects of administrative culture in countries and contexts ranging from Bangladesh, Bulgaria, Fiji and Ghana, to Mexico and Saudi Arabia. The articles fall into two main groupings. In terms of content specificity, the first loose grouping presents three articles that mainly deal with theoretical and contextual aspects relevant to the discourses and practices of administrative culture.

INTRODUCTION

This special issue on administrative culture explores and charts administrative culture in developing and transitional countries. It builds on the recognition that culture is a complex concept which is understood and explained differently from discipline to discipline. "Administrative culture" refers to the culture of public administration in a country. Often not explicitly recognized in organizational analyses is the fact that this type of culture has consequences for the ways in which public policies are adopted and implemented, as well as for how public officials relate to themselves and to society in general. It is a phenomenon that challenges researchers as they attempt to conceptualize and design studies for penetrating deep recesses of the administrative mind set.

In the context of public administration and management, although scholars like Fred Riggs (1964) emphasized the role of culture in public administration, it was not until the 1980s that culture became an important variable in analyzing and explaining institutional behavior (Hatch, 1993,

p. 657). Putnam, in his seminal book *Making Democracy Work* (1993), concluded that culture was at the root of variations in political institutions' performance in northern and southern Italy. Northern Italy developed a culture of trust and civic associationism that made democracy work better there than in the country's southern region. Given the primacy of culture, Daniel Etounga-Manguelle (cited in Harrison & Huntington, 2000, p. xxxviii) says that "Culture is the mother; institutions are the children."

Recently, there has been a global trend to implement organizational reforms. This has been inspired by good governance and New Public Management's (NPM's) efforts to introduce best practices based on market principles and private sector management. As a consequence of this trend, administrative culture has become more relevant than ever before (Jabbra & Dwivedi, 2004; Farazmand, 2009; Verhoest, 2011). This prompts some important questions: to what extent are specific administrative cultures compatible with these global reform initiatives, and to what extent do they allow for new ideas and recipes for managerial change?

Various countries' experiences of reform differ because the different cultural contexts and administrative developments have taken different historical paths, leading to differences in administrative norms and values (Christensen & Lægreid, 2011). "History matters," argues Cheung (2011, pp. 132–133), when referring to the administrative reforms of Asia, for these have been shaped by local history and cultural contexts that make them different from those in Western Europe, North America, and Australia. In each and every country, an understanding of administrative culture is a precondition for choosing from the range of options for the design of public administration, and it is crucial for the successful implementation of reform measures (Schedler & Proeller, 2007).

THE RESEARCH THEMES AND SCOPE OF THIS SPECIAL ISSUE

This special issue includes empirical and theoretical articles that are relevant to this broadly defined topic of administrative culture. It explores the theoretical and methodological underpinnings of administrative culture as well as the prospects and challenges associated with it. It reviews various perspectives on knowledge claims, the moral foundations of administrative culture, and the ways in which these are studied. A key aim of this symposium edition is to approach administrative culture from different angles in order to observe agreements and disagreements among scholars. Such an exercise is likely to offer a better understanding of administrative culture.

To make this special issue more inclusive and diverse in scope, we chose not to focus on any specific aspects of administrative culture and instead sent out a "general" call for papers. After the peer review and editorial review process, the papers were selected for publication. Most articles in this issue analyze administrative culture either as a dependent or an independent variable. As a dependent variable, the focus is on how political and social developments in the pre-colonial, colonial, and post-colonial eras have influenced the development of administrative values and norms in the developing and transitional countries. As an independent variable, administrative culture is analyzed as a source of bureau pathology. The authors have also studied how administrative culture influences changes that have been inspired by NPM-based reforms, and to what extent these reforms have been adopted. Are NPM-inspired reforms superior and desired choices?

The articles published in this special issue are genuinely international in scope. They include a myriad of perspectives for exploring aspects of administrative culture in countries and contexts ranging from Bangladesh, Bulgaria, Fiji and Ghana, to Mexico and Saudi Arabia. The articles fall into two main groupings. In terms of content specificity, the first loose grouping presents three articles that mainly deal with theoretical and contextual aspects relevant to the discourses and practices of administrative culture.

The first article, by Ishtiaq Jamil, Steinar Askvik, and Farhad Hossain, introduces the concept "administrative culture" and how it is understood and explained from different perspectives within the philosophy of science. In the second article, Loredana Di Pietro and Francesca Di Virgilio seek to understand one of the roles of organizational culture by examining the contexts and behavioral norms in workplaces where conflict exists. They focus on the specific domain of culture pertaining to the management of conflict. An intensive questionnaire survey provides the basis for their examination and analysis of aspects of conflict in organizations. Di Pietro and Di Virgilio investigate the relationship between organizational culture and the behavioral norms used to informally manage conflict. Their findings suggest that there is a clear relationship between culture and behavioral norms, which is relevant for understanding the challenges and the evolution of conflict-filled situations.

In the third article, Goran Hyden argues that in the past, very little attention has been paid to the role of local administrative culture in reforming and developing public administration in Africa. The article identifies institutional conditions, derived from pre-colonial and colonial days, which have shaped behavior and attitudes in government services. It shows how African countries differ from other regions of the world, and how administrative reforms have been difficult to implement in the politico-administrative circumstances of the region. To facilitate an understanding of administrative culture in the African context, Hyden's article presents and discusses differences among three competing models of administration in Africa.

The second group of articles offers six papers with country-specific analyses of administrative culture. To begin with, Habib Zafarullah identifies some of the principal characteristics of administrative culture in Bangladesh, as the bureaucracy there tends to quash reform and retain its independent character. The article shows how bureaucracy looks after itself and safeguards some of its unethical practices by maintaining a close connection to political processes and by dominating the policy making structures. Zafarullah claims that these peculiar aspects of bureaucracy resist change and pose a threat to democratic governance and development. David Arellano-Gault, in his article, explores changes in the administrative culture of Mexican public administration. He examines and analyzes the impact of the Civil Service Law of 2003 on professionalism and morale aspects of Mexican bureaucracy.

Turning to Ghana, Justice Nyigmah Bawole et al. carry out empirical research on local and regional government, examining the practice of performance appraisal as a critical element of administrative culture in the country's civil service. The article shows how a certain negative administrative cultural trait has evolved in Ghana's public administration, and it points out the implications of the practice for civil service performance. Deyana Marcheva, in her article, examines how historical incidents in Bulgarian society have shaped administrative culture in the country. She explores the tension between traditional and modern structural drivers in the re-established Bulgarian state and demonstrates how socio-political transitions in Bulgaria have reinforced duality at the core of the national administrative culture.

The next essay spotlights Saudi Arabia. In doing empirical research on King Abdul Aziz University, Abdulrahaman Ali Alhazemi, Christopher Rees, and Farhad Hossain examine the role of leadership, culture, and learning in the implementation of organizational reforms in the country's public sector. The study identifies barriers to the effective implementation of strategic reforms, including adherence to the status quo, resentment towards standard human-resource processes, and a certain degree of inflexibility in management and leadership. In the context of Fiji, Mohammad Habibur Rahman, Rafia Naz, and Alka Nand probe how the island nation's recent public-sector reform initiatives have largely failed to bring about the expected results. Based on case studies of two organizations, the article explains how the implementation of policies has both succeeded and failed. This brings to light a multitude of challenges, including cultural changes and the lack of a well-prepared implementation framework.

Finally, Sk. Tawfique M. Haque and Sheikh Noor Mohammad analyze the potential link between administrative culture and corruption in Bangladesh. Some cultural features more dominant in Bangladesh society such as the high degree of collectivism, steep hierarchy, and large uncertainty avoidance norms make administrative culture rigid, patron-clientelistic, centralized, and less user friendly. All these lead to abuse of discretionary power and widespread corruption in the public sector.

ACKNOWLEDGMENTS

We are grateful to all those who have contributed articles to this special issue. We also appreciate and acknowledge the valuable contributions made by the guest reviewers throughout the peer review process. As guest editors, we would like to thank Colin Talbot, Richard Common, and Carole Talbot, formerly of the *International Journal of Public Administration* for their cooperation. They have given us a great opportunity to develop the scholarship on administrative culture in the developing and transitional countries. We also acknowledge the assistance of Ali Farazmand and Michael Macaulay, the new editors of *IJPA*, for their kind cooperation during the publication process of this special issue.

REFERENCES

Cheung, A.B.I. (2011). NPM in Asian countries. In T. Christensen & P. Lægreid (Eds.) *The Ashgate research companion to New Public Management* (pp. 131–144). Farnham, UK: Ashgate.

Christensen, T., & Lægreid, P. (2011). Introduction. In T. Christensen & P. Lægreid (Eds.), *The Ashgate research companion to New Public Management* (pp. 1–13). Farnham, UK: Ashgate.

Farazmand, A. (2009), Building administrative capacity for the age of rapid globalization: A modest prescription for the twenty-first century. *Public Administration Review, 69,* 1007–1020.

Harrison, L.E. (2000). Why culture matters. In L.E. Harrison & S.P. Huntington (Eds.) *Culture matters: How values shape human progress* (pp. xvii–xxxiv). New York: Basic Books.

Hatch, M.J. (1993). The dynamics of organizational culture. *Academy of Management Review, 18*(4) 657–693. Retrieved from http://www.jstor.org/stable/258594

Putnam, R.D. (1993). *Making democracy work.* Princeton, NJ: Princeton University Press.

Riggs, F.W. (1964). *Administration in developing countries: The theory of prismatic society.* Boston: Houghton Mifflin.

Schedler, K., & Proeller, I. (2007). Public management as a cultural phenomenon: Revitalizing societal culture in international public management research. *International Public Management Review, 8*(1) 186–194. Retrieved from http://www.ipmr.net

Verhoest, K. (2011). The relevance of culture for NPM. In T. Christensen & P. Lægreid (Eds.), *The Ashgate research companion to New Public Management* (pp. 47–64). Farnham, UK: Ashgate.

Understanding Administrative Culture: Some Theoretical and Methodological Remarks

Ishtiaq Jamil and Steinar Askvik

Department of Administration and Organization Theory, University of Bergen, Bergen, Norway

Farhad Hossain

Institute for Development Policy and Management, School of Environment and Development, University of Manchester, Manchester, United Kingdom

The article highlights five aspects of administrative culture. It first describes different ways of conceptualizing administrative culture. The second aspect is the ontology of administrative culture, two views of which are presented. The first of these sees organizational culture as a dependent variable that can be manipulated and altered to reflect management and leadership preferences; the other views organizations as miniature societies reflecting broader societal culture. Change is more path dependent than rationally arranged at will. The third aspect of administrative culture concerns epistemology, focusing on how knowledge about culture is created, how a researcher may carry out inquiry, and what the inquiry is about. The fourth aspect – the axiology of administrative culture – concerns the appropriate administrative norms and ethical standards of public officials. Finally, the methodological aspect points to how to study and capture different aspects of administrative culture.

Administrative culture draws major inspiration from cultural theory, more specifically, from theories of organizational culture. The relationship between culture and social organization has been "a recurring theme in the social sciences for the last 50 years" (Denison & Mishra 1995, p. 204), but to sociologists, social anthropologists, and organization psychologists, the term *culture* has different connotations. Anthropologists tend to define it as the "way of life in a given society" (Dwivedi & Gow, 1999, p. 18) while an organization psychologist like Schein (1992, p. 12) defines it as "a pattern of shared basic assumptions in a group." Further, Martin (2001, p. 4) defines it as "metaphor, a lens for examining organizational life." According to Hofstede et al. (2010, pp. 4–5), culture is "the collective programming of the mind which distinguishes one group of people from another," but Tayeb (1988, p. 42) defines it as "a set of historically evolved learned values, attitudes, and meanings shared by members of a given community." Kluckhohn (1951, cited in Verhoest, 2011) seems to synthesize several of the above definitions: "Culture consists in patterned ways of thinking, feeling and reacting, acquired and transmitted mainly by symbols, constituting the distinctive achievement of human groups, including their embodiments in artifacts; the essential core of culture consists of traditions (i.e., historically derived and selected) ideas, and especially their attached values" (p. 48).

The definitions above emphasize that some core values and basic assumptions are fundamental and influence the way a group of people think, feel, and act, and distinguish them from other groups.

This article provides a theoretical and methodological background for studying administrative culture. It focuses on five aspects of the subject, and each of these is discussed in a separate section.

THE CONCEPT OF ADMINISTRATIVE CULTURE

We begin by presenting our view on what *administrative culture* means. According to Sharma (2002, p. 65), "administrative culture must necessarily be the culture of administrators, more specifically the culture of those participants whose activities are restricted to the administrative environment."

Broadly defined, administrative culture is associated with the dominant values and norms in public organizations. These influence interpersonal relations both within and beyond the organization, thus impacting performance and outcomes for the wider society. Administrative culture defines what acceptable and legitimate behavior is and therefore provides a framework for behaving, acting, and forming preferences (Jamil, 1994; Lam 1994; Denison & Mishra 1995; Jabbra & Dwivedi, 2004). In analyzing administrative culture, researchers have usually focused on the central bureaucracy and top civil servants, profiling their traits and behavior, and examining the consequences of this for organizational performance (Jabbra & Dwivedi, 2004, p. 1110; Lam, 2004, p. 194).

Other studies have had a narrower focus on deviant behavior, corrupt practices, and the irregular, unpredictable behavior of bureaucrats, all of which result in unanticipated, even disastrous consequences (Islam, 2004; Jamil, 2007). Deviant behavior points to a gap between rational and non-rational behavior, but more specifically, it refers to deviance from a certain Weberian model of a legal rational bureaucracy (Islam, 2005, p. 1016). Rational behavior is formal, prescribed in rules and laws, and based on moral and ethical standards, while non-rational behavior is informal and reflects familial ties or kinship and narrow personal interests. In South Asia, for instance, *Sifarish* (a Persian word denoting *recommendation*) or *Tadbir* (though literally means looking after and using prudence in daily affairs but it is mostly used in relation to persuasion (e.g., in Bangladesh) is a popular mechanism employed frequently to get things done in public offices by bypassing, bending, breaking, or delaying what might be termed a rational approach to decision making. Bribing is usually associated with this act (Islam, 2004, p. 322; Jamil & Huq, 2005, pp. 175–176). Studies in this realm have mapped bureau pathologies by analyzing the extent to which public and private lives of officials are blurred, thereby leading to policies often not in accordance with formal policy objectives.

According to Henderson (2004): "At its most basic, administrative culture may be thought of as general characteristics of public officials (i.e., shared values, attitudes, beliefs)–federal, state, and local. Administrative culture is related to the broader political culture, from which it derives, and can be further discussed in terms of sub-cultures" (pp. 238–239).

Jamil (1994, p. 275), in his study of administrative culture, argues that "public administration as part of the national political system possesses cultural traits that are not well captured by the existing theories of organizational culture" (Exceptions to this observation are Riggs' (1964) book *Administration in Developing Countries: The Theory of Prismatic Society* and Ott's (1989) *The Organizational Culture Perspective*). To fill the gap, Jamil suggests establishing a dialogue between political theories and organizational culture theories. In this regard, he adds three more dimensions to the study of administrative culture: political responsiveness, which maps the politics-administration interface; social responsiveness, which focuses on the (civil) society-administration interface; and cohesiveness, which analyzes internal sources of control and the exercise of authority and power within a bureaucracy. Similarly, Lam (1994), in his study of Hong Kong's civil service, suggests there is a need to study the political orientation of civil servants that is, to what extent the civil servants are tolerant of different opinions and interests. As is evident from the last few paragraphs, the conceptualization of administrative culture, while concerned with values and norms within bureaucracy, is also concerned with political orientation and the responsiveness of public officials to society. In this regard, researchers who study professional neutrality ask whether bureaucratic actions are based on merit, skills, and the rule of law, or whether they are based on political loyalty, and to what extent public servants' lives and careers depend on responding to narrow political interests. The politics-administration dichotomy appears to be less valid than formerly thought. Both sets of actors are increasingly involved in policy making and implementation, including jointly committing to New Public Management (NPM) in the push for structural and functional reforms. The process of globalization is causing paradigm convergence in the public sector, and this in turn is making the system of public administration increasingly complex; there is now more use of network governance than there is of hierarchic or rule-based or market-based and corporatized coordination (Farazmand, 1999, 2012).

From the above, we see that the classical role of bureaucracy based on Weberianism, understood as rule orientation or rule following, is in transition. Researchers are now increasingly focusing on the bureaucrats' current and normative roles in a globalized world where markets and networks play important roles in governance. Administrative culture, like other constructs in the social sciences, is in a state of flux because the values in organizations are subject to change. What concepts are pertinent for studying administrative culture in a state of transition, and in a new scenario with multiple actors at multiple levels? Does NPM, with its emphasis on market liberalism and managerial efficiency, offer a solution to this dilemma? Should not public administrations be careful about instituting these values without critical analysis?

Some developed countries were quick out of the starting block and have had relative success in instituting NPM measures in their systems of public administration, while other countries, such as Norway, are "slow reformers" (Christensen & Lægreid, 2008, pp. 12–13). The experiences in the developing countries have been variable (Samaratunge et al., 2008, p. 27), and any claimed victory over traditional management practices has been partial, even though NPM has broadened the menu of managerial choices (Manning, 2001, p. 298). According to Schick (1998), developing countries need to be careful in introducing market principles in their administrative practices because, in the absence of the rule of law and a strong legal system, the introduction of market-based principles might do more harm than good. In response to the primacy of the market paradigm, "Asian NPM which is a hybrid of Western and Eastern traditions combining state-led development strategies and instrumentalities of public administration" may be an alternative for the developing countries (Cheung, 2011, p. 132).

THE ONTOLOGY OF ADMINISTRATIVE CULTURE

The ontological debate ("what there is" from the Greek word for *being*) in administrative culture is based on two contrasting views of social phenomena. It concerns the distinction between an organization's structure and the individual actors working within that structure (Jamil, 2010, pp. 41–42). The *structural view* emphasizes that individual action is only meaningful within a social context; individual actors are socially embedded and hence their actions are socially governed. In contrast, the *individual view* is based on the assumption that social phenomena are created by actors' responses, preferences, and ideas (Gilje & Grimen, 1993, pp. 184–185). However, at times the individual's freedom to act is curtailed by the dominant, powerful actors. In the case of public administration, these may be political leaders or top civil servants who may influence and form the preferences of subordinates. At other times, as Dowding (2006, p. 137), explains, dominated actors can willingly acquiesce within a given social structure.[1]

In the context of organization, an important ontological debate concerns whether culture in organization can be

created or whether culture in organization is more persistent and path-dependent (March & Olsen, 1989, 1995). This debate is also highlighted in a seminal article by Smircich (1983) and recently by Alvesson in the book *Understanding Organizational Culture* (2012) focusing on "culture is what an organization has" in contrast to the idea that "culture is what an organization is."

Organizational Culture as Dependent Variable

Within this school (both the old management school such as Taylorism and the new approach dominated by the NPM doctrine), organizational performance and effectiveness are given a central place in the study of organizations. Organizational culture stands out as one among several factors that may make an impact on the performance of organizations. If an organization's leaders determine that the prevailing culture is not producing intended outcomes, they may resort to reforms to instill an appropriate culture for producing desired goals. This is a functionalist approach to build "strong" organizational culture to improve productivity and profitability (Martin, 2001, p. 8). Leadership or management strategies are independent variables that are concerned with producing desired cultural norms and values in organizations. Organizational cultural values are dependent variables that can be manipulated, altered, and modified to create the appropriate norm. Many contemporary reforms inspired by NPM are introduced in public administration in recent years to instill norms borrowed from the private sector management (Christensen et al., 2007). Organizations' leaders customize these recipes to fit into their organizations. This is an instrumental approach, calculating causal relationships between means and desired ends with the assumption that the best outcome will be introduced in the given organization. According to Schedler and Proeller (2007, p. 189), "organizations not only possess culture, but also can create culture, and moreover, that the right culture is a trigger for efficiency and effectiveness." In this regard, power is an important variable that influences decision making, either to promote individual self-interest or to achieve favorable outcomes for all in the organization (Hatch, 1997, p. 283).

ORGANIZATIONAL CULTURE IS WHAT AN ORGANIZATION IS

In contrast to the above, this school argues that organizations are miniature societies. Drawing on ideas from social anthropology, it claims that organizations reflect dominant assumptions, values, and norms that cannot be easily manipulated or changed. Accordingly, organizations should be seen basically as social cultures that need to be interpreted. Here the concept of culture signifies the patterns of meaning given to actions understood as rituals, and with this signification there comes a recognition of physical artifacts as

---

[1] According to Scott (cited in Dowding, 2006, p. 137), domination may take place in both thick and thin senses. Thick domination is when one is subjected to subordination by others, while thin domination indicates a situation where one acquiesces voluntarily to social structural norms. In this regard, Nussbaum and Sen (cited in Dowding, 2006, p. 137) give an example of "the Indian woman who gives up food and her health for her husband and male children," and she does so willingly.

symbols of meaning. Since organizations operate and interact with the surrounding environment, they cannot guard against the influx of societal values. Consequently, such values are not external to the organization; they are part of an integrated totality that makes up the organization as a culture.

These two schools imply different notions of policy making and organizational change (Christensen et al., 2007). From the first school, policy making is unproblematic and exogenous–that is, leaders choose a course of action based on means-end rationality and aim to alter organizational behavior at will. Organizational change is, therefore, based on rational adjustment. Here power is an important variable for it enables leaders (or whoever holds the reins of power) to influence organizational culture. In this view, a change of leadership may bring about changes in organizational strategies and policy making which may in turn change organizational values.

By contrast, according to the school of "culture is what an organization is," goals must be compatible with administrative values and organizational culture *before* they are legitimized, supported, and accepted. The more the goals are attuned to cultural values, the greater the possibility for their successful implementation without opposition. According to Lægreid and Verhoest (2010, p. 8), "cultural sensitivity and compatibility are important when introducing reforms," since the reforms are then more easily accepted. Organizational change, therefore, is gradual because organizational values are persistent, stable, and deep rooted and change does not come readily. The more organizational values are institutionalized, the less the possibility for rational change or changes according to some imposed objectives. In this regard, history and experiences are important for organizations, and over time these are retained in organizational memory and transformed into rules, laws, norms, and values, all of which give a basis for organizational actions of a persistent and durable nature. The older the organization, the more it is infused with values that guide individual actions (Selznick, 1984).

The second school offers an explanation of why public organizations develop distinct cultures of their own, and why they are more concerned with survival, continuity, and consistency of behavior than with efficiency. They can be more concerned with legitimacy and acceptance in their respective societies than with making functional and rational choices. In fact, attaining identity and becoming socializing within an organizational culture is itself a goal of organization members. This socialization legitimizes whatever is considered appropriate action. It is therefore based on the logic of appropriateness and not on the logic of calculation (i.e., organizational values once created are persistent and cannot readily be changed) (Scott, 1995, pp. 37–40; March & Olsen, 1989, p. 54; Hall & Taylor, 1996, pp. 937–942; Christensen & Lægreid, 1998; Peters, 1999, pp. 62–65; Christensen et al., 2007).

EPISTEMOLOGY AND CLAIMS OF KNOWLEDGE

Epistemology is concerned with the nature of knowledge, how it is created, and how and what researchers will learn about reality from their inquiry. Creswell (2003, pp. 6–13) discusses four ways in which knowledge claims are generated.

Post-Positivism

It challenges the traditional idea of the absolute truth of knowledge, as in classical Positivism, yet it derives from a tradition which argues that scientific knowledge is constructed through a deterministic relation between cause and effect. The goal of a post-positivist inquiry is to correlate causes with outcomes. This is done in a reductionist manner, with one or a few ideas or causes being tested to examine their effect on a phenomenon. In this regard, hypotheses are formulated and tested through scientific observations and experiments. Finally, the major concern of this school is to test or verify theories or laws to understand a specific social reality better.

In the context of administrative culture, theory testing and verification are quite common, as is illustrated by Hofstede (1991) and those who followed his method of inquiry. This is a variable-focused inquiry in which a particular variable is assumed to affect another variable in a fully measurable manner. In those cases where a post-positive position is applied to the study of administrative culture, it will frequently be linked to the above-discussed notion of culture as dependent variable. The rational conclusion of such an approach is that if appropriate management actions are imposed, then performance improvement is the natural result.

Constructivism

The assumption here is that the researchers are seeking understanding about a social phenomenon and are trying to be receptive to different meanings about why things happen, rather than narrowing the explanation of a phenomenon down to just a few variables. The constructivist approach is not concerned with a causal explanation of a phenomenon but stresses that individuals develop subjective meanings of the world in which they live, and that these are varied and multiple, usually being formed through interaction with others. It "seeks answers to questions that stress how social experience is created and given meaning" (Silverman, 2005, p. 10). A constructivist approach implies an induction-based research process, as the analyst tries to interpret meanings from observations and interactions with other individuals, and then tries to relate findings to established theories (Symon & Casell, 1998, p. 2).

Many researchers prefer a phenomenological approach to the study of culture and are concerned with meaning formation and interpretation as a basis for understanding it. Phenomenology provides a critique of the post-positivist approach to studying culture with pre-identified variables and has "thus discouraged the integration of culture research with other constructs of organization theory which are primarily discussed in terms of variables, dimensions, causes, or effects" (Denison & Mishra, 1995, p. 205).

Advocacy/Participatory Perspective

It highlights the problems of marginalized groups and is primarily concerned with social justice. Those who follow it claim that neither Post- positivism nor Constructivism stretch far enough to advocate for or activate agendas that would help marginalized groups. In order to change the lives of these people, the essential tools are political discourse, debate, and agenda-setting. To achieve change, research from this perspective focuses on actions whereby people can be empowered and freed from social exploitation. It is concerned with reforms and programs that can change existing practices in order to foster better lives (Gaventa, 2004).

The advocacy perspective is concerned with changing administrators' values and dispositions, so that they become socially responsive to the way programs are implemented and consequently perceived by citizens. Researchers who hold this view live in expectation of doing away with bureau pathology and inculcating values that are oriented towards change and development, especially for vulnerable groups. They therefore study administrative systems from the perspective of action research. Here the neutrality constraints imposed by both Post-positivism and Constructivism give way to the idea of the researcher as an activist in pursuit of change (Creswell, 2003).

Pragmatism

Pragmatism is concerned with applications and solutions to problems. The researcher forms a claim of knowledge by studying actions, situations, and consequences rather than identifying antecedents, as in the case with Post-positivism. A mixture of methods is used to collect and analyze data (Creswell, 2003) which would lead to understanding a problem. Putnam (1993) provides a prime example of this approach in his study of institutional performance in Italy based on social capital. He combines both qualitative and quantitative methods. His qualitative method includes historical evidence that helps him map civic involvement and set up contrasts between northern and southern Italy. By conducting historical analysis and disciplinary field observations and case studies, he demonstrates that social contexts matter for institutional performance more in northern Italy than in the southern districts. His quantitative study includes a number of surveys conducted in different time periods. These provide *moving pictures* of institutional performance and confirm that civic involvement matters for democratic performance.

THE AXIOLOGY OF ADMINISTRATIVE CULTURE AND POLICY IMPLICATIONS

Axiology, which covers the domains of ethics and aesthetics, can be described as a theory of value (Weinberg, 1970, p. 612) that provides a basis for understanding organizational values. The axiological approach prompts questions such as the following: What values do public organizations nurture, especially in relation to society? Are some values more important or somehow better than others? What should be the appropriate administrative norms and ethical standards of public officials? To what extent should their behavior coincide with citizens' expectations? The issues of ethics and the code of conduct are important here because they define the moral and professional standards for carrying out public offices. They prompt the question of the extent to which administrative culture inspires those who occupy public office to consider community service an ideal form of duty and a calling that is more important than individual desires and material gain. From the researcher's perspective, the code of conduct for officials in public organizations is important to analyze since such officials exercise authority, wield power, allocate and reallocate public funds and resources, implement policy decisions, and make development plans. In this respect, three more questions arise: What constitutes accountability? What makes public officials accountable for their actions? Should officials be controlled by some external agency that oversees their ethical conduct, or should some professional norms and standards be developed for self-imposed control (Dwivedi & Gow, 1999, p. 25)?

March and Olsen (1989, pp. 119–134) in analyzing democratic governance, differentiate between public officials' *aggregative* and *integrative* roles, both of which relate to axiology. The aggregative role entails responding to the interests of stakeholders, some of whom are quite powerful. The official enters into exchange relationships similar to economic transactions. In this process we observe trading, negotiation, coalition building, promises, and so forth. In contrast, the integrative role involves being more concerned with fairness, justice, the awarding of rights, and with the idea that once a right is given, it is irrevocable; those who receive the right think of themselves as being naturally entitled to it. In the aggregative process, rights have to be earned and not given, and the official's role is to respond to the various interests that mandate these rights. The integrative process calls for moral responsibility and accountability, justice, and an honest effort to achieve the common good and the welfare of citizens rather than aggregating interests. The integrity of public officials is driven by a logic of unity rather than a logic of exchange; it is based on a process stemming from mutual understanding, consensus, trust, collective will, sympathy, and identity.

Although the aggregative and integrative roles of officials stand in contrast to each other, they nevertheless mesh together to form the norms of democratic governance. Officials play an aggregative role when they are geared towards individual interests and preferences in society; they play an integrative role when promoting citizen participation in the pursuit of solidarity, justice, fairness, and the common good. The challenge is to know how to instill integrative norms into an institutional framework in order to achieve democratic ideals. And the challenge for the researcher is to know how to access and read what the actual administrative norms are; to separate intellectually espoused values from those that exist in reality.

Research in this domain concerns seeking to understand the moral education of bureaucrats and how this relates to accountability. What are the normative roots of accountability measures? How are public officials made accountable, and to whom? With regard to the study of accountability, we observe three key areas of tension discussed below.

Legal-Rational Authority Versus Informal Authority

According to a certain understanding of the Weberian ideal type, public officials' authority must be based on their being accountable to rules. The extent to which public officials follow legal procedures is thus a key. It is postulated that legitimacy is achieved when public officials can claim to be neutral, non-partisan, and make impartial decisions. However, extreme cases of upholding such values have also been associated with inflexibility, rigidity, and less autonomy for stakeholders. Bureaucrats typically find themselves in situations where rules precede results and top-down hierarchy dominates decision making (Dwivedi & Gow, 1999)

Weberianism is typically understood as being based on formal rule following and rationality, but these values are lacking in many developing nations and transitional societies where informal relations based on lineage, kinship, "old boy" networks, and regional ties dominate administrative culture and are more important than formal rules and procedures. As a result, we observe two trends. First, public administrations persistently display norms and values that reflect traditional social norms and that fail to adapt and become responsive to the trends of globalization, modernization, institutional change, and democratic principles (Jamil, 2007). Second, in the absence of the rule of law and the lack of a clear distinction between public and private life, public offices and positions are frequently abused for private gain. Informal relations then become important for gaining access to public services, and official rules are frequently violated or neglected. Lobbying and personal cajoling become part and parcel of administrative cultural norms and become essential mechanisms in getting things done or in gaining access to services.

Professional Norms Versus Performance Based Orientation

Norm-based accountability is common in professional organizations such as hospitals, law firms, engineering departments, and agricultural offices. Here employees are motivated by prescribed professional norms. Nevertheless, the norms often lead to conflicts between different hierarchical levels in organizations.

In contrast to norm-based accountability, NPM emphasizes performance- and results-based accountability. Here the focus is on results rather than conformity to rules, especially the type of roles found in the legal-rational model of accountability. On the basis of performance, incentives are given and contracts are renewed–although renewed contracts may also depend on competitive advantage. This kind of accountability must thus also tangle with negotiation and bargaining between a principal and an agent. Bureaucrats are managers who act on behalf of the principal (that is, the political leaders), and they are accountable to the rule of law. They work within a culture of both moral obligation and market-based imperatives. However, in a society where the rule of law is frequently violated by officials, and where a large informal economy exists, unaccountable behavior may grow because of limited checks and balances. At its worst, autonomy coupled with significant informal relations leads to corruption. Thus a strong warning: to introduce NPM in a culture that lacks a well-functioning rule of law is to ask only for more trouble (Schick, 1998).

Professional Neutrality Versus Political Loyalty

Many developing and transitional societies have now introduced democratic forms of decision making. This means politicians are important actors in the process of governance. In this scenario, politicians expect bureaucrats to be accountable to political leaders and sensitive to political signals. Democratic accountability requires political loyalty, but at the same time, bureaucrats as professionals must maintain professional neutrality. This is a difficult balance to achieve. In many developing nations, bureaucrats are increasingly politicized and their careers, promotions, and postings depend on their allegiance to political masters. Maintaining a balance between professional standards and political motives becomes a difficult equation where a public official's personal convictions may either reward him or her profusely or cost him or her dearly. At one extreme in an administrative culture, much of the bureaucracy's attention is directed toward pleasing political leaders. When this happens, we may observe a serious erosion of neutrality and universality in bureaucratic actions. Clientelistic and partisan behavior may then become important ingredients of administrative culture, with different camps vying for influence through increased lobbying (Haque & Zafarullah, 2001, pp. 1088–1090; Jamil & Dangal, 2009, p. 206).

Two trends can be observed in how politics can impact bureaucracy, particularly in developing and transitional societies. First, political loyalty, especially among senior bureaucrats, is now a qualification for being promoted and given lucrative posts and other benefits according to the nature of loyalty. Merit and performance measurement remain mostly in the background when political leaders make decisions about bureaucrats' careers and promotions. Second, this practice can eventually fragment the bureaucracy. An example of this can be seen in Bangladesh, a country whose civil service may no longer claim to be a coherent group based on the principle of esprit de corps. Political loyalties have divided the bureaucracy into two camps: one group is loyal or friendly to the party in power; the other group favors the opposition and waits for when the party it supports will come to power and bestow benefits (Jamil & Haque, 2005). But there are also bureaucrats in an in-between position, caught in the tug-of-war between the two factions. These people would like to remain neutral and professional but find it difficult to do so because they are neglected by the political masters, deprived of due promotions and effective postings. A study by Jahan and Shahan (2008) has revealed that Bangladesh's Public Service Commission (the sole agency for recruiting aspiring civil servants to various government services) is, during the recruitment process, more politically influenced by the democratically elected governments than it was in earlier periods when the country was under military and authoritarian regimes.

The above discussion about the normative orientation of administrative values reveals at least three main discourses which are significant for researchers who investigate administrative culture (Dwivedi & Gow, 1999, p. 175):

1. Weberianism as traditionally understood, with emphasis on formalism, hierarchy, uniformity, merit, competence, and professionalism;
2. NPM and market values, which focus on results, performance, competition, effectiveness, efficiency, quality, and service; and
3. democratic values, which include equality, representativeness, participation, transparency, inclusiveness, and responsiveness.

These three categories of values relate to the different forms of accountability elaborated above.

We may also observe a patrimonial administrative culture especially in the case of Africa where informal institutions have become a threat to formal institutional mechanisms such as rule of law and instituting NPM measures (Hyden, 2012, p. 6). Therefore, a hybrid administrative culture is likely to be more dominant where one or the other dominating forms may characterize public administration. These together form a complex river-like system for researchers to navigate, explore, and map. These values are well represented in the legal-bureaucratic, managerial,

and contemporary political literature of public administration. In this regard, the literature on new public management argues that national variations in terms of introducing NPM-inspired reforms in contemporary public administrations may depend on different administrative cultures (Christensen & Lægreid, 2011, p. 2).

METHODS FOR STUDYING ADMINISTRATIVE CULTURE

The development of public administration–from Weberianism to market-based managerialism, both of which are combined with the influence of politics and societal culture–causes administrative culture to display diverse aspects and values. How is it possible to study these? What methods are appropriate and relevant?

Following Creswell (2003), we can distinguish among three main types of research designs, each of which adopt different strategies of data collection: (1) quantitative research designs use statistically based methods for describing and analyzing social phenomena, that is, data collected through experiments and surveys in which observations are intended to measure how concepts and variables are linked to each other in certain patterns; (2) qualitative research designs are based on phenomenological methods where the primary task is to observe, interpret and understand the meaning of social processes. Here extensive descriptions and narratives are important for understanding what is going on within a given social group. (3) The third type of research design is to combining quantitative and qualitative approaches in order to present a more complete picture of the phenomena in question. Sometimes qualitative and quantitative data are gathered concurrently, at other times sequentially.

In studies of administrative culture, the use of survey methodologies has been important. This seems particularly to be the case in comparative studies of how national societal cultures affect the value systems of national state bureaucracies. Also, survey methods are useful in longitudinal studies. Here Hofstede's (1991, 2010) methodology has become popular, insofar as it demonstrates how a limited number of dimensions in a culture can be operationalized and measured through the use of questionnaires. Survey methods for measuring administrative culture have also become popular in studies of different branches of civil service in a country (e.g., Christensen & Lægreid, 2008). In both cross-sectional and longitudinal studies on culture (World Values Survey, 1990–2012; Hofstede, 1991, 2010; Schwartz, 1992; Jamil, 2007), the preferred methodology has been quantitative: surveys and questionnaires are considered useful tools for investigating cultural traits such as attitudes, values, and perceptions of organizational practices. Numerical measurements seem to map national cultural trends in a manner that allows for diverse analytical possibilities.

When it comes to qualitative methods, the concept of culture central to anthropological and folkloristic studies has been influential (Hatch, 1993, p. 697). This method is more difficult to put into operation, and the results from it can be interpreted and studied in multiple ways. Because anthropologists try to understand culture holistically, they do not want to separate a culture from its context. In order to understand both hidden and visible culture, they admonish researchers to live within the community they study participate in it, and experience it from a more internal perspective. Similarly, the phenomenological approach to culture emphasizes a qualitative understanding of meaning and interpretation, and its practitioners therefore argue that culture should not be studied as a *variable* with *outcomes* (Denison & Mishra, 1995, p. 205). Culture, according to anthropologists and phenomenologists, is better understood through a qualitative approach where culture becomes more meaningful when studied in relation to a context and on the basis of respondents' own words. In the context of organization studies, therefore, the focus has been on symbols, processes, and symbolic behavior in organizations, and in interpreting these phenomena in a variety of ways. This approach emphasizes that any attempt to conceptually understand an organization's complex phenomena is necessarily an oversimplification of that organization's culture.

The choice between qualitative and quantitative research methodology in studying administrative culture depends on the research objectives, research questions, and design. In this regard, how administrative culture is conceptualized and how different types of knowledge claims are generated and constructed may decide the choice of whether a deductive or inductive study is more desirable. A deductive study with the objective of hypothesis testing may opt for a quantitative research method while inductive study with the objective of interpretation and meaning formation relating observations to some general patterns or theories may choose a qualitative approach (Martin, 2011, p. 6).

Also the choice of methodology may depend on the number of cases or respondents and the number of variables included in the study of administrative culture. As Table 1 illustrates, if the research design includes few cases and few variables, researchers are more likely to adopt a qualitative method. This is more common in ethnographic or case studies adopted to understand administrative culture. In contrast,

if the number of respondents is numerous and they are measured on a large number of variables and concerned with testing deductively derived hypothesis, a quantitative method is likely to be used. A number of databases such as the World Values Survey and the Afro or Asianbarometer include a number of variables measured for a number of countries. Further, if the number of respondents is large and measured on few number of variables such as the study of Hofstede, who studied four dimensions (later expanded these to six dimensions, see Hofstede et al. 2010) of culture in many countries, an adoption of quantitative study method is more likely. On the other hand, if the number of variables is many and few respondents we may also observe a preference for the qualitative study method. This type of interpretive study in contrast to hypothesis testing study explains contexts in details in order to develop context-specific understandings rather than testing generalizable theory (Martin, 2001, p. 6).

However, in the study of administrative culture, the mixed-method approach has been used less frequently. Yet what we sometimes see is a kind of historical approach where researchers use a mixture of data to describe and analyze the historical development of administrative culture in a particular country. In such studies, analyses are based on historical documents and information about how public administration has developed. In general, however, we tend to conclude that due to the limited number of empirical studies, methodological issues in the analysis of administrative culture have not been fully exposed and discussed.

CONCLUSION

This article has focused on aspects of administrative culture that pose challenges for researchers: how to conceptualize administrative culture; how different types of knowledge claims can be generated and can point to a range of phenomena, from organizational constructs to explanations; the need to evaluate administrative behavior on the basis of certain moral standards; and finally, how researchers have selected their methods of study.

As a concept, administrative culture is slowly but surely gaining prominence in the study of public administration. This is especially the case in the present age of globalization, e-governance, and in the realm of new management techniques spearheaded by NPM. As a response, administrative values are undergoing transformation. Since successful reforms invariably entail a change of values, studies of administrative culture are relevant *if* the right kinds of reforms are to be introduced. A public administration will develop its own culture, sometimes in accordance with the preferences of political and administrative elites, but it will also always be infused with values from the wider society.

At the same time, the public administration is constantly being challenged by innovative ways of how to think, behave, and respond to complex societal problems. From the

TABLE 1
Choice of Methodology in Conducting Scientific Inquiry
of Administrative Culture

Respondents	Number of variables	
	Few	Many
Few	Qualitative	Qualitative
Many	Quantitative	Quantitative

Source: Authors' construct.

published studies, it is apparent that there is constant tension between existing values and new values that are argued to be more contemporary and modern. Transformations are taking place, but not always in accordance with the reform objectives, or in a coherent relationship to societal demands. In this regard, it is vital to understand why reform measures fail or why a public administration is slow to respond, or what makes a system more compatible with reform measures. Answers to these questions may be sought in studying the administrative culture of organizations in particular contexts. Based on the amount of published research in this area, it can be reasonably claimed that there is at this point a scarcity of empirical studies, and that suitable methodological approaches are still in the process of development.

REFERENCES

Alvesson, M. (2012). *Understanding organizational culture*. London: Sage.

Cheung, A.B.I. (2011). NPM in Asian countries. In T. Christensen & P. Lægreid (Eds.) *The Ashgate research companion to new public management* (pp. 131–144). London: Ashgate.

Christensen, T., & Lægreid, P. (1998). Administrative reform policy: The case of Norway. *International Review of Administrative Sciences*, 64, 457–475.

Christensen, T., & Lægreid, P. (2008). NPM and beyond: Structure, culture and demography. *International Review of Administrative Sciences*, 74(1), 7–23.

Christensen, T. & Lægreid, P. (2011). Introduction. In T. Christensen & P. Lægreid (Eds.), *The Ashgate research companion to new public management* (pp. 1–16), London: Ashgate.

Christensen, T., Lægreid, P., Roness, P., & Røvik, K.A. (2007). *Organization theory and public sector: Instrument, culture and myth*. London: Routledge.

Creswell, J.W. (2003). *Research design: Qualitative, quantitative, and mixed methods approaches* (2nd edition). Thousand Oaks, CA: Sage Publications.

Denison D.R., & Mishra, A.K. (1995). Toward a theory of organizational culture and effectiveness. *Organization Science*, 6, 204–223.

Dwivedi, O.P., & Gow, J.I. (1999). *From bureaucracy to public management: The administrative culture of the government of Canada*. Peterborough, ON, Canada: Broadview.

Farazmand, A. (1999). Globalization and public administration. *Public Administration Review*, 59, 509–522. Retrieved from http://www.jstor.org/stable/3110299

Farazmand, A. (2012). The future of public administration: Challenges and opportunities. *Administration and Society*, 44, 487–517.

Gaventa, J. (2004). Strengthening participatory approaches to local governance: Learning the lessons from abroad. *National Civic Review 93*, 16–27.

Gilje, N., & Grimen, H. (1993). *Samfunnsvitenskapenes forutsetninger: Innføring i samfunnsvitenskapenes vitenskapsfilosofi* [Assumptions in the social sciences: Introduction to philosophy of science in the social sciences]. Oslo: Universitetetsforlaget.

Hall, P.A., & Taylor, R.C.R. (1996). Political science and the three new institutionalisms. *Political Studies 44*, 936–957.

Haque, A.S., & Zafarullah, H.M. (2001). Public management for good governance: Reforms, regimes, and reality in Bangladesh. *International Journal of Public Administration*, 24, 1379–1403. Retrieved from http://pactu.edu.np/downloads/njpg/june-2011/4_muhammad-azizuddin_bangladesh_administrative-reform-in-bangladesh-an-overview-of-political-dynamics.pdf

Hatch, M.J. (1993). The dynamics of organizational culture. *The Academy of Management Review*, 18, 657–693. Retrieved from: http://www.jstor.org/stable/258594

Hatch, M.J. (1997). *Organization theory: Modern, symbolic and postmodern perspectives*. Oxford: Oxford University Press.

Henderson, K.M. (2004). Characterizing American public administration: The concept of administrative culture. *International Journal of Public Sector Management*, 17, 234–250. Hofstede, G. (1991). *Cultures and organizations, software of the mind: Intercultural cooperation and its importance for survival*. New York: McGraw Hill.

Hofstede, G., Hofstede, G.J., & Minkov, M. (2010). *Cultures and organizations: Software of the mind* (3rd edition). New York: McGraw Hill.

Hyden, G. (2012). African politics in comparative perspective (2nd edition). Cambridge: Cambridge University Press.

Islam, N. (2004). Sifarish, sycophants, power and collectivism: Administrative culture in Pakistan. *International Review of Administrative Sciences*, 70, 311–330.

Jabbra, J.G., & Dwivedi, O.P. (2004). Globalization, governance, and administrative culture. *International Journal of Public Administration*, 27, 1101–1127.

Jahan, F., & Shahan, A.M. (2008). Politics-bureaucracy relationship in Bangladesh: Consequences for the Public Service Commission. *Public Organization Review*, 8, 307–328.

Jamil, I. (1994). Administrative culture: A mode of understanding public administration across cultures. In Coyle, C. (ed.) *Research in Urban Policy*, (Vol. 5) (pp. 275–294). Greenwich, CT: JAI Press.

Jamil, I. (2007). *Administrative culture in Bangladesh*. Dhaka: A.H. Development Publishing House.

Jamil, I., & Haque, M. (2005). The culture of Tadbir: The "building block" of decision-making in the civil service of Bangladesh. In R.B. Jain (Ed.), *Globalization and good governance: Pressure for constructive reforms* (pp. 175–203). New Delhi: Deep and Deep Publications.

Lam, J.T.M. (1994). Administrative culture and democracy in Hong Kong. *Asian Affairs*, 21, 166–181. Retrieved from http://www.jstor.org/stable/301722

Lægreid, P., & Verhoest, K. (2010). Introduction. In P. Lægreid & K. Verhoest (Eds.), *Governance of public sector organizations: Proliferation, autonomy and performance* (pp. 1–18). Basingstoke, UK: Palgrave Macmillan.

Manning, N. (2001). The legacy of the new public management in developing countries. *International Review of Administrative Sciences*, 67, 297–312.

March, J.G., & Olsen, J.P. (1989). *Rediscovering institutions: The organizational basis of politics*. New York: The Free Press.

March, J.G., & Olsen, J.P. (1995). *Democratic governance*. New York: The Free Press.

Martin, J. (2001). *Organizational culture: Mapping the terrain*. London: Sage.

Ott, S.J. (1989). *Organizational culture perspective*, Belmont, CA: Dorsey Press.

Peters, G.B. (1999). *Institutional theory in political science: The "new institutionalism."* London: Pinter.

Putnam, R.D. (1993). *Making democracy work: Civic traditions in modern Italy*. Princeton, NJ: Princeton University Press.

Riggs, F.W. (1964). *Administration in developing countries: The theory of prismatic society*. Boston: Houghton Mifflin.

Samaratunge, R., Alam, Q., & Teicher, J. (2008). The new public management reforms in Asia: A comparison of South and Southeast Asian countries. *International Review of Administrative Sciences*, 74, 25–46.

Schedler, K., & Proeller, I. (2007). Public management as a cultural phenomenon: Revitalizing societal culture in international public management research. *International Public Management Review*, 8, 186–194. Retrieved from http://www.ipmr.net

Schein, E.H. (1992). *Organizational culture and leadership* (2nd edition). San Francisco: Jossey-Bass Publishers.

Schick, A. (1998). Why most developing countries should not try New Zealand's reforms. In *The World Bank research observer*, *13*, 123–131. Retrieved from http://www1.worldbank.org/publicsector/pe/befa05/NZReforms.pdf

Schwartz, S.H. (1992). Universals in the content and structure of values: Theory and empirical tests in 20 countries. *Advances in experimental social psychology* (vol. 25). New York: Academic Press Retrieved from http://lepo.it.da.ut.ee/~cect/teoreetiline%20seminar%2023.04.2013/Schwartz%201992.pdf

Scott, W.R. (1995). *Institutions and organizations*. London: Sage.

Selznick, P. (1984). *Leadership in administration: A sociological interpretation*. Berkeley: University of California Press.

Sharma, R.D. (2002). Conceptual foundations of administrative culture: An attempt at analysis of some variables. *International Review of Sociology: Revue Internationale de Sociologie*, 12, 65–75.

Silverman, D. (2005). *Doing qualitative research*, 2nd edition. London: Sage.

Smircich, L. (1983). Concepts of culture and organizational analysis. *Administrative Science Quarterly*, *28*(3), 339–358. Retrieved from: http:www.jstor.org/stable/2392246

Symon, G., & Casell, C. (1998). *Qualitative methods and analysis in organizational research: A practical guide*. London: Sage.

Tayeb, M.H. (1998). Organizations and national culture: A comparative analysis. London: Sage.

Verhoest, K. (2011). The relevance of culture for NPM. T. Christensen & P. Lægreid (Eds.) The Ashgate research companion to new public management (pp. 47–64). London: Ashgate.

Weinberg, A.M. (1970). The axiology of science: The urgent question of scientific priorities has helped to promote a growing concern with value in science, *American Scientist*, *58*, 612–617. Retrieved Dec. 19, 2012, from http://www.jstor.org/stable/27829310

World Values Survey (1990–2012). http://www.worldvaluessurvey.org/index_surveys

The Role of Organizational Culture on Informal Conflict Management

Loredana Di Pietro and Francesca Di Virgilio

Department of Management, University of Molise, Campobasso, Italy

Many researchers and scholars would without hesitation justify the role of formal processes to manage the conflict in the workplace. The conflict process is greatly influenced by organizational culture. A number of researchers have explored the influences of organizational culture on the different ways of handling conflict. But the organizational culture and conflict management research has often ignored the examination of the impact and implications of culture on informal conflict management in organizations.

In this article we take a narrower approach that focuses on the specific domain of culture pertaining to the management of conflict. The purpose of this study was to analyze the amount and types of conflict in organizations with the aim of investigating the relationship between organizational culture and the behavioral norms used to informally manage conflict by examining the results of a survey questionnaire given to 168 employees of a Public Administration. The results indicate that there is a relationship between culture and behavioral norms. In this scenario, formal processes of conflict management become prescriptions and lose their relevance for understanding the challenges and the evolutions of conflict situations.

We demonstrate that the practice of conflict management is more problematic, especially in that it brings the topic of organizational culture into the discussion of conflict theory literature.

INTRODUCTION

Over the last 20 years, organizational culture has been a topic of significant interest in the organizational studies literature. Despite scholarly debates about the conceptualization and measurement of organizational culture, many agree that organizational culture is shared, is socially constructed, is transmitted across organizational generations, and contains multiple layers (Ostroff et al., 2003; Schein, 2000).

This research analyzes the ties between organizational culture and its effect on how conflict is handled within the workplace. This study seeks to understand the context and the behavioral norms in which workplace conflict exists in order to understand the role of organizational culture. So we strive to identify the real context that generates conflict, context that is typically not visible to the naked eye. The effects of organizational culture on conflict and conflict management are analyzed by asking 168 employees of a Public Administration about their perceptions of the amount and types of conflict within their organization and how they normally go about handling conflicts that arise. To manage the inadequacies of the organizational procedures and align with the organizational culture, employees develop ways of behaving consistent with the culture of an organization (Isenhart & Spangle, 2006).

Additionally, employees will most likely know both the informal and formal processes of handling conflict within their organizations. By asking them how they usually behave in a conflict situation, it's possible to understand how culture contributes to the collective behavioral norms of conflict management within organizations. This research uses these concepts through a survey tool that assesses not only individual beliefs about their own conflict behaviors, but also their perceptions of their co-workers' behaviors and their organization's practices.

The following section reviews the literature on the role of culture in organizational context and the importance of informal management conflict. The research questions have been included in the third section. A description of the research methodology and empirical findings of the study are then provided. The final section offers a discussion, limits and future research.

LITERATURE REVIEW

The Role of Culture in Organizational Context

According to the branch of cognitive anthropology referred to as ethnoscience (Goodenough, 1971), culture is a system of shared cognitions or a system of knowledge and beliefs (Rossi & O'Higgins, 1980; Rashid et al., 2003). A culture is seen as a unique system for perceiving and organizing material phenomena, things, events, behavior and emotions (Rossi & O'Higgins, 1980). A cognitive perspective is increasingly being applied to the study of organizations (Bougon, 1983; Harris & Cronen, 1979; Wacker, 1981). The cognitive emphasis leads the researchers to view organizations as networks of subjective meanings or frames of reference that organization members share to varying degrees and which, to an external observer, appear to function in a rule like, or grammar like manner. Some of these research efforts document how organization members conceive of themselves as a collectively. They are also often diagnostic, in that they assess the extent to which there is a shared basis for action or grounds for conflict (Wacker, 1981). In this scenario, culture is usually defined as social or normative glue that holds an organization together (Tichy, 1982). It has an emphasis on what an organization *is*, rather than what the organization *has*, a reflection of the values embedded within modern corporate society, the context in which corporate society is meaningful. It expresses the values or social ideals and the beliefs that organization members come to share (Siehl & Martin, 1981; Smircich, 1983a,b). These values or patterns of belief are manifested by symbolic devices such as myths (Boje et al., 1982), rituals (Deal & Kennedy, 1982), stories (Mitroff & Kilmann, 1976), legends (Wilkins & Martin, 1980), and specialized language (Andrews & Hirsch, 1983). Schein (1992) defined culture as a pattern of shared basic assumptions that the group learned as it solved its problems of external adaptation and internal integration that has worked well enough to be considered valid and, therefore, to be taught to new members as the correct way to perceive, think, and feel in relation to those problems. Thus, organizational culture is shared, is socially constructed, is transmitted across organizational generations, and contains multiple layers (Hofstede, et al., 1990; Mohan, 1993; Ostroff et al., 2003; Rowlinson & Proctor, 1999; Schein, 1992, 2000). It serves as a powerful social control function, limits the range of acceptable behavior, and hence, restricts individual differences in organizations (O'Reilly & Chatman, 1996).

The literature of Organization Development (Argyres & Silverman, 2004; Bate et al., 2000) state the concept of culture can be seen also as an internal organizational variable conceived as shared key values and beliefs that fulfills several important functions. First, it conveys a sense of identity for organization members (Deal & Kennedy, 1982). Second, it facilitates the generation of commitment to something larger than the self (Siehl & Martin, 1981). Third, culture enhances social system stability (Kreps, 1981). And fourth, culture serves as a sense-making device that can guide and shape behavior (Pfeffer, 1981; Siehl & Martin, 1981). This line of research offers a tantalizing prospect that organization culture may be another critical lever or key by which strategic managers can influence and direct the course of their organizations (Tichy, 1982).

In this article the organizational culture is seen as the amount of social interaction already present in the organization, as a context within interpretations of organizational identity are formed and the way in which individuals interpret events and how they react to events, it strongly influences how employees are likely to act as well as how they understand their own and others' actions (Helms & Stern, 2001). These patterns of behavioral assumptions perpetuate and continue to influence behaviors because they persistently lead people to make decisions that have traditionally worked for the organization (Ott, 1989; Sweeney & Hardaker, 1994). According to Sweeney and Hardaker (1994), we consider the organizational culture that affects the way in which people consciously and subconsciously think, make decisions and ultimately the way in which they perceive, feel and act towards opportunities and threats presented by the internal and external environments, which can include conflict. We use a perspective for understanding what is occurring in an organization and refers to a collection of theories that attempt to explain and predict how the people in organizational contexts act in different circumstances (Ott, 1989). This perspective was developed in response to researchers feeling that the more conventional structural and systematic perspectives of organizations did not include a human factor that acknowledged life within organizations. The organizational culture perspective suggests that the personal preferences of organizational members are not restrained by the systems of formal rules, authority, and norms of rational behavior unlike the structural and systems perspectives of organizational theory. Instead, they are controlled by cultural norms, perceptions, artifacts, values, beliefs, and assumptions (O'Reilly et al., 1991; Ott, 1989; Schein, 2000).

This article work stemmed from this foundation and according to Goffee and Jones's (1998) "Sociability" and "Solidarity" model. Goffee and Jones (1998) categorized organizational culture based on two dimensions: sociability and solidarity. Sociability describes the friendliness of relationships between people in an organization. Ideas, attitudes, interests and values are shared through friendships. On the other hand, solidarity describes the ability of people to pursue shared goals of the organization without much regard for the impact on individuals and the relationships between them.

Organizational Conflict and the Importance of Informal Management Conflict

Most literature on organizational conflict addresses the types of conflict organizations encounter, the effects of such conflicts and what strategies should be put to use in order to resolve the conflicts (Jehn et al., 2010; Lee & Yu, 2004; Lewis et al., 1997; Thatcher et al., 2003; Wallace et al., 1999). Anyway, the ties between organizational culture and its effect on how conflict is handled within the workplace lacks in the literature.

Organizational cultures set the culture of conflict in an organization. This means that there is a conflict set of words, ideas, values, behaviors, attitudes, archetypes, customs and rules that powerfully influence how an organization's members think about and respond to conflict (Cloke & Goldsmith, 2000). They set parameters for what we believe is possible when we are in conflict and define what we can reasonably expect, both of ourselves and of others. They shape our capacity to ask questions, alter how we see our opponents and ourselves, and tell us what is or is not acceptable (Cloke & Goldsmith, 2000).

Lewis et al. (1997) argue that conflict in organizations become institutionalized through common attitudes, values and rituals. As a result, conflict can become part of the culture of an organization without members being aware of its presence. Morgan (1988) suggests that conflict ingrained within the culture of an organization can be extremely hard to identify and thus break down. On the other hand, many organizational cultures place a premium on conflict avoidance, where others reward accommodation or compromise. Most possess a subtle set of rules regarding who can behave how, with whom, and over what.

The mainstream literature have come to the conclusion that employees are unable to handle conflict on their own and must be told how to manage it in a positive way (Cloke & Goldsmith, 2000; Eisaguirre, 2002; Hiam, 1997; Thomas, 1992; Weiss & Hughes, 2005). Weiss and Hughes (2005) suggest people lack an innate understanding of how to deal with conflict effectively. Although this topic is certainly important in ascertaining conflict behavior in a company, what needs to be studied is how organizational members perceive and informally act as a whole in conflict situations.

In the organizational conflict literature lacks systematically a focus on informal norms, routines, and processes that develop in organizations regarding conflict management (for exceptions, see Costantino & Merchant, 1996; Slaikeu & Hasson, 1998). As Kolb and Putnam (1992) argued, it is unlikely that these formal channels constitute the only, or even the major, location where conflict and grievances are worked out. The informal processes of an organization, outside the formal policies and rules, create shared values that unconsciously govern behavioral norms of employees. It is argued (Slaikeu & Hasson, 1998) that, with time, such informal norms drop out of people's consciousness; they become so powerful, underlying and unquestioned, that they continue to influence organizational behavior and strategic decision making even when the organization's business environment changes (Ott, 1989; Sweeney & Hardaker, 1994).

In this scenario, the informal conflict management will be strongly influenced by organizational culture because organizational culture controls behavioral norms. For example, informal norms of conflict management might sanction hidden agendas, "bitching," ignoring requests, and other ideographic practices. In the informal setting, every day practices govern the way issues evolve and the way conflict roles emerge to manage these issues. De Dreu et al. (2004) also speculated that units within organizations or even entire organizations develop over time a relatively stable set of orientations toward, and strategies to manage conflict, and specifically called for more research on cultures of conflict.

Thus to provide insight into conflict management in organizations, understanding the informal processes in which features of organizations constrain or enable how conflict is managed should be an important conceptual territory in the conflict scholarship landscape (De Dreu et al., 2004; De Dreu & Gelfand, 2008; Jehn & Bendersky, 2003; Kolb & Putnam, 1992).

According to Donais (2006), in this study we categorize the sources of workplace conflict into two categories: organizational and interpersonal conflict. Interpersonal conflict is the most apparent form in the workplace in gossip and rumors. The disputes that result from interpersonal conflicts include harassment and discrimination. In addition, stresses from home often spill over into the office causing interpersonal conflict between employees. Organizational conflict focused on the specific features of conflict of persons at different hierarchical levels (Xin & Pelled, 2003). Existing studies have focused on conflict among managers (Ensley et al., 2000; Floyd & Lane, 2000; Massey & Dawes, 2007; Mohr & Puck, 2007), among employees (Tjosvold et al., 2003) and between managers and employees (Schaubroeck et al., 1993; Xin & Pelled, 2003). There may also be work style clashes and seniority and pay equity conflict. Conflict can arise over resource allocation, distribution of duties, workload and benefits, tolerance for risk taking, and varying views on accountability. In addition, conflict can arise where there are perceived or actual differences in treatment between departments.

For the purpose of this study, conflict is defined as the interpersonal interaction of organizational actors with different hierarchical levels that perceive opposition in goals, aims, and values and who perceive the other entity or entities as potentially interfering with the realization of these goals and creates tension (Thomas, 1992). Conflict is defined in terms perception, that is, one entity perceives interference with its goals.

Methodology

In this study, we investigated the effects of organizational culture on informal conflict management by asking employees about their perceptions of the amount and types of conflict within their organization and how they normally go about handling conflicts that arise.

The intent of the present study is to answer the following main research question:

RQ_1:   What is the relationship between organizational culture and informal conflict management?

To answer the main research questions, we were guided by three derived research questions:

RQ_{1a}:   What types of conflict and how much conflict exists in organizations?
RQ_{1b}:   What are the behavioral norms for handling conflict and do they differ from formal methods?
RQ_{1c}:   What is the relationship between the types and amount of conflict in organizations and the behavioral norms used to informally manage conflict?

Participants

The ideal method to go about attaining the information to answer the above research questions is to do an in-depth study of two or three public organizations. This would involve spending months with each organization observing behavioral norms in conflict situations and interviewing both leaders and employees of an organization regarding conflicts within their organization and how they handle the conflicts. However, this method may be too sensitive and may cause social harm to the employees. The potential harm this type of study may have for lower-level employees, especially, is too great to risk. As a result, we choose to conduct an exploratory study to obtain information about our research questions by interviewing a non-random quota convenience sampling of the public.

The participants are 168 employees belonging to a territorial Public Administration in the region of Molise (Italy). It's a government authority centrally concerned with the organization of government policies and programs which includes 412 human resources. To investigate organizational culture, a crucial question is what represents "an organization" from a cultural point of view. One organization may include several culturally different departments and these departments may consist of culturally different work groups. Determining what units are sufficiently homogeneous to be used for comparing cultures is both a theoretical and an empirical

problem. We took the pragmatic approach to accept as units of study entire organization as a unit culturally homogeneous. In a few cases, the research results later gave us reason to doubt a unit's cultural homogeneity, but it is unlikely that the results have been substantially affected by this.

We administered a survey questionnaire to a convenience sample which includes people approached in the offices, consisting of 84 managers (head officers, directors, and senior executives) and 84 college-level non managers (professionals). A criterion in their selection was that they were assumed to be sufficiently reflective and available. Participants were approached and asked to complete surveys within a period of three months from March 2011 to June 2011.

Direct surveys are a method used to gain information by contacting respondents personally and surveying them face-to-face. We asked the questions on the survey and gave the respondents the choice of answers. This method usually gets a good response rate and information is more reliable and corrects (Singh & Mangat, 1996).

Measurement Items of the Questionnaire

We designed a survey questionnaire in order to gather the information needed to answer the above research questions. We administered a survey questionnaire by asking participants about various aspects of the culture of participants' organization as well as conflict and conflict management in their organizations. The survey consisted of 20 items including yes/no, scaled, multiple choices and closed-end. The survey gave us information regarding the respondents' employment status and position. The rest of the questionnaire addressed amount and typologies of conflict, the informal processes used by employees at the organization, whether a formal conflict management process is used at the organization and the culture of the organization.

The survey included 6 items on conflict (Jehn & Mannix, 2001), 4 items on formal conflict management (Rahim 1983), 4 items on informal conflict management (Costantino & Merchant, 1996; Scott, 2001; Shapira, 2000), and 4 items on organizational culture (Goffee & Jones, 1998).

The reason we decided to give a direct survey (asking the questions ourselves) is that we wanted to make sure the delivery of the survey was consistent. We could ensure that every respondent understood each question the way we wanted.

The first section of the survey gave us respondents' demographics regarding their employment status (part-time/part-time) and position (employee/manager).

The second section addressed conflict behaviors of the individual and their co-workers to assess the organizations' conflict behavior as a whole. Conflict was measured by the amount and type of conflict present in the organization according to Jehn and Mannix (2001) past research. We adapted the past conflict scales (Ensley et al., 2000) so that the conflict type scales would reflect only conflict content level (Barki & Hartwick, 2004). The respondents could choose a scale for the amount of conflict: a lot (so that the conflicts interfere with work on a regular basis), some (there is conflict, but not enough so that it interferes with work on a regular basis), and little (it is rare that conflicts occur). The question asked the types of conflict occurring in respondents' organization. They could choose any number out of 8 responses: personality incompatibility, status conflict, miscommunication, resources (money, office space, staplers, etc.), attitude, perception of goals, different backgrounds or values, different expectations, or other, therefore making this question the only one that is not mutually exclusive.

The third section asked if there was a formal and informal conflict management and whether or not organizational members followed it. Formal Conflict Management in the organization was measured by four questions in the survey questionnaire, adapted from previous measures (Rahim, 1983), which asked employees to call whether their organization has a formal conflict management process. Two items inquired respondent's own behaviors, and two items asked about the behaviors of the other co-workers. If respondents responded yes, they were asked if members of the organization usually follow the process on an always/sometimes/never scale.

Given the lack of reliable and validated measures of Informal Conflict Management, items were measured by asking what the respondents usually do in a conflict and what they believe their co-workers usually do in conflict situations. The purpose of these questions is to show the behavioral norms of members of an organization in a conflict (Costantino & Merchant, 1996; Slaikeu & Hasson, 1998).

The final section asked the respondents to classify the culture of the organization via social interaction. Organizational Culture was measured in relation to conflict by the amount of social interaction already present in the organization. The respondents were asked if outside activities were held for organizational members (such as happy hour, work parties, lunch outings, etc.) and if they participated in the activities. Both of these questions were on a scale of always, sometimes and never. This measure is based on Goffee and Jones' (1998) model of culture on sociability. Sociability describes the friendliness of relationships between people in an organization. It is valued for its own sake and independent of its impact on the performance of the organization. Ideas, attitudes, interests and values are shared through friendships. This study is based on the specific topic of sociability of this model because it refers to how people relate to each other, especially in conflict situations. We specifically focused on the relationship between the employees as Goffee and Jones (1998) suggest that through relationships and friendships ideas, attitudes, interests and values are shared.

Data were analyzed using the SPSS 18.0 software applying various statistical analysis techniques as contingency tables and frequencies. The data were edited by checking and adjusting for errors, omissions, legibility and consistency in order to ensure completeness, consistency, and readability.

The first step of the analysis was to test the reliability of the data using Cronbach's alpha value investigation (Cronbach and Shavelson, 2004). According to Peterson (1994), a value of 0.7 can be considered as cut-off point for evaluating the research reliability, even if also lower value (between 0.65 and 0.7) can be considered reliable for preliminary research (Peterson, 1994). Table 1 summarizes the alpha value for each dimension of the collected data. The results imply that the measurement scale is reliable.

Key Findings

In order to answer the research questions listed above, we looked at the relationship between numerous parts of the data.

First, respondents were asked to choose the level and types of conflict presented in their organization. The majority of the respondents asserted that some conflict exists in their organization. Interestingly, when position is cross tabulated with the amount of conflict, it results in a relationship that is statistically significant at $\alpha = .05$ level using Chi-Square (see Table 2). This shows that a manager is more likely to perceive a lot of conflict in the workplace than an employee.

They were also able to choose as many of the type of conflict as they felt are in their workplace, resulting in overlapping categories. The type of conflict that is most predominant in organizations is miscommunication (77 percent). The next types of conflict are personality (69 percent) and attitude (62,5 percent).

The research question RQ_{1b} inquiries into the behavioral norms organizational members use to handle conflict. It also questions whether the informal methods differ from any formal methods, if they exist. The survey questions

TABLE 1
Cronbach's alpha value

Factors	Items	α Cronbach
Conflict	6	0,848
Formal Conflict Management	4	0,859
Informal Conflict Management	4	0,862
Organizational Culture	4	0,894

TABLE 2
How Respondents Perceive the Level of Conflict in Their Workplace

Emp/Mgr Position	Amount of conflict			Total
	A lot	Some	Little	
Employee	3	52	29	84
Manager	14	44	26	84
Total	17	96	55	168
Chi-Square	7.948 (value), 0.019 (sig)			

regarding informal conflict management had two separate categories – what the respondent does and what the respondents' co-workers do – and two sets—what people do in conflict, and who people talk to first in conflict. The responses showed that there is quite a difference between their own behaviors and their co-workers behaviors. The majority (42 percent) of respondents said they would usually talk to the person they are in conflict with in a conflict situation. The second most popular reply was talking to a different co-worker about the conflict (33 percent). Respondents, however, said that their co-workers usually (44 percent) consult another co-worker when in conflict rather than talking to the person, avoiding the conflict, talking to their manager or a HR representative (21 percent).

There was a strong statistical significance at the $\alpha = .05$ level when these two variables were cross tabulated using Chi-Square (Table 3).

The positive relationship between the respondents' actions and their co-workers' actions imply that the participants' responses accumulatively results in behavioral norms for conflict behaviors within organizations. If the majority of participants are consulting another co-worker in a conflict repeatedly, then eventually consulting a co-worker will become the expected norm.

The second aspect of behavioral norms is who respondents talked to first in conflict situations and who they perceived their co-workers to talk to first. The reason this is a part of the informal conflict management section is because it is our assumption that there is often one or two people that employees go to in conflict situations. Since the majority of respondents said they talk to a non-manager co-worker first (73 percent) and perceive their co-workers to talk to a non-manager co-worker first (81 percent), we can assume that this is a behavioral norm in most conflict situations for employees to talk to another co-worker who is not their manager regarding the conflict before talking to the person they are in conflict with or a manager regarding the situation.

This was found statistically significant at the $\alpha = .05$ level using Chi-Square (Table 4).

The final aspect of the informal conflict management section of the survey is whether the behavioral norms of conflict management differ from the formal methods present in an organization. We asked respondents first if a formal process existed in their organization and then whether they and their co-workers utilize the formal process. Sixty-six percent of respondents confirmed that there was a formal conflict management process in their organization that they knew of. Of those participants that responded yes, only seven percent said that employees in the organization always followed the formal process. The majority of respondents (62 percent) said that they only sometimes followed the formal process, while the rest responded that no one ever followed the formal process of conflict management in their organization. These findings support that informal conflict management exist in organizations.

The research question RQ_{1c} asks to examine the relationship between the amount and types of conflict in organizations and the behavioral norms used to informally manage conflict. A few things have to be assumed from the above data in order to interpret and understand the following cross tabulations. First, the data show that employees in organizations do participate in behavioral norms that are outside of formal conflict management systems. Second, the behavioral norms are likely to consist of employees consulting each other regarding a conflict rather than seeking advice from a manager or someone from Human Resources.

TABLE 4
Who people talk to first when facing a conflict

Respondents talk to first	Co-workers talk to first			
	Another Co-worker	Manager	HR	Total
Another co-worker	114	9	0	123
Manager	22	21	0	43
HR	0	0	2	2
Total	136	30	2	168
Chi-Square	205.544 (value), 0.000 (sig)			

TABLE 3
How Respondents and Their Co-workers Usually Act in Conflict Situations

Respondents do when in conflict	Co-workers usually do in conflict					
	Consult friend/ co-worker	Avoid	Talk to manager	Talk to person	Talk to HR	Total
Avoid	5	11	1	3	1	21
Consult friend/co-worker	33	13	5	5	0	56
Talk to person	30	16	14	9	1	70
Talk to manager	6	1	10	0	0	17
HR	0	0	3	1	0	4
Total	74	41	33	18	2	168
Chi-Square	48.721 (value), 0.000 (sig)					

When we examined the relationship between the amount of conflict and the informal conflict management in organizations, we found that there is not a significant relationship between the two variables at the $\alpha = .05$ level. The amount of conflict respondents said is present in their organization does not have a significant impact on what the respondents and what their co-workers do in conflict situations. The amount of conflict also does not impact who the respondents and their co-workers talked to first. As a result, the amount of conflict in an organization does not impact how employees handle the conflicts in an informal manner.

The second part of this research question asked to look at the relationship between the type of conflict and the behavioral norms used by respondents. We had to split question number into eight separate variables of respondents saying yes or no as to whether that particular type of conflict exists in their organization.

In order to determine the relationship between the types of conflict and its impact on informal conflict management, we cross tabulated the type of conflict that is most predominant in the organization, miscommunication, with respondents' answers to the behavioral norms questions on the survey. There is a statistical significance between miscommunication and what respondents do in conflict of a .015 at a $\alpha = .05$ level (see Table 5).

However, there was no statistical significance between miscommunication and what respondents' co-workers do in conflict. Again, there is a difference between the respondent's self-perception and the perception of their co-workers when it comes to who they talk to first. When a respondent said there was miscommunication as a cause of conflict there was a statistically significant probability of .017 impacting who the respondent talks to first in a conflict (see Table 6).

However, there is no statistical significance between miscommunication and who the respondents' co-workers talk to first. None of the other types of conflicts had any statistically significant relationship with the informal conflict management. As a result, the relationship between the type of conflict and informal processes in use within organizations is quite minimal.

After the analysis between numerous parts of the data, we answered the main research question (RQ_1) that involves

the relationship between culture and the informal conflict management. Before examining this particular relationship, we cross tabulated the culture questions on the survey with the respondents' answers regarding the amount and type of conflict in their workplace. We found a strong, positive statistically significant relationship between the existence of outside activities and the amount of conflict in the organization of .002 at the $\alpha = .05$ level (see Table 7).

This means that if respondents answered "always" to the existence of outside activities in their organizations, then they were likely to answer "little" for the amount of conflict present in the organization. In contrast, if they responded that there are "never" outside activities in their organization, then they were likely to perceive "a lot" of conflict. Interestingly, there was no significant relationship between the existence and participation in outside activities to promote sociability and the type of conflict existing within an organization.

The existence of activities outside of the workplace does have a statistically significant relationship with who

TABLE 6
Who respondents talk to first in "Miscommunication" conflicts

| Conflict is a Miscommunication | You talk to first | | | |
	Another co-worker	Manager	HR	Total
Yes	102	27	2	131
No	21	16	0	37
Total	123	43	2	168
Chi-Square	8.094 (value), 0.017 (sig)			

TABLE 7
How the existence of outside activities interacts with the amount of conflict

| Outside activities | Amount of conflict | | | |
	A lot	Some	Little	Total
Always	5	8	17	30
Sometimes	8	71	34	113
Never	4	17	4	25
Total	17	96	55	168
Chi-Square	16.818 (value), 0.002 (sig)			

TABLE 5
How respondents react in "Miscommunication" conflicts

| Conflict is a Miscommunication | You do what in conflict | | | | | |
	Talk to person	Consult friend/co-worker	Avoid	Talk to manager	Talk to HR	Total
Yes	60	46	13	9	3	131
No	10	10	8	8	1	37
Total	70	56	21	17	4	168
Chi-Square	12.390 (value), 0.015 (sig)					

TABLE 8
How the existence of outside activities interacts with who
respondents talk to first in conflict situations

Existence of outside activities	Respondents talk to first			
	Another co-worker	Manager	HR	Total
Always	21	7	2	30
Sometimes	80	33	0	113
Never	22	3	0	25
Total	123	43	2	168
Chi-Square	12.519 (value), .014 (sig)			

TABLE 9
How the existence of outside activities interacts with whom
co-workers talk to first

Existence of outside activities	Co-workers talk to first			
	Co-worker	Manager	HR	Total
Always	21	7	2	30
Sometimes	94	19	0	113
Never	21	4	0	25
Total	136	30	2	168
Chi-Square	10.364 (value), .035 (sig)			

TABLE 10
How participation in outside activities interacts with whom
respondent talks to first in conflict situations

Participate in outside activities	Respondents talk to first			
	Another co-worker	Manager	HR	Total
Always	40	11	2	53
Sometimes	74	28	0	102
Never	9	4	0	13
Total	123	43	2	168
Chi-Square	5.710 (value), .058 (sig)*			

*significance at the $\alpha = 0.10$ level.

respondents and their co-workers talk to first (Tables 8, and 9) which suggests that the existence of outside activities in the workplace does in fact influence who co-workers talk to first in a conflict situation.

However, there was no statistically significant relationship between sociability (measured by outside activities) and what respondents and their co-workers *do* in conflict.

Since both interactions show statistically significant relationships, it can be concluded that participation in outside activities does in fact influence who co-workers talk to first in a conflict situation. Tables 10 and 11examined the interaction between respondents' participation in outside activities and who they and their co-workers talk to first in a conflict situation.

The overall results, therefore, suggests that organizational culture, in terms of sociability, influences informal conflict management.

TABLE 11
How Participation in outside activities interacts with whom
co-workers talk to first

Participate in outside activities	Co-workers talk to first			
	Co-worker	Manager	HR	Total
Always	40	11	2	53
Sometimes	88	14	0	102
Never	8	5	0	13
Total	136	30	2	168
Chi-Square	9.813 (value), .044 (sig)			

DISCUSSION

The data of this study suggest that there is a positively significant relationship between the position of an employee (manager or non-manager) and the amount of conflict the employee perceives is present in the organization. As we mentioned earlier, this may be a result of managers seeing more conflict since some employees go to their manager to discuss conflict situations. Our findings showed that conflict does indeed exist within organizations at a medium level of "some." We found also that the types of conflict present in the Public Administration do not necessarily have to do with lack of physical resources like so many researchers suggest (Bannister, 2001; Peters & Pierre, 1998; Starling, 2011). The most common type of conflict found is caused by miscommunication. Additionally, respondents did not find conflicts such as resource conflict and status conflict, to be prevalent in organizations. This finding differs from previous research that states that conflicts on resources are prevalent in organizations (Pondy, 1969; Thomas, 1992).

The data of this study suggest that while formal conflict management systems exist in the workplace, employees tend to handle conflict using other informal processes. In fact, 93 percent of respondents said that employees in their organization only "sometimes" or "never" follow the formal conflict management system in workplace. Despite, employees prefer to talk to each other about a conflict situation or speak to the person with whom they are in conflict. Since the majority of respondents felt their co-workers talk to another co-worker first in a conflict situation, we can assume that a behavioral norm of handling conflict is talking to a co-worker that employees trust and feel comfortable confiding in.

Next, our findings showed statistically significant relationships between what respondents say they do regarding informal conflict management and what they say their co-workers do. In addition, there was a statistically significant relationship between a type of conflict (miscommunication) and some aspects of informal conflict management. By understanding what people do in conflict situations that are different from the formal structures and processes, we analyze conflict management systems that are supported by and embrace informal.

Finally, our findings showed that culture, defined by sociability, do have an impact on the amount of conflict and a statistically significant relationship with informal conflict management, specifically who respondents and the co-workers talk to first.

The final main research question looked into the relationship between culture and informal conflict management. In this study, we used Goffee and Jones' (1998) dimension of sociability to define culture. We found that for the most part organizations only "sometimes" had activities to form and maintain social relationships and employees only "sometimes" participated in these activities. And yet, there was a statistically significant relationship between sociability and the informal conflict management, specifically who respondents talked to first and who their co-workers talked to first. So we conclude that a strong culture of sociability will inevitably impact the informal conflict management, specifically who employees talk to in conflict situations.

The results suggest that relationships between organizational culture and conflict are more complex than previously theorized. Mainstream have considered the theoretical and practical implications of studying only organizational culture or conflict management. Since our approach focus on the relationship between the two factors, it's necessary to understand the informal conflict management that are created by organizational members along with the organizational culture. Since the members are behaving repeatedly in ways that modify conflict, they are basically creating rules or behavioral norms for conflict management behavior. These rules become engrained in the organizational culture and are passed through and among organizational members.

IMPLICATIONS AND RECOMMENDATIONS

This study presents both academic and practical implications.

On one hand it has opened the door to a whole new relationship not previously explored in-depth within organizational and conflict literature. There is a need, upon expanding on this study, for more operational and inclusive measurable definitions of the variables. Researchers have the opportunity to play with the relationship between the type of culture and the type of conflicts present in the organization. They can study the difference between those conflict management systems that embrace cultural cues of conflict management and those organizations whose conflict management systems ignore cultural clues. Also, researchers have the opportunity to compare and contrast different organizational cultures and their impact on conflict management.

On the other hand, often managers feel that conflict is destructively rampant throughout an organization and hire someone to create a formal conflict management process that is truly just a rubber stamp for management. The formal process does not actually change the culture of the organization regarding conflict. Informal processes most likely already exist, so it is duty of managers of Public Administrations to recognize the informal processes and embrace them in order to create a truly effective formal conflict management system. The ideal role of management in this instance is for managers of Public Administrations to be perceptive and sensitive to informal processes and use them to effectively manage conflict behaviors.

This study shows that managers of a local Public Administration should identify naturally occurring processes and determine whether or not they will be congruent with constructive conflict management. Managerial definitions of conflict will not necessarily be helpful and in some cases may be downright deceptive. Interviewing and anonymous feedback from employees will probably surface system and processes that are operational. Additionally, awareness of organizational goals and values will facilitate the interveners understanding of how to build on and expand constructive systems. It is essential to recognize that organizational culture has an impact on conflict management processes. By embracing and channeling the naturally occurring processes of conflict management, as this research shows, public managers can begin to align cultural recommendations for conflict management and formal conflict management systems to make them constructive all of the time.

The traditional orientation in management philosophy is to reduce conflict or, even better, to avoid conflicts in organizations. This has led management and organizations to devote significant resources to conflict resolution and avoidance activities.

By contrast, our research leads to recommend that companies and managers actively explore informal conflict management processes that already exist among employees and use these processes to aid in the development or existence of formal conflict management processes.

LIMITATIONS AND FUTURE RESEARCH

Although this study offers important issues in the field, there are some limitations which should be taken into account.

The methodology used for this study is not the ideal. We have done an in-depth study of a public organization involving spending months interviewing both leaders and employees regarding conflicts within their organization and how they handle the conflicts. But it would be ideal also to spend time observing behavioral norms in conflict situations and doing a comparative analysis of the behavioral norms in contrast to the formal processes and systems in place at the organization. It would be essential to study the cultural norms and cues regarding conflict. However, this method is too sensitive and may cause social harm to the employees. As a result, the ideal method is not achievable in this case. Consequently, the results of this study cannot possibly meet all of the requirements we originally set out to meet.

A few interesting psychological phenomena became apparent during the analysis of our data. First, many of the respondents tended to give answers that put them in a favorable light and their co-workers in a less favorable light. The data show that 44 percent of respondents said they talk to the other party to the conflict, while only 10.7 percent of respondents felt their co-workers did the same. These data support a psychological phenomenon called false uniqueness bias. This is defined as the tendency to see ourselves as better than others (Campbell, 1986). Additionally, the fundamental attribution error has become apparent in the interview process.

Despite, another limitation emerges from the lack of the role of time in order to analyze the strengths of interpersonal and organizational conflicts both in terms of recency error (respondents tend to remember the most recent events) and in term of comparability among answers. So, for our future research we'll introduce the role of time.

Our measures for each variable should be more appropriately viewed as global measures for the phenomena. In this study we have excluded the possible role of sub—culture. It is argued that the strength and intensity of the culture variables (i.e., the type of leadership, prevailing stories and myths, or accepted ritual and symbols) do not provide employees with as much opportunity to interact personally on a regular basis; therefore, they are unable to co-create the culture through communication and interactions (Sweeney & Hardaker, 1994).

Future research should use or develop more in-depth, multidimensional measures for each variable. We are going to use more relevant demographic variables such as gender of participants and their contractual position (to be full-time employees defined by working 32 or more hours a week). We are going to introduce also the "solidarity" based on Goffee and Jones' (1998) model of culture and to compare the public-and private-sector workers' results.

CONCLUSION

Organizational culture literature and workplace conflict literature are important bodies of research when studying organizations. This study combines those two fields of research. We examined the amount and types of conflict in organizations, the processes used to informally manage conflict, and the relationship between culture and informal conflict management through surveying a sample of the working population. We found that informal conflict management arises from organizational members along with the organizational culture. Employees create these informal systems with behavioral norms to deal with conflict.

The purpose of the study is to alert academic word to an approach of conflict management already in place within organizations that can be found through the examining organizational culture and through the behavioral norms.

Furthermore, an intriguing issue for informal conflict management is the culture of the organization. We suggest that it can also influence the way in which employees naturally handle conflict within their organization. We are not suggesting that there is a good culture or a bad culture regarding conflict management. Instead, we believe that the issues is how employees, managers, and consultants understand and interpret the organizational culture to give clues and guidelines as to how employees should and do act in conflict so that their actions align with the organizational culture.

We conclude that a strong culture of sociability will inevitably impact the informal conflict management, specifically who employees talk to in conflict situations. Although we are unable to generalize these findings in order to make a statement such as all culture will impact the informal conflict management, but in this first study we are able to state that there is an inextricable tie between organizational culture and informal conflict management.

REFERENCES

Andrews, J.A.Y., & Hirsch, P.M. (1983). Ambushes, shootouts, and knights of the roundtable: The language of corporate takeovers.*In* L. R. Pondy, P. Frost, G. Morgan, & T. Dandridge (Eds.), *Organizational Symbolism.* Greenwich, CT: JAI Press.

Argyres, N., & Silverman, S. (2004). R&D, organization structure, and the development of corporate technological knowledge. *Strategic Management Journal, 25*, (8/9), 929–958.

Bannister, F. (2001). Dismantling the silos: Extracting new value from IT investments in public administration. *Information Systems Journal, 11*, (1), 65–84.

Barki, H., & Hartwick, J. (2004). Conceptualizing the construct of interpersonal conflict. *International Journal of Conflict Management, 15*, (3), 216–244.

Bate, P., Khan, R., & Pye, A. (2000). Towards a culturally sensitive approach to organization structuring: Where organization design meets organization development. *Organization Science, 11*, (2), 197–211.

Boje, D.M., Fedor, D.B., & Rowland, K. M. (1982). Myth making: A qualitative step in OD interventions. *Journal of Applied Behavioral Science, 18*, 17–28.

Bougon, M. (1983). Uncovering cognitive maps: The self-q technique. *In* G. Morgan (Ed.), *Beyond method: Social research strategies*, Beverly Hills, CA: Sage.

Campbell, J.D. (1986). Similarity and uniqueness: The effects of attribute type, relevance, and individual differences in self-esteem and depression. *Journal of Personality and Social Psychology, 50*, (2), 281–294.

Cloke, K., & Goldsmith, J. (2000). *Resolving conflicts at work.* San Francisco, CA: Jossey-Bass.

Costantino, C. A., & Merchant, C. S. (1996). *Designing conflict management systems: A guide to creating productive and healthy organizations.* San Francisco, CA: Jossey-Bass.

Cronbach, L., & Shavelson, R. (2004). My current thoughts on coefficient alpha and successor procedures. *Educational and Psychological Measurement, 64*, (3), 391–418.

De Dreu, C. K. W., van Dierendonck, D., & Dijkstra, M. T. (2004). Conflict at work and individual well being. *International Journal of Conflict Management, 15*, 6–26.

De Dreu, C. K.W., & Gelfand, M. J. (2008). Conflict in the workplace: Sources, functions, and dynamics across multiple levels of analysis. *In* C. K. W. De Dreu, & M. J. Gelfand (Eds.), *The psychology of conflict and conflict management in organizations* (pp. 3–54). New York: Lawrence Erlbaum.

Deal, T. E., & Kennedy, A. A. (1982). *Corporate cultures*. Reading, MA: Addison-Wesley.

Donais, B. (2006). *Workplaces that work*. Aurora, Ontario, Canada: The Cartwright Group.

Eisaguirre, L. (2002). *The power of a good fight*. Indianapolis, IN: Alpha Books.

Ensley, M.D., Pearson, A.W., & Amason, A.C. (2000). Understanding the dynamics of new venture top management teams. Cohesion, conflict, and new venture performance. *Journal of Business Venturing, 17*, 365–386.

Floyd, W., & Lane, P.J. (2000). Strategizing throughout the organization: Managing role conflict in strategic renewal. *The Academy of Management Review, 25*, (1), 154–177.

Goffee, R., & Jones, G. (1998). *The character of a corporation: How your company's culture can make or break your business*. London: Harper Business.

Goodenough, W.H. (1971). *Culture, language and society*. Reading, MA: Addison-Wesley.

Harris, L., & Cronen, V. (1979). A rules-based model forth analysis and evaluation of organizational communication. *Communication Quarterly, 12*, 12–28.

Helms, M., & Stern, R. (2001). Exploring the factors that influence employees' perceptions of their organization's culture. *Journal of Management in Medicine, 15*, (6), 415–429.

Hiam, A. (1997). *Assessing behavior in conflict*. Amherst, MA: Trainer's Spectrum.

Hofstede, G., Neuijen, B., Ohayv, D.D., & Sanders, G. (1990). Measuring organizational cultures: A qualitative and quantitative study across twenty cases. *Administrative Science Quarterly, 35*, 286–316.

Isenhart, M., & Spangle, M. (2006, October). Flying Below the Radar: System Changes Made Informally. Paper presented at the Conference of the Association for Conflict Resolution, 25–29.

Jehn, K.A., & Bendersky, C. (2003). *Intragroup conflict in organizations: A contingency perspective on the conflict–outcome relationship. In* B. Staw, & R. Kramer (Eds). *Research in organizational behavior* (pp.187–242). Oxford, UK: Elsevier Science Inc.

Jehn, K.A., & Mannix, E.A. (2001). The dynamic nature of conflict: A longitudinal study of intragroup conflict and group performance. *The Academy of Management Journal, 44*, (2), 238–251

Jehn, K., Rispens, S., & Thatcher, S.M.B. (2010). The effects of conflict asymmetry on workgroup and individuals outcomes. *Academy of Management Journal, 53*, 67–89.

Kolb, D. M., & Putnam, L. L. (1992). Introduction: The dialectics of disputing. *In* D. M. Kolb, & J. M. Bartunek (Eds.), *Hidden conflict in organizations: Uncovering behind the scenes disputes*. Thousand Oaks, CA: Sage.

Kreps, G. (1981, July). Organizational folklore: The Packaging of Company History at RCA. Paper presented at the ICA/SCA Conference on Interpretive Approaches to Organizational Communication, Alta, UT.

Lee, S.K.J., & Yu, K. (2004). Corporate culture and organizational performance. *Journal of Managerial Psychology, 19*, 340–359.

Lewis, D.S., French, E., & Steane, P. (1997). A culture of conflict: Effects affective conflict within an organization. *Leadership and Organization Development Journal, 18*, 275–280.

Massey, G.R., & Dawes, P.L. (2007). The antecedents and consequence of functional and dysfunctional conflict between marketing managers and sales managers. *Industrial Marketing Management, 36*, 1118–1129.

Mitroff, I. I., & Kilmann, R. H. (1976). On organizational stories: An approach to the design and analysis of organizations through myths and stories. *In* R.H. Kilmann, L.R. Pondy, & D.P. Slevin (Eds.), *The management of organization design* (pp. 189–207). New York: Elsevier-North Holland.

Mohan, M. L. (1993). *Organizational communication and cultural vision: Approaches for analysis*. Albany: State University of New York Press.

Mohr, A.T., & Puck, J.F. (2007). Role conflict, general manager job satisfaction and stress and the performance of IJVs. *European Management Journal, 25*, (1), 25–35.

Morgan, G. (1988). *Images of organization*. London: Sage Publications.

O'Reilly, C., & Chatman, J. (1996). Culture as social control: Corporations, cults and commitment. *In* B. Shaw, & L. Cummings (Eds). *Research in organizational behavior* (pp.157–200). Stamford, CT: JAI Press.

O'Reilly, C.A., Chatman, J., & Caldwell, D. (1991). People and organizational culture: A profile comparison approach to assessing person-organization fit. *Academy of Management Journal, 34*, (3), 487–516.

Ostroff, C., Kinicki, A.J., & Tamkins, M.M. (2003). Organizational climate and culture. *In* W.C. Borman, D.R. Ilgen, & R.J. Klimoski (Eds). *Handbook of psychology: Industrial and organizational psychology* (pp.565–593). Hoboken, NJ: John Wiley & Sons.

Ott, J.S. (1989). *The organizational culture perspective*. Pacific Grove, CA: Brooks/Cole Publishing Company.

Peters, B.G., & Pierre, J. (1998). Governance without government? Rethinking public administration. *Journal of Public Administration Research Theory, 8*, (2), 223–243.

Peterson, R.A. (1994). A meta-analysis of Cronbach's coefficient alpha. *Journal of Consumer Research, 21*, 381–391.

Pfeffer, J. (1981). Management as symbolic action: The creation and maintenance of organizational paradigms. *In* L.L. Cummings, & B.M. Staw (Eds.), *Research in organizational behavior* (pp. 1–52). Greenwich, CT: JAI Press.

Pondy, L.R. (1969). Varieties of organizational conflict. *Administrative Science Quarterly, 14*, 499–505.

Rahim, M.A. (1983). A measure of styles of handling interpersonal conflict. *The Academy of Management Journal, 26*, (2), 368–376.

Rashid, M.Z.A., Sambasivan, M., & Rahman, A.A. (2003). The influence of organizational culture on attitudes toward organizational change. *Leadership & Organization Development Journal, 25*, (2), 161–179.

Rossi, I., & O'Higgins, E. (1980). The development of theories of culture. *In* I. Rossi (Ed.), *People in culture* (pp. 31–78). New York: Praeger.

Rowlinson, M., & Proctor, S. (1999). Organizational culture and business history. *Organizational Studies, 20*, 369–396.

Schaubroeck, J., Ganster, D. C., Sime, W. E., & Ditman, D. (1993). A field experiment testing supervisory role clarification. *Personnel Psychology, 46*, 1–25.

Schein, E. H. (1992). *Organizational culture and leadership: A dynamic view*. San Francisco: Jossey-Bass.

Schein, E.H. (2000). Sense and nonsense about culture and climate. *In* N. M. Ashkanasy, C. P. M.Wilderom, & M. F. Peterson (Eds.), *Handbook of organizational culture and climate*. Thousand Oaks, CA: Sage.

Scott, W.R. (2001). *Institutions and organizations*. Thousand Oaks, CA: Sage Publications.

Shapira, Z. (2000). Governance in organizations: A cognitive perspective. *Journal of Management and Governance, 4*, 53–67.

Siehl, C., & Martin, J. (1981). Learning Organizational Culture. Working Paper, Graduate School of Business, Stanford University.

Singh, P., & Mangat, N.S. (1996). *Elements of survey sampling*. Dordrecht, Netherlands: Kluwer Academic Publishing.

Slaikeu, K. A., & Hasson, R. H. (1998). *Controlling the costs of conflict: How to design a system for your organization*. San Francisco, CA: Jossey-Bass.

Smircich, L. (1983a). Organizations as shared meanings. *In* L.R. Pondy, P. Frost, G. Morgan, & T. Dandridge (Eds.), *Organizational symbolism*. Greenwich, CT: JAI Press.

Smircich, L. (1983b). Studying organizations as cultures. *In* G. Morgan (Ed.), *Beyond method: Social research strategies*. Beverly Hills, CA: Sage.

Starling, G. (2011). *Managing the public sector*. Wadsworth Cengage Learning, USA.

Sweeney, E.P., & Hardaker, G. (1994). The importance of organizational and national culture. *European Business Review, 94*, 3–14.

Thatcher, S.M.B., Jehn, K.A., & Zanutto, E. (2003). Cracks in diversity research: The effects of diversity faultlines on conflict and performance. *Group Decision and Negotiation 12*, 217–241.

Thomas, K.W. (1992). Conflict and conflict management: Reflections and update. *Journal of Organizational Behavior, 13*, 265–274.

Tichy, N.M. (1982). Managing change strategically: The technical, political, and cultural keys. *Organizational Dynamics, 9*, 59–80.

Tjosvold, D., Hui, C., Ding, D.Z., & Hu, J. (2003). Conflict values and team relationships: Conflict's contribution to team effectiveness and citizenship in China. *Journal of Organizational Behavior, 24*, (1), 69–88.

Wacker, G. (1981). Toward a cognitive methodology of organizational assessment. *Journal of Applied Behavioral Science, 17*, 114–129.

Wallace, J., Hunt, J., & Richards, C. (1999). The relationship between organizational culture, organizational climate and managerial values. *The International Journal of Public Sector Management, 12*, 548–564.

Weiss, J., & Hughes, J. (2005). Want collaboration? Accept- and actively manage- conflict. *Harvard Business Review, 83*, (3), 1–12.

Wilkins, A., & Martin, J. (1980). Organizational Legends. Working Paper, Graduate School of Business, Stanford University.

Xin, C.R., & Pelled, L.H. (2003). Supervisor-subordinate conflict and perceptions of leadership behavior: A field study. *The Leadership Quarterly, 14*, 25–40.

Culture, Administration, and Reform in Africa

Goran Hyden

Department of Political Science, University of Florida, Gainesville, Florida, USA

Research on public administration in Africa has been prescriptive rather than analytical. Solutions have been provided in search of problems. Little, if any, attention has been paid to the role of local administrative cultures. This article problematizes public sector reform efforts on the African continent by identifying the cultural realities in which administration is being pursued and how the practices differ from the prescriptions offered by consultants. A principal distinction is made between a "civic" and an "affective" cultural model. The conclusion is that any reform efforts in the future need to start from what is on the ground rather than trying to impose something from outside that does not match existing administrative practices.

INTRODUCTION

Ever since the 1990s, public sector reform has loomed large on the African development agenda. Better service delivery and greater efficiency have been two major concerns driving this reform process, which continues across the continent. Bold initiatives have been taken in conditions where the odds of success must be considered low. African countries typically lack an independent middle class that can place meaningful policy demands on the government and get a response because of its own influence and power in society. Many countries still struggle with a socialist government legacy and a dominant political party that is little interested in challenges to its power. Others are recovering from civil conflicts. On top of all that, many countries face a shortage of trained manpower. Still, governments are expected to deliver services and goods and much of a regime's legitimacy—and stability—relies on this ability to satisfactorily implement public policies.

There has been little interest in trying to understand where organizations in Africa come from and how they are embedded in social and cultural contexts with distinct operational implications. The technocratic way of approaching public sector reform in Africa has been dominant, leaving a trail of grey literature that continues to be the main source of interpreting public administration in the region. The result is that there is a shortage of independent research that problematizes the issues of public management. Although there are a few notable exceptions, for example the overview of public administration in Africa by Adamolekun (1999), most of what is being written on public administration in Africa tends to be prescriptive rather than analytical. It pays no attention to how administrative and political legacies shape choice and behavior. Nor does it consider the conflicts that exist between norms that are indigenous to African societies, those that were introduced by the colonial powers, and the contemporary reform agenda with its inspiration from New Public Management.

The purpose of this article is to discuss why the administrative culture is an important but overlooked factor. It begins by tracing the institutional conditions derived both from pre-colonial and colonial days that have shaped behavior and attitudes in government services. It shows how African countries differ from other regions of the world and how administrative reforms have been difficult to implement in the politico-administrative circumstances in the region. It ends with a discussion of how three models of administration compete with each other and how it is difficult to capture administrative culture in the African context in a single formula.

THE COLONIAL LEGACY

The world of public administration is a product of a dual process involving indigenous institutional development and/or a transplantation from one country context to another. Europe, and much of Asia, offer examples of indigenous growth of administrative institutions while the other regions rely much more extensively on transplanted institutions. Wherever institutions were transplanted long time ago, the issue arises—sooner or later—whether or not they should be treated as indigenous rather than transplanted. The point is that whether an administrative set-up is the result of an organic growth or subject to transplantation from another source, institutionalization takes time. Indigenous development is typically organic involving incremental changes over time before durable structures have been achieved. Such a development usually reflects changes in society and economy. The evolution of a rational-legal form of administration is, as Weber and others have shown, the result of such changes as the rise of capitalism, urbanization, and other aspects of modernity. Transplantation implies a radical break with existing norms and values but it takes time to take root and mature. In Africa, transplantation was initially associated with colonial conquest. In recent decades transplantation has also been linked to benevolent development practices by Western donor institutions. The introduction of new institutions in Africa by external agents, therefore, has relied on both the whip and the carrot.

An analysis of administrative culture in Africa must consider two important facts. The first is that the colonial interlude was quite brief, spanning over only a few generations. For example, Jomo Kenyatta, who became Kenya's first president in 1963 and died in office in 1978, was born before the British had established control of the territory in the early 20th century. The second is the timing of the imperial conquest. Unlike Latin America which was colonized in the 16th century and countries seized their independence as early as the beginning of the 19th century, colonialism in Africa is almost exclusively a 20th century phenomenon. This means that not only did Latin American countries have much longer time to shape their administrative institutions from within but they could also face modernization while being independent countries. This is a significant difference from Africa where modernization was a colonial and foreign project that clashed with indigenous pre-modern values. Africans, therefore, have always had an ambivalent attitude toward modernity. They embrace many of its outcomes, notably improved healthcare and formal education, but they are more skeptical of the process and mechanisms that produce modern goods and values. For all these reasons, it is no surprise that pre-modern values continue to be significant in shaping political and administrative behavior in these countries.

The persistence of pre-modern values in African countries is not only the result of an aborted colonial project but also the nature of its own political economy. Most importantly, the technological innovations that historically helped propel agriculture in a more productive direction in Asia

and Europe, notably the draught animal, the wheel and the plough, never came to Africa for reasons relating to its isolation (Goody, 1971). Agricultural technology in Africa remained simple, farmers relying almost exclusively on manual tools. The result was that farms were inevitably small. Any social differentiation reflected the size of the household. Heads with many wives and children were typically able to produce more and enjoyed a level of status that smaller households could not reach. Whatever differentiation that did exist never stood in the way of sharing resources with others. There was no private ownership of land. Clans and lineages were the authoritative entities for deciding any dispute over land. This form of social organization did not crystallize into social classes of rich and poor. Cleavages were not lateral between the haves and have-nots but vertical among families, lineages, and clans.

If freedom and equality are the guiding principles for social action in modern society, reciprocity was the legitimate norm in pre-colonial Africa. Reciprocity did not necessarily imply an even playing field, only the obligation that a favor had to be returned within an unspecified time frame. Although conflicts did occasionally arise, they were settled by the contending parties. There was never a need for a third party to judge. Institutions were informal and deeply immersed in the social structure of society. Individuals were never integrated into corporate or bureaucratic structures with a common goal. Instead, individuals approached each other with the shared expectation of reciprocity.

I have referred to this as the "economy of affection" (Hyden, 1980). It is an economy without public or corporate goals. Instead, it relies on sharing and distributing resources in such a way that all those in need are satisfied. It is not socialist, but it is communalist or communitarian. It is micro-rational, although not in the sense that public choice theory implies with its assumption of the autonomous individual in pursuit of utilitarian ends. Its rationality is embedded in social network or community relations. Calculations include consideration of what a particular action means to those on whom an individual is dependent.

During colonial days the metropolitan governments in Europe were not anxious to spend more than necessary on administering their African territories. Their ideology was that as much as possible, these territories should pay their own expenses. This meant collecting revenue from people and commercial transactions in these territories. Taxation, however, was not just a fiscal matter. It had implications for how these territories were being governed.

Two distinct ideologies evolved among the colonizers. One relied on "direct" rule in which the colonial service was an extension of the system at home. It was a unified career system in which all designated officers in a single hierarchy reported to a central office. This "integrated prefectoral" model of administration (Smith, 1967) was much preferred by the French, but it was adopted also by the British, especially in places where there were no traditional African authorities to rely on. The other system has been referred to as "indirect rule." It implied the use of indigenous institutions as the lowest organs of administration. For example, local kings or chiefs, together with the rudimentary system of administration that they had created under their rule were adopted by the colonial administration, adjusted to serve its objectives, and formalized by law. This model was applied especially by the British who tried to save the number of servants that they had to send to Africa. Its architect was Lord Lugard who as early as 1906 had made an initial pitch for this model of administration (Lugard, 1965). It really took off, however, only in the late 1920s and became an inspiration to many young colonial servants who ventured to Africa in the 1930s and 1940s. One of the most committed practitioner of indirect rule—Sir Donald Cameron—concluded, following his long-time career: "Build from the bottom; do not attempt as I found in Nigeria when I returned there in 1931 to make as it were, a crown or a king at the top and then try to find something underneath on which it might—perhaps—appropriately be placed" (Cameron, 1937, p. 4)

Indirect rule was not just an approach with administrative implications. Historians of British colonialism have also pointed to its political implications. It gave priority to "native" interests and the doctrine of native paramountcy. Although this argument was couched in a patronizing fashion by most people at the time, it provided a rationale to support a common belief among many colonial officers on the ground in Africa that the progress of people on the continent would be best served by an "organic growth," which would be upset if there were too much outside interference (Lee, 1967, p. 44).

This was quite a radical position in the 1930s and 1940s but it became less so after the Second World War when the British began implementing the Colonial Development and Welfare Act which had been adopted in 1940. This piece of legislation obliged the colonial service to enter into more actively promoting social development in the education and health sectors and providing an infrastructure that fostered local development. This placed the British in a more direct tutelary relation with their African subjects. This new relationship generated benefits in terms of better health and more educated Africans, but it also led to a greater realization among them that they were being treated as subjects and not citizens (Mamdani, 1996). Their political awareness, therefore, came as a result of being increasingly exposed to more direct forms of rule. The notion of an organic growth of indigenous institutions under indirect rule was replaced by the notion that Africans have to be made ready for democracy the way this concept was understood and practiced back in Britain.

The picture that emerges of public administration in the former British colonies is one where at the level of formal institutions distinct features of the British model can be identified but where these institutions are permeated by local norms that make its mode of operation quite different from the original model. There are at least three of explanations of this hybridity. One line of argument is that the colonial interlude was too short to result in a social transformation of African society and, by extension, the rise of a modern bureaucracy. A second line is that the British preference for indirect rule legitimized indigenous African norms of rule that in the end undercut the growth of a civil society as well as a Weberian type of rational and purposive administration. Yet another line is that the original model was upheld by British civil servants in the colonies and when they departed at or around independence there was not enough of a critical mass of senior African civil servants to reproduce it. Was the experience in other African countries colonized by the French, Portuguese, or Belgians any different?

The main difference is that the other colonizing powers relied foremost on direct rather than indirect rule. The French, in particular, but also the Portuguese, approached colonization with an organizational blueprint that in essence was a replica of what existed on the ground at home. They were more deliberate than the British in achieving a full transplantation of new institutions to the African scene. It was a centralized system of administration in which "prefects" served as heads at different levels of the government hierarchy. It rested on a coherent system of laws and procedures that made it more autonomous of society than the British system ever was but also more rigid and dependent on legal rather than political opinions. The French and Portuguese systems of administration tended to be even more alien bodies in African society than the British system was. At the same time, Africans who have taken over administrative positions after independence have tended to imitate the hauteur of their colonial predecessors. Administrators in the former French and Portuguese colonies have reproduced the elitist dispositions that can be found among practitioners of these models also in the metropolitan contexts.

If there are differences with regard to the way the colonial model of administration was introduced, there is more similarity with regard to how the state as a governing institution relates to society in Africa. Because political considerations tend to dominate economic and administrative ones, the administrative—and economic—sphere cannot be analyzed without reference to the qualities of the state. The administrative norms that the British and French brought to Africa have been undermined not by the lack of understanding on the part of those Africans who occupy positions in government bureaucracies but by the political leaders for whom the reversal of the norms associated with colonial rule has been a priority. To this day, African government leaders remain skeptical of the wisdom and value of models that are being brought by international agencies. This has implications for public sector reform.

ADMINISTRATIVE DEVELOPMENT AFTER INDEPENDENCE

There were two reasons why the institutions that had been put in place by the colonial administration were called into question after independence. One was their lack of grounding in African society. According to Dia (1995), African countries at independence found themselves saddled with a hybrid and disconnected system in which formal institutions transplanted from the outside had been superimposed upon indigenous informal institutions reflecting the cultures and traditions of these societies. The other was the revolution of rising expectations that political independence brought to the African scene. The rapid constitutional developments that paved the way for independence within a few years outstripped the development of the public services as local institutions. As Adu (1969, p. 14) writes, the civil services in African countries were unable to respond to the national aspirations of independence and the progressive realization of these aspirations. Africanization of the civil services was an attempt to deal with this challenge but it was not enough. Those Africans who were rapidly promoted to senior and leading positions in the civil service were often seen as colonial "leftovers" with orientations on the job that nationalist politicians perceived as being out of date.

The allegations of being disconnected, irrelevant, and lacking capacity for administering new development policies became too much to ignore. Even Western scholars got involved in the debate about the future of African civil services by beginning to argue for a special type of public administration that was attuned to the development needs of the new states (e.g., Thompson, 1964; Schaffer, 1969). This "development administration movement" became influential in the 1960s and added weight to the political calls for a transformation of the institutions inherited from the colonial powers. This movement was an attempt to generate a progressive administrative culture through changes in the behavior and attitude of the civil servants themselves.

Little came out of this attempt at transforming the civil service in a progressive direction. Instead, administrative changes were driven by politics. The ambition after independence has largely been one of dismantling the formal institutions that were inherited from the colonial powers. This process of institutional change—achieved both by design and by default—has not been confined to changes in administrative practices. It has also affected the underlying state structures. In fact, it has been a matter of attuning the state to the norms and values of African society, many of which have their origin in pre-colonial society. It becomes necessary to trace this process in greater detail with respect to three key relationships:

1. politicians and administrators,
2. staff inside the service, and
3. bureaucrats and the public. This framework builds on previous efforts, e.g., by Peters (1988) and Pierre (1995), to create a pragmatic, middle-range theory for the study of administration.

Politicians and Administrators

During the colonial period, the politicians that controlled the colonial service were not on the ground in Africa, but located in the metropolitan capitals. This physical distance created an organizational distance that mattered. Administrators in the colonies enjoyed a definite degree of autonomy and could make discretionary decisions with important ramifications for the indigenous population. This changed with independence and the emergence of an African cadre of nationalist politicians. The latter clearly wanted to create a new order by reversing many of the principal features of colonial administration. Although the extent to which this ambition was put into practice varied from one country to another (e.g., Hyden, 1995), the tendency in that direction was ubiquitous across Africa.

At the rhetorical level, this widespread political effort to revamp the civil service was driven by a well-intended aspiration to do what the nationalist politicians believed the colonial administration had ignored: benefit the majority of the indigenous population. As a result, populist development policies were pursued regardless of cost and feasibility. The views of civil servants were largely ignored and they had little choice but to comply with the whims of the politicians. The alternative was losing their job. A study that reviewed the first ten years of public administration, reflecting the views of senior civil servants, drew attention to "undue" politicization as the most serious issue affecting civil service performance in Anglophone African countries (Rweyemamu & Hyden, 1975).

To promote their development aspirations, politicians became increasingly interested in using affective or ascriptive rather than professional criteria for hiring and promoting civil servants at the senior level. The formal relations that had been laid down in constitutions, laws, and procedures were thrown to the side in favor of a set of informal rules that made the politicians undisputed rulers and confirmed a number of other pre-modern features of African society, notably patriarchy. For instance, it was not unusual that the head of state insisted that he be referred to as the Father of the Nation. This "Big Man" approach has been identified as a principal characteristic of African politics. It is at the root of clientelism and the "weak state" syndrome that so many observers and analysts have identified (e.g., Chabal & Daloz, 1999; Herbst, 2000; Hyden, 2006).

Because power is being held in a personal rather than official capacity in these societies, it is being exercised in a dispersed and unpredictable manner. The civil service which was the backbone of the state in colonial days has been broken. The informal institutions that have replaced the formal relations between politicians and administrators tend to dominate the outcome of what government does. It is not policy but patronage that determines these outcomes. Growing involvement by international agencies in economic policy and governance reforms has only marginally helped to create a more predictable policy environment. The very institutional foundation on which a professional civil service can be built has been undermined.

Staff Relations

The internal administration of the public service provides another measure of how individual officers behave. The academic debate on this issue has centered largely on how much behavior is shaped by universal organizational norms or by factors external to the organization. The former suggests that organizational behavior is the same regardless of culture while the latter implies that it is a reflection of structures in society.

Among the latter, Price (1975) has argued that policies based on purposive rationality will emerge in Africa only when administrative elites become isolated from the rest of society in the same way as Calvinists and Leninists did in European countries. This argument is in line with a historicist approach that sees the character of administration being a reflection of the broader development of society (cf. also Riggs, 1964; Hyden, 1983). Advocates of this approach have also been generally skeptical toward effective transplantation of institutions and management approaches derived from experiences in developed societies.

The organization theorists, on the other hand, point out that African subordinates respond to administrative systems in very much the same way as they do in Western societies. The pressure of authority in organizations is such a dominating reality that it evokes a universal, cross-cultural response (Leonard, 1977). Managers may exercise their authority differently, but the result is the same as Dzakpasu (1978) demonstrated in a study of an African public company. Protagonists of this approach are generally optimistic about the prospect for improving administrative performance. Instead of assuming that improved performance has to await social and political changes in society, they tend to look for organizational enclaves where managers enjoy enough autonomy from political interference to actually engage in effective management (Leonard, 1991).

These two approaches are not necessarily mutually exclusive and the image of administration and management of African public services is both more complex and differentiated as a study of high-level civil servants in nine eastern and southern African countries indicates (Montgomery, 1987). The author tests five different assumptions that have been made about relations between senior and junior officers in African administrations:

1. African administrative systems are more like personal fiefdoms than modern organizations;
2. African managers are indifferent to policy issues;
3. these managers are driven more by ideological fantasies than performance issues;
4. public managers tend to denigrate private sector entrepreneurship; and
5. African administration is too rigid to change.

When probing these theses in the nine countries, the study revealed four of them emerged in recognizable form. Even if the personalistic interpretation of African administration may be oversimplified, it manifests itself in various forms, both positive and negative. For instance, personalism at least in part explains why African managers showed real concern with the incompetence of their subordinates. At the same time, these managers turned a blind eye to corruption and concerned themselves much less with national goals and public welfare than checking on how colleagues and subordinates behave. Much of what these managers were asked to record of their daily schedule was quite trivial, like expressing disapproval of specific behavioral attributes of their subordinates. The study also shows that internal organizational matters far outweigh other considerations in the day-to-day management of public organizations. Managers devote far more attention to issues of internal resource distribution than on trying to achieve policy objectives. Policy issues filled only a minor part of the agenda of top public servants in the nine countries. Turf battles and "bureaucratic politics" occupied much more of their time.

The only image of African administration that was not supported by the data was that these senior managers are driven by ideological or political fantasies. Interaction with cabinet ministers rarely involved the discussion of political issues. By contrast, administrative arrangements feature quite often in these conversations. Negotiations were almost always internal with little or no pressure group politics influencing resource allocation. Dealings with the private sector, at least at that time, were almost non-existent. The relative unimportance of the private sector was confirmed by the study. This conclusion may not stand up to closer scrutiny today, but it does suggest that with the exception of multinational corporations, the managerial competence of the growing private sector is an issue.

Finally, the study confirmed that senior managers in the public service in Africa are reluctant to take innovative measures to change the incentive structure and the existing assignment of tasks. These managers showed much greater readiness to resolve issues than to deal with process matters that typically involved appeals to higher authority or coordination with senior colleagues. Again, the image of the African administrator is that he or she is most comfortable when acting alone. The "publicness" of the role is often deliberately avoided.

Relations between senior and junior officers in the public service in African countries is a topic in need of further study, but whatever subsequent evidence available tends to confirm Montgomery's findings. Appiah (2004), for example, found that the dominance of generalists tend to have detrimental effects on professionalization of the public service. He sees the top civil servants being too rule-oriented at the expense of being concerned with the interests and welfare of clients. Even when hired on professional grounds they get caught in neo-patrimonial arrangements that limit their own development and service to the public (Gran, 2004).

At least one other study, however, suggests that staff relations based on personal acquaintance are not inevitably harmful to performance. Umeh and Andranovich (2005, p. 129) conclude that in the African administrative context, it is not uncommon to find two individuals (senior and junior cadres) maintaining a highly paternalistic and trusting relationship simply because they both, for instance, attended the same educational institution or were colleagues in some capacity prior to joining the organization they both work for. The power distance between senior and junior staff in Africa, to borrow the concept developed by Hofstede (1991), is quite long but it functions in a benevolent manner.

Bureaucrats and the Public

The public service is meant to be a means to an end, not an end in itself. Civil servants are hired in order to deliver services and amenities to the public. Historical experience has confirmed, however, that bureaucrats easily ignore their role in society, especially if there are no pressures on them to perform the role as servants of the public. This problem has been addressed in developed societies through democratic means. Citizens are allowed to organize with a view to lobbying government as well as holding officials accountable for their decisions and actions. The evolution of a purposive bureaucracy that is also responsive to public demands has taken place parallel to the institutionalization of democracy. The African region lacks a democratic legacy. A client-oriented bureaucracy operating in a civic context, therefore, should not be expected.

Civic space is the outgrowth of a society in which thinking long-term, accepting abstract rules, and acknowledging interdependence comes naturally to individual actors. Such a society is inevitably modern, relies on a market-based economy, and rests on the principle of rule of law. Furthermore, it is typically a society of relative plenty. "Civicness" is more easily pursued in conditions of plenty than poverty. It encourages discourse on issues of principle with a claim to universal validity.

Affective space is prominent in societies like those in Africa that are still characterized by pre-modern features. The formal institutions of a market economy are weak and the idea that rules are independent of human agency is not widely embraced. Such space tends to foster compliance and

TABLE 1
Comparison of Civic and Affective Spaces of Communication

Type of Space	Action level	Interaction behavior	Claims of validity	Effects
Civic	Principles	Discursive	Universal	Enhancing citizen voice
Affective	Concrete action	Compliant	Local	Strengthening loyalty

a preference for claims of validity based on concrete and tangible results. Adhering to the norm of reciprocity, people want to see that what officials promise is also delivered. How it is achieved does not matter. The differences between civic and affective space are summarized in Table 1.

Because affective space dominates over civic space in Africa associational life tends to be different from the civil society known from Western societies. The public's emphasis on immediate and tangible results makes associations vulnerable to failure. Because the existence of an organization is not dependent on a universal cause, but serving a particular local interest or preference, its legitimacy rests on a shallow and temporary foundation. Furthermore, organizations are often dominated by a single individual with persuasive personal qualities. Because of the dominant role of such an individual, relations in most of these organizations tend to be personalized. Criticism is discouraged and viewed as a sign of disloyalty. Rules and procedures are often ignored in order to make things work the way the leader wants it. In short, many of the features that are associated with the Big Man syndrome in politics can be found also in associational life outside government in African countries.

There is no denying that African countries have a rich associational life of their own but the vast majority of organizations are community-based and focused on local problem-solving. They serve an important role in local communities and contexts but they have little, if any, influence on how government bureaucrats operate. These organizations do not operate according to a particular plan but instead function in response to need. Holding public officials accountable is not what these organizations are all about. International non-governmental organizations operating in Africa try to take this accountability relation seriously but their ability to be effective is hampered by the perception in government circles that as foreign entities they have no right to question local officials. The result is, as Montgomery's study indicates, that African bureaucrats are quite aloof from public interests and responses (Montgomery, 1987, p. 916). They are demonstrably less public-oriented than they are concerned with personal matters.

Foreign donor governments have tried to step in and strengthen public accountability by not only insisting on it in their own relations with African counterpart institutions but also help fostering the growth of local accountability

31

mechanisms. Support of parliament and national audit offices are cases in point. Such initiatives notwithstanding, local capacity for holding government officials accountable remains weak. African governments continue to see their accountability relationship with donors as more significant than the one with local constituencies.

IMPLICATIONS FOR PUBLIC SECTOR REFORM

Because the administrative realities in African countries constitute an intractable mixture of formal and informal rules, with the latter often determining choice and behavior, ever since independence there has been plenty of calls for reform. It is possible to identify three generations of administrative reform. The ideas of the development administration movement translated into the recommendations of the first-generation reforms in Africa during the late 1960s and early 1970s.[1] They focused on reforming organizational structures and management practices and creating new and more favorable incentive structures. The reforms that took place in the former British colonies were also influenced by the Fulton Commission in the United Kingdom which submitted its report in 1968 on reforms in the British civil service. Despite their high profile, these first-generation reforms resulted in few sustainable changes. Many recommendations were simply shelved. The introduction of fresh career lines did little to boost motivation and performance. The quality of African public services deteriorated throughout the 1970s (Hyden, 1983; Balogun, 2003).

A second generation of reforms began in the 1980s in the wake of the Structural Adjustment Programs (SAPs) that African governments were obliged to adopt in order to obtain further credit from the international finance institutions (The International Monetary Fund and the World Bank). Because of the over-extended, inefficient, and unproductive nature of African public services, this generation of reform focused on downsizing government and relying on a greater role of the private and voluntary sectors in generating business and delivering services. Over a period of a decade beginning in the mid-1980s, employment in public services was significantly reduced, in some countries as much as by one-third. With privatization of public corporations, however, came problems of a different kind: transfer of ownership to foreign owners, quarrels over public-private partnerships, and a rise in graft, a form of corruption that had been virtually absent before this time in Africa (Ouma, 1991; Awortwi, 2004).

The second generation of reforms was relatively easy in an administrative perspective. Downsizing meant attention had to be paid to compensation schemes, but the issue was more economic and political than it was administrative. The same effort also generated the need for restructuring departments along fresh functional lines. Again, this was relatively straightforward.

It is the third generation of reforms that began in the late 1990s which have proved particularly challenging because they aim at reversing negative performance trends in a positive direction within the public services. Although much has been made of the origin and inspiration of these reforms in New Public Management (NPM) that began in New Zealand and spread to many other developed countries around the world before becoming "mainstream" in public sector reforms also in developing countries, the reform agenda sounds like an echo of the past. The expected outcomes of the reforms are

1. improved delivery of services to the public;
2. improved economic and financial management;
3. better public resource utilization;
4. the adoption of new management techniques; and
5. decentralization of authority to local government entities (Larbi, 1995; Olowu, 1999; Awortwi, 2003).

None of this is really new and the question is whether circumstances are more congenial for success this time around.

Public sector reforms are difficult and challenging in any environment. A study of the political economy of administrative reform in six middle-income countries in Asia, Central Europe, and Latin America[2] revealed that political factors are very important in shaping the outcome of reforms (Heredia & Schneider, 2003). Two specific observations are of interest here. One is that the prospects for administrative reform are dimmer in countries where the bureaucratic and political elites are fused (as they were for decades in Mexico and Thailand). The other is that when a new generation of political leaders come to power they are more likely than their predecessors to embark on reform. This "New Broom" argument has also been made with reference to a study of civil service reform in Uganda (Kjaer, 2002). A change of regime may create opportunities for reform that would otherwise not exist.

The third generation of reforms is wide-ranging and includes several dimensions. Heredia and Schneider (2003, p. 3) distinguish among three models of reform:

---

[1] Most Anglophone countries had major reviews of their own. The most notable in terms of their political visibility were the Ndegwa Commission in Kenya, the Udoji Commission in Nigeria, the Mills-Odoi Commission in Ghana, and the Wamalwa Commission in Swaziland. Interestingly, the persons after whom these commissions were named were all senior civil servants who had been trained in colonial days and promoted to top positions following independence. They also had one other thing in common: they became founding members of the African Association for Public Administration and Management (AAPAM) in 1971.

[2] The six countries included are Argentina, Brazil, Chile, Hungary, Mexico, and Thailand.

1. civil service reforms;
2. accountability reforms; and,
3. managerial reforms.

Each requires a bit of elaboration. The first type of reform is aimed at reducing particularism and politicization of the bureaucracy by enhancing the role that merit plays in recruitment, promotion, and tenure in the service. The second aims at strengthening legislative oversight and transparency in the service. The third aims at making the service more efficient and service-oriented through decentralization and more attractive incentives in pay and employment schemes. Each one of them carries a definite NPM signature.

The experience of the middle-income countries is that managerial reforms tend to be the easier, with accountability reforms, especially those focusing on transparency, being more problematic. The most difficult ones to implement, however, are the civil service reforms. The basic difficulty facing those seeking to professionalize the civil service is that moving from discretionary to merit-based recruitment and promotion deprives superiors of one of their crucial levers of power (Heredia & Schneider, 2004, p. 22). This loss of power, in conjunction with the technical and administrative complexities inherent in setting up and operating a merit-based personnel system make the enforcement costs of civil service reform particularly high.

It would be wrong to reduce the character of the administrative reforms in the middle-income countries to just "fine-tuning," but all six have a long legacy of public administration with roots in the country's culture and economy and there has been something solid to build upon. The reforms that have been attempted in Africa include more basic reforms such as controlling the numbers and costs of employment in the public services and rationalizing and restructuring of the service. For instance, despite the successful downsizing in the 1980s, public services across Africa have begun to grow again. Similarly, despite commitment to decentralization, the power of the ministerial headquarters continues to weigh heavy on local government level personnel. Presidents have been reluctant to reduce the number of ministerial positions that they use as patronage. For example, Kenya and Uganda have governments with 70 ministers; the Tanzanian Government has 60[3] (Kiragu & Mutahaba 2006, p. 6).

The strategy among reform-sponsoring agencies has been to launch system-wide projects. They have adopted the conventional rhetoric of administration which proclaims that explicit, comprehensive planning of administrative structures is possible and necessary and that piecemeal change only creates chaos (March & Olsen, 1983, p. 282). It is not clear, however, how effective such a strategy is in situations where the administrative realm tends to be driven by factors over which civil servants have little control, notably political decisions. Some analysts have suggested an alternative approach that considers identifying opportunities for improvement in organizational settings where the chances for making a difference are great. There is evidence from around Africa that even in the face of an overall dismal record governments have at least some agencies that function well enough to serve as models for others (Daland, 1981; Strauss, 1998). Daland refers to such agencies as "pockets of productivity" and believes that they can be used for spreading reforms to other agencies.

The reason why there are relatively few such pockets of productivity in African governments is because clientelist relations and patronage politics are so pervasive. Reformers continue to fail bringing about durable change of institutional rules to enhance performance. Their efforts may spur some changes in the short-term but they are very hard to sustain and institutionalize. A main reason why reforms falter is that political office-bearers are more interested in the status quo because it perpetuates clientelism and rent-seeking. Thus, champions of reform have to be found elsewhere, notably among the professional ranks within the civil service. Experience from countries like Mozambique and Tanzania, which have been relatively successful in reforming their public sector, confirms that such champions have been in the forefront of these efforts. The problem with reliance on such outstanding individuals is that because of their success they are easily recruited by international agencies for work at a different level. This is what happened to the reform champions in Mozambique and Tanzania. The lack of continuity at the top level is a serious problem because judging from experience in other countries, e.g., the United States bureaucratic reform requires long-term commitment, patience, and perseverance (Brown, 1977).

The emphasis that the World Bank and other donors have placed on "quick-wins," i.e., reforms that can be implemented quickly and at little cost, is important for getting a momentum but the real challenge is how to sustain the reform process when resistance is becoming more explicit.

As long as such resistance is championed by political leaders who view administrative reforms as threats to their control of patronage, this challenge remains overwhelming. It gets no easier from the fact that many civil servants prefer to hide behind the security that hierarchical relations of authority inside ministries and departments offer. The model of administration that was inherited from the colonial powers is not wholly irrelevant. It serves the interest of those civil servants who fear change.

Even though it may be argued that administrative reform ought to be easier in African countries than elsewhere because the civil service is less rigidly institutionalized and competition between different modes of organizational behavior creates unexpected opportunities for change, the situation is more accurately described as "conflict-ridden" (Kayizzi-Mugerwa 2003, p. 346). The politicians have their

---

[3]These figures include deputy and/or assistant ministers.

TABLE 2
Differences Between Competing Models of Administration in Africa

Dimension/source	Neo-Patrimonialism	Colonial Model	New Public Management
Organizational Objective	Power maintenance	Law-and-order	Development
Service rationale	Ruler	Rule	Result
Organizational Structure	Patriarchal	Hierarchical	Team-based
Operational mode	Discretionary	Mechanistic	Organic
Staff orientation	Upward	Inward	Outward
Career System	Favoritist	Fixed and closed	Flexible and open
Handling of wrongs	Blaming others	Denying responsibility	Learning lesson

own neo-patrimonialist approach that calls into question the forms associated with the model inherited from the colonial powers. In addition, there are the reformers who wish to introduce a results-oriented way of organizing the public sector. The difference between these models or approaches is summarized in Table 2.

These competing models are responsible for producing a hybrid administrative reality where norms shift and it is difficult to know which one is decisive where and when. Administrative culture in African countries, therefore, is not captured in one formula.

CONCLUSION

In trying to understand administrative culture, Africa is not an exception but is, instead, an outlier. Many of the features that have been described here as typical of African systems of administration are found elsewhere. Political interference in administrative organization is not unique to Africa, n is the lack of a long-term commitment to administrative reform. What makes African countries different, however, is the absence of an indigenous state and administrative tradition to build on.

The efforts by political leaders since independence to reshape the government structures that they inherited from the colonial powers could be described as a process of manufacturing a set of alternative norms derived from African society. This process, however, has focused more on changing the broader state-society relations and the result has been a subversion of the norms associated with the colonial administration. It has also limited the extent to which administrative reforms are feasible because the conflict between indigenous and foreign norms makes it very difficult to know where to start and how to proceed. That is why administrative reform efforts that build on the conventional rhetoric that it must be comprehensive rather than piecemeal, standardized rather than adapted to local circumstances, tend to fall short of their objectives.

Foreign consultants serving as advocates of administrative reform in Africa have been reluctant to consider the complex character of administrative culture and have acted as if change could come both quickly and widely. Given the dismal record of such reform efforts, it may be important to remember that the long-term development of political and administrative institutions is typically less a product of intentions, plans, and consistent decisions than incremental adaptation to changing problems and circumstances. The implication, as one observer has noted, is that administrative development is less a matter of engineering than of gardening; less a matter of hunting than of gathering (Szanton, 1981, p. 24). African countries are still in the process of growing, if not manufacturing, their own administrative culture.

REFERENCES

Adamolekun, L. (1999). *Public administration in Africa*. Boulder, CO: Westview Press.

Adu, A.L. (1969). *The civil service in Commonwealth Africa*. London: Allen & Unwin.

Appiah, F. (2004). The politics of professionalization, Africanization and reorganization of the post-colonial Ghanaian civil service. In F. Appiah, D.P. Chimanikire, and T. Gran (Eds.), *Professionalism and good governance in Africa* (pp. 87–120). Copenhagen: Liber.

Awortwi, N. (2003). *Getting the fundamentals wrong: Governance of multiple modalities of basic services delivery in three Ghanaian cities*. Maastricht: Shaker Publishing.

Awortwi, N. (2004). Getting the fundamentals wrong: Woes of public-private partnerships in solid waste collection in three Ghanaian cities. *Public Administration and Development*, 24(3), 213–224.

Balogun, J. (2003). Leadership and agency governance: The search for the common cause of excellence in the African public service. In United Nations, *Leadership and social transformation in the public sector: Moving from challenges to solutions*. New York: United Nations.

Brown, D.S. (1977). Reforming the bureaucracy: Some suggestions for the president. *Public Administration Review*, 37, 163–170.

Cameron, D. (1937). Native administration in Nigeria and Tanganyika. *Journal of the Royal African Society*, 36(November), 1–16.

Chabal, P., & Daloz, J.-F. (1999). *Africa works: Disorder as political instrument*. Oxford, UK: James Currey.

Daland, R. (1981). *Exploring Brazilian bureaucracy: Performance and pathology*. Washington, DC: University Press of America.

Dia, M. (1995). *Africa's management in the 1990s and beyond: Reconciling indigenous and transplanted institutions*. Washington, DC: The World Bank.

Dzakpasu, C. K. (1978). Modern management techniques in public enterprise and training in Africa. *African Administrative Studies*, 19, 65–70.

Goody, J. (1971). *Technology, tradition and the state in Africa*. Cambridge: Cambridge University Press.

Gran, T. (2004). In conclusion: Resistance to 'traditional' modernization, deconstruction of the modernizing state and the increased importance of cultured professionalism. In F. Appiah, D.P. Chimanikire, & T. Gran (Eds.), *Professionalism and good governance in Africa* (pp. 293–303). Copenhagen: Liber.

Herbst, J. (2000). *States and power in Africa: Lessons in authority and control*. Princeton, NJ: Princeton University Press.

Heredia, B., & Schneider, R.B. (Eds.). (2003). *Reinventing Leviathan: The politics of administrative reform in developing countries*. Miami: North-South Center.

Hofstede, G. (1991). *Cultures and organizations: Software of the mind*. New York: McGraw-Hill.

Hyden, G. (1980). *Beyond Ujamaa in Tanzania: Underdevelopment and an uncaptured peasantry*. Berkeley: University of California Press.

Hyden, G. (1983). *No shortcuts to progress: African development management in perspective*. London: Heinemann Educational Books.

Hyden, G.(1995). Public administration in developing countries: Kenya and Tanzania in comparative perspective. In J. Pierre (Ed.), *Bureaucracy in the modern state* (pp. 161–184). London: Edward Elgar.

Hyden, G. (2006). *African politics in comparative perspective*. New York: Cambridge University Press.

Kayizzi-Mugerwa, S. (Ed.). (2003). *Reforming Africa's institutions: Ownership, incentives, and capabilities*. Tokyo: United Nations University Press.

Kiragu, K., & Mutahaba, G. (2006). *Public service reform in Eastern and Southern Africa—Issues and challenges*. Dar es Salaam: Mkuki na Nyota Publishers.

Kjaer, M. (2002). *The politics of civil service reform: A comparative analysis of Uganda and Tanzania in the 1990s*. Aarhus: Politica.

Larbi, G.A. (1995). The role of government in adjusting economies: Implications and impact of structural adjustment on the civil service: The case of Ghana. London: Overseas Development Administration.

Lee, J.M. (1967). *Colonial development and good government*. London: Oxford University Press.

Leonard, D. K. (1977). *Reaching the peasant farmer: Organization theory and practice in Kenya*. Chicago: University of Chicago Press.

Leonard, D. K. (1991). *African successes: Four public managers of rural development*. Berkeley: University of California Press.

Lugard, F. D. (1965) (1922). *The dual mandate in British Tropical Africa*. London: Frank Cass.

Mamdani, M. (1996). *Citizen and subject: Contemporary Africa and the legacy of late colonialism*. Princeton, NJ: Princeton University Press.

March, J. G., & Olsen, J. P. (1983). Organizing political life: What administrative reorganization tells us about government. *American Political Science Review, 77*(2), 281–296.

Montgomery, J. (1987). Probing managerial behavior: Image and reality in Southern Africa *World Development, 17*(7), 911–929.

Olowu, D. (1999). Redesigning African civil service reforms. *Journal of Modern African Studies, 37*(1), 1–23.

Ouma, S.O.A. (1991). Corruption in public policy and its impact on development: The case of Uganda since 1979. *Public Administration and Development, 11*(5), 472–490.

Peters, G. (1988). *Comparing public bureaucracies*. Tuscaloosa: University of Alabama Press.

Pierre, J. (1995). *Bureaucracy in the modern state: An introduction to comparative public administration*. London: Edward Elgar.

Price, R. (1975). *Society and bureaucracy in contemporary Ghana*. Berkeley: University of California Press.

Riggs, F. (1964). *Administration in developing countries*. Boston: Houghton Mifflin.

Rweyemamu, A. H., & Hyden, G. (eds.), (1975). *A decade of public administration in Africa*. Nairobi: East African Literature Bureau.

Schaffer, B. (1969). The deadlock of development administration. In C. T. Leys (Ed.). Politics and change in developing countries. Cambridge: Cambridge University Press.

Smith, B.C. (1967). *Field administration*. London: Routledge & Kegan Paul.

Strauss, J. (1988). *Strong institutions in weak polities: State building in Republican China 1927–1940*. Oxford, UK: Clarendon Press.

Szanton, P. (ed.) (1981). *Federal reorganization: What have we learned?* Chatham, NJ: Chatham Press.

Thompson, V. (1964). Administrative objectives for development administration. *Administrative Science Quarterly, 9*(1), 91–108.

Umeh, O. J., & Andranovich. G. (2005). *Culture, development and public administration in Africa*. Hartford CT: Kumarian Press.

Bureaucratic Culture and the Social-Political Connection: The Bangladesh Example

Habib Zafarullah

Department of Sociology and Criminology, University of New England, Armidale, Australia

This article identifies some of the principal attributes of bureaucratic culture in Bangladesh from historical, social and political standpoints. The Bangladesh case is placed within a broad conceptual perspective that relates to the developing world situation. The peculiar traits of the Bangladesh bureaucracy epitomize a close connection with the political process, an inclination for self-preservation, domination of the policymaking structures, and a propensity to maintain clientelism in society. While working behind a façade of legal-rationalism, bureaucrats are not reluctant to indulge in unethical practices. Efforts at reform have been quashed or delayed, as the bureaucracy tends to retain its autonomous character. The peculiarities of the bureaucracy serve to deter change and development and pose a problem for democratic governance.

INTRODUCTION

A theme widely deliberated and revisited is bureaucratic culture—a manifestation that exists in every society with organized political and administrative systems. The attributes of this culture, which generally mirror wider social values, obviously vary from one society to another being conditioned by general societal mores, norms, customs and traditions as well as by bureaucrats' orientations, beliefs, and propensities which they acquire through education, training, and professional development and intellectual and ideological persuasions. Apart from external stimuli, certain variables internal to the bureaucracy, such as structure, authority relationships, rules, and procedures, also shape bureaucratic culture. Thus, the concept may be redefined as configurations of behavior that typify the totality of distinctive values, beliefs, assumptions, sentiments, orientations, and attitudes shared by members of a bureaucracy (Waldo, 1965; Almond & Powell, 1966; Smith, 1974; Nachmias & Rosenbloom, 1978).

In post-colonial societies where the development of political institutions is delayed or is still in a nascent stage, the bureaucracy, because of its colonial legacy and institutionalized status, has taken advantage of the inexperience and imprudence of parties and politicians in gaining the upper hand in governing. The "overdeveloped" institutionalized bureaucracy is in a much stronger position to provide vital inputs to the governmental process in relation to other lesser-developed institutions in the political and civil space by virtue of its stability, expertise, and control over resources (Smith, 2003; Peters, 2009).

Most institutional bureaucracies have pronounced sub-system autonomy and a remarkable ability of adapting themselves to and shaping their environments (Almond & Powell, 1966). This endows them with an unmistakable distinctiveness, which accompanied by their propensity to directly involve themselves in political affairs, including an obvious role in statecraft in some cases, can make them a highly politicized institution in society. The bureaucracy then becomes a zealous participant in the political process especially if it "can accommodate its values in harmony with greater political influence" (Smith, 1974, p. 36).

For a bureaucracy to be a major partner in the political process it must be in accord with the political elite on key governance and policy issues and have the capacity to work together with it either for the public good or to promote its parochial interests. The level of political involvement would depend on bureaucrats' perceptions, political beliefs, judgments, and values about the political system in which they operate as well as the degree of external influences. As Wilson (1993, p. 435) argues: "The long-term character of a bureaucracy is not determined by the technical tasks it confronts but by the political and social forces operating on it."

While societal and political cultural factors shape the mind-set of bureaucrats and define the relationship of the bureaucracy with the political structures and the general public, the interplay between this relationship with the internal operational forms and organizational dynamics of the public administrative system actually determine the nature of bureaucratic culture. However, while insight into bureaucratic orientations and perceptions may provide indicators about the cultural traits of a bureaucracy, this may not always reflect the manner in which civil servants actually behave at the organizational level and the nature of their relationship with the political system or the general public. Indeed, bureaucratic schizophrenia can be both chronic and acute in any administrative system and the syndrome can have contagious effect and overpower, in varying degrees, almost every member of the bureaucracy. Thus, the actual behavior of bureaucrats may not reflect their professed wisdom conditioned by their orientations, perceptions, and so on. Some bureaucrats may portray themselves to be one in thought and another in action. Thus, any objective study of bureaucratic culture needs to examine discrepancies between these two behavioral manifestations.

This article explore and assess the cardinal cultural properties of the bureaucracy in Bangladesh.[1] However, this is not a detailed exposition of the syndrome, but rather it provides a synoptic perspective of the main themes that epitomize its character.

ESSENCE OF BUREAUCRATIC CULTURE IN BANGLADESH

The Historical Bequest

The British colonial legacy and the patterns of government administration in post-colonial Pakistan have significantly influenced the cultural makeup of the bureaucracy in Bangladesh. The bureaucracy, especially the Civil Service of Pakistan (CSP), an elitist-generalist corps with an "ICS-steel frame" pedigree and bred in the Oxbridge tradition,

assumed virtual control over the governmental process in the absence of effective political institutions in the country. Military intervention in politics provided the bureaucracy the opportunity to take on extra-bureaucratic roles and carry on tasks normally assigned to political representatives. The bureaucratization of politics was ingeniously perfected by the military-turned-civilian regime, which was mainly concerned with entrenching itself in power. Politics and bureaucracy were entwined and served as an impediment to democratic governance rather than altruistically addressing goals of nation building and development.

The bureaucracy was the exclusive source for inputs into the policy process—from problem identification and agenda setting to implementation and evaluation—and its dominance over state affairs stemmed from a unique ethos that nurtured elitism, conservatism, and inertia. Bureaucrats were highly motivated to advance their power and authority in the command structure and to maintain their social "prestige" and "esteem." Over-commitment to career concerns and an extraordinary appetite for greater control over the state apparatus drove them to adopt tactics that transformed the bureaucracy into a self-regulatory institution largely insulated from political control. Their penchant for self-preservation aborted every concerted move by political executives (both parliamentary and presidential) to reform the administrative system and guaranteed the retention of the status quo until the dismemberment of the country (Pakistan) in 1971 (Khan, 1980). Concurrently, the contradictions between the value patterns of the bureaucracy and those of the political elite in the opposition camp sharpened.

Society-Bureaucracy Connection

Like other post-colonial developing societies, Bangladesh was bequeathed a bureaucratic apparatus founded on the Weberian style and procedures that conflict with prevailing indigenous societal values and norms and, therefore, unable to cope with the demands of the community it serves. The degree of incongruity between norms and realties is fairly high; what is actually prescribed often remains unenforced (see Riggs, 1962). Laws made with good intents and based on apparent sound reasons, are forsaken because of bureaucratic failures or abused to accommodate cliquish or partisan demands.

In independent Bangladesh, the "new" bureaucracy, crystallized from the remnants of the CSP and other central services in Pakistan as well as the old provincial services, failed to abandon the ingrained cultural traits acquired through the internalization of values from the past and the contemporary societal environment. In fact, the bureaucracy acquired new characteristics that reflected prevailing social, political, administrative, and economic realities. Structural and procedural changes to the political-administrative system, the transformation of the public sector, fierce competition for

---

[1]This article is based on two spells of surveys of civil servants' perceptions undertaken in Dhaka (Bangladesh). These surveys were based on structured questionnaires and respondents were randomly chosen from several ministries. See Zafarullah (1991, 2000). These were followed up with sporadic interviews with senior civil servants during yearly field trips to the country. In these unstructured interviews, interviewees were given leeway to give their personal views on several issues raised in this article and about future directions. Several civil servants in key positions and some retired ones were randomly interviewed.

civil service positions, economic liberalization programs, the growth of the private sector, growing unemployment, fall in real income, rising poverty among the masses, increasing delinquency, the primacy of the black market economy, unproductive government spending, and social degeneration have resulted in significant changes in the bureaucratic value system.

Bureaucratism and Social/Community Obligations

The social-cultural-political architecture of many so-called "Third World" countries manifests certain traits, historically acquired and socially embedded, that have had remarkable influences on bureaucratic demeanor. One such attribute is "clientelism" or patron-client relationship that has existed in almost all societies since time immemorial. It is a form of "asymmetric but mutually beneficial relationships of power and exchange, a non-universalistic quid pro quo between individuals or groups of unequal standing" (Roniger, 2004, p. 353). In administrative systems, it involves distribution of patronage or favors of officials to citizens or clients in return for support or pecuniary gains.

In Bangladesh, such objectivity of the legal-rational administrative system is often compromised when bureaucrats are entrapped in clientelism. Decisions are then subjected to personal negotiations and bargaining, and policies and rules are twisted to satisfy family and community obligations. Traditional loyalties expect public officials to be more accommodating towards "a law of social conduct" or religious order than being deferential towards formally stipulated roles. Clearly, the norms of impersonality injected by Western ideas and entrenched by colonialism are undercut by social compulsions. The bureaucracy and the public are socialized into a barter culture regulated by clientelism. Presumably, bureaucratic patronage and nepotism generate positive outcomes in maintaining family and social ties but their implications for bureaucratic ethics can be extensively damaging.

People who derive benefits from their transactions with public organizations by applying personalistic and fraudulent techniques are comfortable with the bureaucracy, but those who are unable to establish a rapport with officials generally approve of the impersonal application of rules. A majority of higher civil servants in post-independence Bangladesh view the administrative system as exceedingly rigid to effectively respond to citizens' demands. They also approve of lower officials exercising greater discretion in decision-making. Bureaucrats prefer wider citizen influence in public policy and are clearly supportive of the free flow of information between the government and the public. Administrative performance, they maintain, is impaired by the wide gap between the bureaucracy and the people. Apparently, they prefer more egalitarianism in the government-citizen equation (Zafarullah, 1991, 2000; Jamil, 1999).

Influence of Legal-Rationalism

Patron-client relationships contravene the expected norm of "legal-rationalism" in a formalized bureaucracy based on a predetermined legal order enforceable equitably and without discrimination in engagements between bureaucrats and citizens. Then again, "bureaucratism" or officials' excessive preoccupation with formalism (strict adherence to rules and regulations) can lead to rigidity, red tape, and denial of special needs of certain clients under extraordinary circumstances. Notions of equity and equality are often eschewed for the sake of maintaining a legal-rationalistic ethos.

Thus, in the Bangladesh bureaucracy, egalitarian sentiments, however, are not clearly reflected in the behavioral mannerisms that bureaucrats display in real life. Being intensely obsessed with procedural nitty-gritty in a highly centralized governmental framework, public officials are inclined to be overly bureaucratic and insensitive to citizens' needs (World Bank, 1996, 3–4; Zafarullah, 2002; Zafarullah & Khan, 2005). Public officials respond only when they have something to gain from the service they offer to individuals or groups (UNDP, 1993, 52). On most occasions, they portray themselves as administrative puritans strictly adhering to official norms and regulations and dispassionate in applying them regardless of the merit of specific circumstances. Clients consider such apathetic behavior as unaccommodating and unfair (Zafarullah et al., 2001). In the words of a senior bureaucrat: "Suspicion, disbelief, misbehavior and throwing about rules are the common weapons [a bureaucrat] generally employ[s] in treating the *lungi*-clad person daring to come up to him" (Siddiqui, 1996, p. 13). Specific instances and encounters by particular groups also highlight attitudinal problems in the bureaucracy (UNDP, 1993). This has caused a decline in the level of people's trust and confidence in the administrative system in providing basic services to the community (Consumark, 1995).

Penchant for Orthodoxy

The preference for traditional authority relationships—obedience and loyalty to and respect for superiors—and exacting compliance to rules in the bureaucracy are influenced by family and social mores. Bureaucratic structures conform to a strict pecking order rather than being egalitarian. Decision-making being concentrated at the highest levels of the administrative hierarchy, there is very little opportunity for junior officers to provide any input into the process. However, some balance in power distance and hierarchic relationship is restored when superiors reciprocate by being compassionate towards junior officers' needs and aspirations. This form of "personalised . . . interpersonal relations fosters group cohesion and solidarity" (Jamil, 1998, p. 416) and can be an important factor in reinforcing bureaucratization and bureaucratic elitism.

In general, Bangladesh bureaucrats' propensity towards the maintenance of the status quo is influenced by social traditions. Traditionally, people who are by nature lukewarm to change or modernization fear the possibility of the dismantling of traditional structures and resultant social dislocation. Bureaucrats mirror a similar kind of unease in approaching their work. As one study reports, "There is low tolerance for ambiguity among bureaucrats . . . [and they] are more concerned with rules than results. [T]here is not enough flexibility and room to adjust goals and procedures, and innovation in their place of work" (Jamil, 1998, p. 416).

Thus, bureaucratic resistance or inertia has foiled attempts at comprehensive administrative reform and democratic governments have succumbed to civil service pressures in waiting around or marking time.

Bureaucratic Autonomy

Bureaucracies, in general, are often self-governing and self-regulated, inherently geared to realize specific goals that serve bureaucratic interests with the support of complementary networks. They act and react on their own volition and pursue a course of action that is consistent with their thinking and independently of other social, political, and economic institutions (Skocpol, 1985; Carpenter, 2001).

The Bangladesh bureaucracy displays the attributes of an institutionalized entity. For years, the bureaucracy has preserved itself as an exclusive group. Its modes of operation and procedures of interaction gained acceptance in society despite its value system being generally dissimilar from those attributable to the political elite or the general populace. These values along with the goals it pursues and sorts of social relationships it engages in have enabled its institutionalization within the political system and conditioned its interactions with other groups and institutions in society. Frequent regime interruptions in the past and discouraging performance of successive political leadership unwittingly have induced citizens to rely on the enduring bureaucracy.

Historically, people are more acquainted with governmental organizations than representative institutions such as parliament. For instance, people in the rural areas can easily relate to the more visible local council officers than those who represent them in parliament. Indeed, the bureaucracy,

with its distinctiveness as a special social group, . . . maintains itself as a subsystem with pronounced autonomy. A permanent career with scope for continued advancement affords bureaucrats opportunities to effectively utilize their expertise, specialization and professionalism in the governing process. There is a general conviction among a large number of civil servants about their "capability." While they do not champion themselves as guardians of the public interest, they firmly believe that the bureaucracy can better manage the problems of the country and that administrative decisions

they make should be insulated from political considerations. (Zafarullah, 2007, p. 166)

There is a general scorn toward politicians because of the way they handle political management. Bureaucrats consider their role as critical in governance and this is engendered by their perception of themselves "as the highly specialized exclusive source of policy advice and guidance for the government with "proven" experience and proficiency in accomplishing policy goals" (Zafarullah, 2007, p. 166). Yet, insofar policy making serves as a critical element in governance, a perception of "extreme political pressure" runs through the senior levels in the bureaucracy. This leads to the diminishing of bureaucratic autonomy as political demands sweep over policy imperatives (Aminuzzaman, 2012). Nonetheless, bureaucratic autonomy is also strengthened by the several bureaucratic cadres' remarkable ability to accommodate each other's interests and to operate as a cohesive group in spite of disagreements on many important policy and career issues.

Bureaucratic-Political "Nexus"

Writing at the end of the 19th century based on his direct experience with the American public administrative system of his time, Woodrow Wilson distinguished between the object of politics and the role of administration. He argued: "Although politics sets the tasks for administration, it should not be suffered to manipulate its offices" (Wilson, 1966, p. 371). The central thrust of his case was the protection of the administrative apparatus from political interference as he was deeply concerned with the politicizing influences of partisan politics and its impact on bureaucratic performance. However, with time, the association between politics and administration became so intense that the dichotomy became an aberration. In the contemporary world, be it in the advanced or developing societies, with the extensive involvement of public servants in governance and the policy process, the magnitude of politicization has ushered in a rethinking of the relationship, particularly its bearings on governmental performance and effectiveness. Despite a mismatch between political and bureaucratic normative styles, there will always remain a deep-rooted connection between the political and bureaucratic domains, be it constructive to realize societal goals or unrewarding insofar as it serves parochial interests, either political or bureaucratic.

The incongruity between the bureaucratic and political value systems manifesting itself after independence of the country led to the estrangement of the bureaucracy from the political hub, essentially to neutralize its power (Ahamad, 1980, p. 154). Soon after, the regime was forced to redefine its relationship with the bureaucracy and increasingly depend on it for its own political survival. The two stints of military-authoritarian rule granted the bureaucracy greater access to power and firmly lodged its members in strategic governmental positions. Consequently, the bureaucracy restored its lost position and made serious encroachments into the core of power politics.

The bureaucracy's political involvement, either direct or indirect, blurs the demarcating line between itself and the political system. The label—"constitutional bureaucracy" — can no longer be applied to the Bangladesh's civil services. It would be wrong to portray it as a neutral instrument of political authority. It has taken on the role of a direct participant in the political process even within a democratic framework. Yet, paradoxically, civil servants, in general, favor bureaucratic neutrality and non-partisanship as well as the separation of administrative functions from the political (Zafarullah, 1991, 2000) and this orientation has enabled the bureaucracy to adjust to political regimes of various complexions since independence.

The politicization of the bureaucracy intensified after democracy was restored in the early 1990s. Both governing parties to date—the Bangladesh Nationalist Party (BNP) and the Awami League (AL) have capitalized on the intense bureaucratic factionalism along functional and political lines, to serve their political interests. The upper echelons of the civil service are highly politicized and there is a strong sentiment running through the lower levels about the inappropriateness of appointing partisan bureaucrats to senior positions. The staffing pattern (especially the promotion process) in the civil service has, to a large measure, become the casualty of political manipulation with partisan bureaucratic support leaving members of the non-generalist cadres to experience the brunt of gratuitous decisions (Zafarullah & Khan, 2001).

The post-1990 BNP government initiated the politicization practice but its moves were subtle being confined to only a few top positions in the civil service. In comparison, the AL government that followed adopted more aggressive maneuvers to reward its adherents in the civil service with accelerated promotions or key positions in almost all state-run organizations. Other public organizations, including universities, regulatory and promotional bodies, nationalized banks, and so on also were not spared. With every alternating government since then the trend has gathered momentum and has now reached a point where almost all sectors of public life are dominated by diehard partisan loyalists keen to preserve and further ruling party interests. Confrontational party politics is mirrored within the bureaucracy with governing party loyalists hostile to those who are not (Zafarullah & Khan, 2001; Osman, 2010; Huque, 2011).

Ethics and Integrity

Civil servants' attitudes towards ethics, integrity, and accountability and their actual conduct or behavior at work and in their dealings with the public provide an interesting dimension of bureaucratic culture. Integrity and ethical conduct in officialdom are significant issues for governmental performance and cannot be compromised. Bureaucratic ethics constitute standards of acceptable behavior informed not only by Weberian ideals but also by traditional social-cultural norms of society. Ethics justify actions and decisions impartially and objectively made in an administrative setting, uphold accountability, promote integrity, challenge unprincipled behavior, and disprove of conflicts of interest. As public servants, bureaucrats are required to honestly, responsibly, and fairly serve the people and to be accountable for their actions.

However, there has been rapid erosion of bureaucratic morality in Bangladesh. Bureaucrats are known for evading responsibility, being self-indulgent, demonstrating capricious behavior in handling clients' needs, under-performing, infringing workplace rules, misusing official power and authority, permitting private considerations to influence decisions, and resorting to other dishonest activities. Corruption is endemic and all-encompassing throughout the administrative fabric (Ahmed, 1992; Kochanek, 1993; Transparency International, 1997; Zafarullah & Siddiquee, 2001). Yet, accountability mechanisms are inadequate and weak in protecting principles of ethics and moral conduct, while political and legal constraints on bureaucratic malfeasance are hard to apply (Siddiquee, 1999; Zafarullah, 2001; Mahmood, 2010; Parnini, 2011).

Determining bureaucratic perceptions on corruption and related issues is a delicate exercise. Public officials are extremely coy and guarded in relating their views on these subjects. However, they do acknowledge the inadequacy and ineffectiveness of existing instruments for addressing citizens' grievances against administrative action and are strong in their opinion about the necessity of creating an ombudsman. On the other hand, they resolutely disprove of external controls on the bureaucracy to ensure responsibility and accountability (Zafarullah, 1991).

Aversion to Change

Like most bureaucracies, in general (Caiden, 1991, p. 1), the civil service in Bangladesh has shown an extraordinary predilection to hang on to the established rather than readily accepting change in its status, structure, functions, and norms of engagement with extra-bureaucratic instrumentalities. It has been more at ease operating in a familiar environment employing conventional practices than embracing anything new or different. Thus attempts at substantial reform have been insidiously thwarted or delayed. Innovative interventions in improving efficiency and effectiveness, ensuring control and accountability, making public servants responsive to citizens' needs, and redefining relationships within officialdom and with external forces, such as the political leadership, have been prevented or restrained (Zafarullah, 2009), although these have attained success in their application in other Asian bureaucracies (Turner, 2002; Sarker, 2006; Samaratunge et al., 2008).

Public management reforms since the mid-1990s in many developing countries have conformed, more or less, with the New Public Management (NPM) paradigm foreshadowed in the changes brought about in Britain and the United States in the late-1980s. In the main, these reforms have focused on fiscal stability, managerial efficiency, state capacity, and public accountability and the means to achieving these included decentralization, privatization, subsidiarity, public sector austerity, public enterprise corporatization, application of information, and communications technology, and so on (Hood, 1995; Pollitt & Bouckaert, 2000; McCourt & Minogue, 2001).

In the early 1990s, very few junior and mid-level civil servants in Bangladesh were aware of these changes occurring elsewhere or about NPM itself. Interestingly, the World Bank had by then initiated its Structural Adjustment Program (SAP) and recommended comprehensive structural changes to Bangladesh's public sector. Surveyed officials indicated that they were only following directions from the top or from external consultants on ways to carry out the SAP. They were not fully made acquainted with the pros and cons of externally induced structural reforms (Zafarullah, 2000). However, a 2000 World Bank survey indicated public officials' concern for over-centralized control, limited delegation of responsibilities down through the hierarchy, and unsound budget management—key issues in the NPM repertoire (World Bank, 2000).

The United Nations Development Program, World Bank, and Public Administration Reform Commission initiatives in reforming the administrative system along NPM lines had little impact on the majority of civil servants in Bangladesh. Bureaucratic inertia accompanied by the lack of political commitment caused the squelching of these initiatives (Zafarullah, 2011). The lack of familiarity with international best practices in public management among the civil servants has had a telling effect on the country's quest for economic development and social advancement. Among the key factors that have inhibited the accomplishment of the civil service's mission and encouraged corruption in the public sector in the perception of public officials themselves, were and continue to be: "political interference by political functionaries from inside the [bureaucracy]; political interference from politicians outside . . . ; micro-management by senior officials inside . . . [and] from outside . . . ; policy [in]consistency; policy [in]stability; [in]adequacy of resources; and resource [un]predictability" (World Bank, 2000, pp. 26–27).

A highly centralized administrative framework is a legacy of the colonial and post-colonial past. The post-independence government squandered the opportunity of dismantling it based on the recommendations of its contrivance—the Administrative and Services Reorganization Committee (1972–73). The military regime's decentralization policy did go a long way in creating a new administrative structure at the local level, albeit with officials representing the civil service. Opportunities were created for them to apply their skills in different functional areas, contribute to local development, and be closer to the people.

However, inter-group factionalism, so conspicuous in the national bureaucracy, along with patronage, is also characteristic of the local government system (Siddiquee, 1997). Junior civil servants assigned to responsible positions there were eager to relocate themselves in the national secretariat or move elsewhere, often pointing to the "overly" dominating role played by the executive officer, a member of the generalist administrative cadre, and political interference of local members of parliament. A general perception among them as well as those in higher positions in the capital indicated support for some form of reform of the system, but they are not too enthusiastic about giving up their authority over local *affairs vis-à-vis* extra-bureaucratic entities (Zafarullah, 1991, 2000). It is hardly surprising that changes proposed by the Local Government Commission in 1997 were either quashed or ignored by bureaucrats unwilling to share power with locally elected representatives (CPD, 2001).

CONCLUSION

Bureaucratic culture in Bangladesh exhibits features that in some sense reflect social-cultural traditions while conforming to Weberian principles that colonial rule introduced. In reality, faith in social traditionalism and informal relations within a neo-patrimonial clientelist order contradicts the Weberian notions of rule of law, formalism, impersonalism, and meritocracy. While the former is still strong in society, the pursuit of bureaucratic rationality and formal relations continue to dominate reform thinking and squelch the much-needed balance between social demands and administrative exigencies. Therein lies the problem. Arguably, bureaucratic pathology derives from structural complexity and procedural rigidity informed by Weberianism and the counter-imperatives of responding to traditional entreaties.

Functioning behind a veneer of neutrality, the bureaucracy is a highly politicized autonomous entity with direct involvement in policymaking—a basic political exercise. Despite frequent regime changes and variations in the political leanings of factions within it, the bureaucracy has been fairly responsive to all successive governments. However, it has not been very receptive to ideas about administrative reform and lacks a service ethos in relating itself to the citizens. It has often faltered in acknowledging and accepting the tenets of democratic governance and in admitting in its operating system norms of ethics, accountability, transparency, probity, and political control. In an era of globalization and sound governance that demands an interactive public management *system vis-à-vis* the state, market, civil society, and the public, the existing bureaucratic culture manifesting a high degree of conservatism serves as a deterrent to democratic rule and social and economic development.

The prevailing culture reflecting the attitudes and orientations of the members of the bureaucracy cannot be transformed by reform or legislation. However, for governance to have a positive impact on society, changes are necessary to promote accountability and probity in government, close the gap between the bureaucracy and the people, improve the politics-administration interface, enhance development management, and create a non-conflicting environment in officialdom. While structural, functional, and procedural amendments based on international best practices fine-tuned to the requirements of the country would be possible with genuine political commitment and affirmative bureaucratic support, attitudinal change will take time to internalize within the bureaucracy. Only through psycho-sociometric learning and widespread socialization can bureaucratic culture and practices change in Bangladesh or, for that matter, in any other post-colonial society.

REFERENCES

Ahamad, E. (1980). *Bureaucratic elites in segmented economic growth: Bangladesh and Pakistan*. Dhaka: University Press Limited.

Ahmed, B. (1992). Government malpractices. In *Report of the Task Forces on Bangladesh: Development strategies for 1990s* (Vol. 2). (pp. 389–407). Dhaka: University Press Limited.

Almond, G.A., & Powell, G.B. (1966). *Comparative politics: A developmental approach*. Boston: Little, Brown.

Aminuzzaman, S.M. (2012). *Dynamics of public policy—Determinants of policy making and implementation in Bangladesh*. Paper presented at the International Conference on Governance and Public Policy in South and Southeast Asia. Dhaka, July 13–14.

Caiden, G. (1991). *Administrative reform comes of age*. Berlin: Walter de Gruyter.

Carpenter, D.P. (2001). *The forging of bureaucratic autonomy*. Princeton, NJ: Princeton University Press.

Centre for Policy Dialogue (CPD). (2001). Policy brief on administrative reform and local government: CPD Task Force report. Dhaka: CPD.

Consumark. (1995). *Users' survey: Bangladesh*. Dhaka: Consumark Ltd.

Hood, C. (1995). Contemporary public management: A new global paradigm?, *Public Policy and Administration, 10*(2), 104–117.

Huque, A.S. (2011). Accountability and governance: Strengthening extra-bureaucratic mechanisms in Bangladesh. *International Journal of Productivity and Performance Management, 60*(1), 59–74.

Jamil, I. (1998). "Good governance": Tensions between tradition and modernity in Bangladeshi Public administration." *Asian Profile, 26*(5), 399–430.

Khan, M. M. (1980). *Bureaucratic self-preservation*. Dhaka: University of Dhaka Press.

Kochanek, S. (1993). *Patron-client politics and business in Bangladesh*. New Delhi: Sage.

Mahmood, S.A. (2010). Public procurement and corruption in Bangladesh confronting the challenges and opportunities. *Journal of Public Administration and Policy Research, 2*(6), 103–111.

Nachmias, D., & Rosenbloom, D. (1978). *Bureaucratic culture: Citizens and administrators in Israel*. London: Taylor & Francis.

Osman, F.A. (2010). Bangladesh politics: Confrontation, monopoly and crisis in governance. *Asian Journal of Political Science, 18*(3), 310–333.

Parnini, S.N. (2011). Governance reforms and Anti-Corruption Commission in Bangladesh. *Romanian Journal of Political Science, 11*(1). Retrieved fromhttp://www.sar.org.ro/polsci/?p=587

Peters, B. G. (2009). *The politics of bureaucracy: An introduction to comparative public administration* (6th edition). London: Routledge.

Pollitt, C., & Bouckaert, G. (2000). *Public management reform: A comparative analysis*. Oxford: Oxford University Press.

Riggs, F. W. (1962). *Administration in developing countries*. Boston: Houghton Mifflin.

Roniger, L. (2004). Political clientelism, democracy, and market economy. *Comparative Politics, 36*(3), 353–375.

Samaratunge, R., Alam, Q., & Teicher, J. (2008). The new public management reforms in Asia: A comparison of South and Southeast Asian countries. *International Review of Administrative Sciences, 74*(1), 25–46.

Sarker, A.E. (2006). New public management in developing countries: An analysis of success and failure with particular reference to Singapore and Bangladesh. *International Journal of Public Sector Management, 19*(2), 180–203.

Skocpol, T. (1985). Bringing the state back In: Strategies of analysis in current research. In P. B. Evans, D. Rueschemeyer, & T. Skocpol (Eds.), *Bringing the state back* (pp. 3–37). New York: Cambridge University Press.

Siddiqui, K. (1996). *Towards good governance in Bangladesh*. Dhaka: University Press Limited.

Siddiquee, N. A. (1997). *Decentralisation and development: Theory and practice in Bangladesh*. Dhaka: University of Dhaka.

Siddiquee, N. A. (1999). Bureaucratic accountability in Bangladesh: Challenges and limitations. *Asian Journal of Political Science, 7*(2), 88–104.

Smith, B.C. (2003). *Understanding third world politics: Theories of political change and development* (2nd edition). New York: Palgrave.

Smith, G. (1974). A model of bureaucratic culture. *Political Studies, 22*(1), 31–43.

Transparency International. (1997). *Survey on corruption in Bangladesh*. Dhaka: Transparency International, Bangladesh Chapter.

Turner, M. (2002). Choosing items from the menu: New public management in Southeast Asia. *International Journal of Public Administration, 25*(12), 1493–1512.

United Nations Development Program (UNDP). (1993). *Report on Public Administration Sector Study in Bangladesh*. Dhaka: UNDP.

Waldo, D. (1965). Public administration and culture In Martin, R.C. (Ed.), *Public administration and democracy* (pp. 39–61). Syracuse, NY: Syracuse University Press.

Wilson, G. K. (1993). Counter-elites and bureaucracies. *Governance, 6*(3), 426–437.

Wilson, W. (1966). *The papers of Woodrow Wilson* (Vol. 5). Princeton, NJ: Princeton University Press.

World Bank. (1996). *Bangladesh: Government that works, reforming the public sector*. Dhaka: World Bank.

World Bank. (2000). *Bangladesh: The experience and perceptions of public officials*. Dhaka: World Bank. Retrieved Jan. 30, 2012, from http://www1.worldbank.org/publicsector/civilservice/countries/bangladesh/bangladesh1113.pdf

Zafarullah, H. (1991, 2000). *Survey of the civil service in Bangladesh: Preliminary findings*. (Mimeo). Armidale, Australia: School of Social Science, University of New England.

Zafarullah, H. (2002). Administrative reform in Bangladesh: An unfinished agenda, In A. Farazmand (Ed.), *Administrative reform in developing nations* (pp. 49–72). Westport, CT: Praeger Publishers.

Zafarullah, H. (2007). Bureaucratic elitism in Bangladesh: The predominance of generalist administrators. *Asian Journal of Political Science, 15*(2), 161–173.

Zafarullah, H. (2009). Reflections on civil service reform in Bangladesh. In R.R. Mathur (Ed.), *Approaches to administrative reform in select countries: A civil service perspective* (pp. 56–78). Punjagatta: ICFAI University Press.

Zafarullah, H. (2011). Public management reform. In I. Jamil, S.M. Aminuzzaman, S. Askvik, & S.T.M. Haque (Eds.). *Understanding governance and public policy in Bangladesh*. Dhaka: North-South University.

Zafarullah, H., & Khan, M.M. (2001). The bureaucracy in Bangladesh: Politics within and the influence of partisan politics. In A. Farazmand (Ed.) *Handbook of comparative and development public administration.* 2nd edition (pp. 981–997). New York: Marcel Dekker.

Zafarullah, H., & Khan, M.M. (2005). *The bureaucratic ascendancy in Bangladesh: Public administration in Bangladesh—The first three decades*. New Delhi: South Asia Publishers.

Zafarullah, H., & Siddiquee, N. A. (2001). Dissecting public sector corruption in Bangladesh: Issues and problems of control, *Public Organization Review, 1*(4), 475–486.

Zafarullah, H., Khan, & Rahman, M. H. (2001). The civil service system in Bangladesh, In J. Burns & B. Bowornwathana (Eds.), *Asian civil service systems* (pp. 24–78). London: Edward Elgar.

The Dilemma for the New Administrative Culture in Mexican Public Administration: Esprit de Corps or Individualist Bureaucracy?

David Arellano-Gault

Centro de Investigación y Docencia Económicas (CIDE), Mexico City, Mexico

Using empirical data from the first survey conducted with certified Civil Service Officials at the federal level in Mexico, this article discusses how a new administrative culture is already rising within this bureaucratic group. The Mexican civil service is a young institution; the law creating the sector was passed in 2003, after the dominant party that controlled the executive branch for more than 70 years (the PRI) lost the presidential elections for the first time in 2000. The general objective of the Civil Service Law of 2003 was to eliminate the spoils system, thus inaugurating a new era for Mexican public administration. However, this law seems to assume that a civil service is primarily a problem of "professionalization" of individuals, not recognizing any attempt to view the civil service as a group of persons developing a group morale and ethos. Still, this article argues that an esprit de corps is an inevitable outcome of the maturity of a civil service, and the Mexican case will not be the exception.

INTRODUCTION

The aim of this article is to explore radical changes in the culture of Mexican public administration due to the creation of a civil service within the federal government in 2003. Mexico's public administration culture can be said to have two critical characteristics: patrimonialism and political dependence. Patrimonialism, which has been present since colonial times (Arellano-Gault, 1999), lies in the assumption that a public position is a privilege and a possession due to the belonging of that public position to a powerful group of persons. Political dependence describes a situation in which public administration is seen as an instrument of political power, so politicians and other powerful groups freely uses public administration as an instrument to advance their personal or collective agendas.

While patrimonialism and political dependence have been two of the most prominent characteristics of public administration in Mexico, they may be on the brink of change due to a law passed in 2003, establishing a professional and meritocratic civil service. This law seeks to create a group of civil service professionals who are not chosen based on political reasons, but rather through merit evaluation. As will be described below, for a country like Mexico this could mean a major transformation of public administration culture. However, this article also argues that the law passed in 2003 seeks to limit the possibility of this civil service from becoming an organized political group with a strong culture on its own.

The Civil Service Law is intended to create a civil service composed of individuals: individuals being evaluated as individuals, not as a group called "the civil service," which might wield its own political power. Given the recent political history of Mexico where unions have been part of the political party in power for more than 70 years, the concern is evident: to avoid the creation of a new politicized union of civil servants. However, this objective of the 2003 law might be destined to fail given that civil services tend to create a separate group of public servants who are in constant need of developing and defending their relative autonomy from politicians. It could even be said that such need is a critical element of any civil service in a democratic context: to develop an esprit de corps or group ethos in order to protect themselves from being dictated by external political influences.

This article explores three interrelated questions:

1. Is public administration culture in Mexico beginning to change due to the creation of a civil service?
2. If this is the case, is such a change creating a more professional public administration? Finally,
3. Is the Mexican Civil Service Law of 2003 succeeding in the creation of an "individualist civil service," as intended, or is it doing the contrary and an esprit de corps is already appearing?

To answer these questions the article analyzes empirical evidence from a survey conducted in 2011 with a group of certified public servants (i.e., those already evaluated and approved by legal procedures to become civil service members) regarding their opinion on the credibility, values, interaction among members, governance structures, and other issues of the civil service system.

This article is organized in six sections. The first is an introduction. The second describes the federal civil service that resulted from the 2003 law in terms of its main intentions, underlying assumptions, and other relevant features. The third section briefly addresses Mexican political history in order to understand the political role of public administration in a country ruled by a single political party for more than 70 years. In light of this history, the fourth section contextualizes the Civil Service Law of 2003, emphasizing the main concerns regarding the civil service becoming a union, and the basic strategy and governance structure created by the law in order to address this concern. With these historical and theoretical frameworks in mind, the fifth section explains the design, purpose, and results of the survey conducted with civil service professionals. As will be described, the survey explicitly seeks to understand whether or not civil servants see themselves as individuals pursuing a career, and if they are concerned about how and by whom the civil service is managed. Finally, the sixth section presents some closing elements for discussion, highlighting the importance of the development of an esprit de corps with both its advantages and its problems.

MEXICAN PUBLIC ADMINISTRATION CULTURE AND THE CREATION OF A NEW ESPRIT DE CORPS

Mexican public administration is contradictory in several ways. The country has formally been a democratic federation since 1917. However, for nearly seven decades the country was ruled by an authoritarian party, many times through allegedly fraudulent electoral proceedings, at all levels. Under these conditions, a civil service had not been an important issue for political groups: there was a stable spoils system, which worked through a strict control of the public apparatus by the president, and the dominant party.

This system was able to develop a relatively professional and loyal bureaucracy, especially within medium-high levels of federal public administration.

It was not until 2000 when an opposition party at last won the presidential elections, and Congress passed a Civil Service Law two years later (LSPC, 2003). The main idea of the law was to create a professional bureaucracy for the federal government, evaluated by performance in accordance with the New Public Management (NPM) (Ingraham, 1995, p. 142). "Professional bureaucracy" here refers to a group of highly prepared individuals who are experts in their field and work in public service offering their expertise as individuals while also offering their services to private or social organizations. However, this law also seeks to create what we can call an "individualist civil service." The central logic of the law is that public officials are individuals placed in a job position in pursuit of a personal career within the public sector. They are individuals within a system and the system treats them as individuals. The political intention of the law is very clear in the Mexican context: to treat them as individuals in order to avoid the creation of an organized group of civil servants that might, in turn, become a new interest group, a group that might begin to behave in a similar fashion as a union of medium- and high-level bureaucrats of the past. From this discussion we can expect that an implicit outcome of the law will be a civil service without the capacity to become organized as a group; a civil service composed of individuals concerned exclusively about their individual careers.

The organization of the civil service seems to fit with the previous assertion, as the federal government structured it in a very centralized and controlled fashion. The Mexican civil service is organized through a formal unit that belongs to the federal Secretary of Public Management. This secretary regulates and manages the Committees of Selection (those who manage the hiring of candidates in each Ministry), the Committees of Professionalization (those in charge of defining the general policies for individual's career development, in each Ministry), and the Advisory Council (those who evaluates the system as a whole) with complete discretion. In order to fully understand the overwhelming power that this Ministry exerts over the civil service we must consider one single fact: there is no way civil servants can participate in these committees, all of which are dominated by designated public officials (positions that are chosen by the superior in the hierarchy and that do not belong to the civil service career).

The Mexican civil service is somewhat unique in terms of the organizational and political terms of the system. As some previous evidence has suggested, a civil service is more than a staff for the management of human resources (Klingner & Arellano-Gault, 2006, p. 36); actually, a civil service is a political institution built in a democracy in order to avoid politicians and designed public officials to *excessively influence* public administration affairs (Cigler, 1990; Silberman,

1993, p. 5; Raadschelders & Rutgers, 1996, p. 86). In this sense, the main assumption of a civil service system is that the administrative career should be separated from a political one, and the main concern is how to actually, in practice, insulate and protect the civil service to prevent politicians from dominating it (Hummel, 1977; Hojnacki, 1996, p. 143).

In the Mexican case, the civil service was supposed to be formed by individuals whose basic characteristic is that they are "professionals." In order to avoid the spoils system, the Civil Service Law does not consider them a group or a political institution, but rather a professional structure whose neutrality is assured because they are professionals, or individuals pursuing a career in the public sector. The most striking element of the law is that political appointees (Secretaries of State) and designated public officials (under-secretaries and other executive positions, for example) are in complete control of the civil service through the committees described above. The fact that these officials control the governance structure of the civil service seems to be a contradiction, or even a paradox: the institution created to control the influence of politicians and designated public officials over the civil service is composed of those same politicians and public officials.

Nevertheless, in 2011, up to 8,500 public officials have obtained the status of Certified Civil Servants, out of the 36,028 public officials who are legally eligible to do so (SFP, 2011). A Certified Civil Servant is one that was selected among many other candidates through a competitive selection process that includes both performance and general knowledge evaluations of his/her job position. As previously stated, a primary question is whether this group, however small, is becoming what the law expected: individuals in pursuit of a career. Or, if they are becoming something else, perhaps a group of persons conscious of their role as civil servants who are different from political appointees or designated public officials. It is interesting to know if they are becoming a more organized group, a group concerned with the governance of the civil service system.

To approximate the current scenario and begin to answer this question, a survey was designed and conducted to explore the perception of Certified Civil Servants (those that through evaluation have acquired such certification) regarding the civil service (Martínez, 2011).[1] From the 8,500 Certified Civil Servants, 2,160 participated in the survey.[2] The complete results are interesting and will be explained in more detail later in this article. However, some of the most important results for our purposes include the

following: The first is that a significant number of Certified Civil Servants declared that they have informal but constant contacts with other certified public servants. They seem to see themselves more and more as a group, separated and different from the "others" (appointed officials or even low-level bureaucrats who are unionized). The second interesting result is that some Certified Civil Servants are beginning to doubt the success of the civil service as it is currently organized. A majority is asking to participate formally as certified members of the civil service in the committees of professionalization and selection, and even in the advisory council that evaluates the system as a whole.

Our main explanation for these results is that a civil service is much more than a system to administer human resources or a collection of individuals in pursuit of personal careers, as the Mexican law seems to assume. A civil service is a political institution created to avoid the spoils system. The question is, once created, who should be responsible for defending the civil service against external political influence? One possible answer could be that in the first place its own members defend the civil service. It is for this reason that a civil service is expected to create an esprit de corps, a group identification that allows a civil service to endure the strong political pressures that it will likely suffer. The *Oxford English Dictionary* defines esprit de corps as "a feeling of pride, fellowship, and common loyalty shared by the members of a particular group." Reisel et al. (2005) define it as the commitment of employees with some common goals and the commitment with other fellow workers in general. Basically we use it as the idea of a common goal and values of a group, which differentiates itself from other groups, obtaining with that identity a motivation to act and defend itself as a group.

It is possible to say that an esprit de corps was already in place in Mexican public administration. An esprit de corps that emphasizes complete loyalty to hierarchy and political bosses (there are no complete and reliable data, but a majority of middle-level public officials had between 8 and 25 years of average experience in public service regardless the fact that Mexico did not have a formal civil service [Arellano-Gault, 2003, p. 181]). Once the Civil Service Law was passed, the idea to create a workforce of individuals who were only concerned with becoming more professional was the attempted solution to preventing the creation of an organized power of public officials.

However, this seems to be an unrealistic solution. A civil service is a political institution, created to avoid the interference of politicians and designated public officials over the administrative apparatus. The substantive characteristic of a civil service is that it protects at least some public officials from being affected by politicized decisions. The primary gain of such a system is the creation of long-term stability within public policy and stronger professional, public organizations. It seems that in order to achieve this, the organizational scheme of a civil service would require the

---

[1] This survey was also conducted with members of two other Civil Service systems: Foreign Affairs Service and Electoral Service. In this article, we use only the one conducted with the Federal Civil Service.

[2] In Mexico, which has a long history of authoritarian management of public service, this level of participation might be considered very high due to the tradition of secrecy and highly vertical hierarchy present in Mexican public administration.

construction of a specific esprit de corps, a group morale and motivation that strengthens its capacity to defend the civil service, as well as the rules and procedures protecting it from political interference. A civil service is a political institution always under attack: politicians have numerous incentives to constantly reduce the power of civil service, tactically speaking at least. The main problem, of course, is that the esprit de corps seems necessary but also it is potentially a problem due to the creation of such a strongly identified and powerful group that might be able to defend itself through rigid regulations and avoiding any external control, evaluation, or accountability.

Thus, this article rises an important discussing regarding the contemporary organizational dilemmas faced in creating congruent, professional, and stable public administration in Mexico. A civil service is indispensable in avoiding a spoils system in a standard democracy. Still the problem is that a civil service can very easily become a rigid, overly politicized, and closed structure (Peters & Savoie, 1994). At the same time, a civil service without an esprit de corps seems to be, organizationally speaking, illogical. No doubt, the dilemma is very complex, and there are no easy solutions for this social paradox. Even the solutions suggested by the New Public Management (NPM) spirit—primarily, to reduce the power of the civil service (through a system of performance evaluation, for example)—seem limited (Laegrid, 2001, p. 147). Such a solution is unviable, due to the likelihood that it would result in a return to a spoils system since evaluation of performance is not necessarily a "neutral" technical activity (Arellano-Gault, 2008). It seems that a civil service is almost always a costly and dangerous institution, but still not as harmful as a spoils system. Creating a political institution based on merit and professional values, nevertheless, requires the development of a viable and stable institution that is able to defend itself. In order to do so, a civil service must become an organized, solid, and firm group. For these reasons, an esprit de corps is likely an unavoidable companion in order to produce a stable civil service able to face the political challenges involved in preventing the return of a spoils system.

To understand the possible implications of the existence of an esprit de corps in the Mexican civil service, in the next section we will briefly address the historical development and main characteristics of Mexican public administration during the seven decades of government of the official political party, the Institutional Revolutionary Party (PRI).

MEXICAN PUBLIC ADMINISTRATION: FROM POLITICAL GAME TO PROFESSIONAL CIVIL SERVICE

A single party dominated Mexico from 1929 to 2000: the Institutional Revolutionary Party (referred to as the PRI in Spanish). This political institution participated in democratic elections every six years (for governors, senators, and the president) and every three years (for municipal mayors and congressmen) and always won almost every position. With few exceptions in the municipal elections, every governor and president came from the PRI structures for decades. Mexico was in this sense a very particular "democratic government" with three main political and administrative characteristics:

1. a federation with continuing elections;
2. a public administration arena in which the PRI dominated and held under strict control all political and administrative positions through a well-developed set of urban and rural corporations (unions and other social organizations of low or middle socioeconomic classes); and
3. a system in which the president was the top of the pyramid and the main chief of party and government.

Actually, the president informally had, and regularly exerted, its political power over decision-making of state governors and members of congress.

But despite regular elections held during this period, the real political arena was not in the electoral process. While the PRI as a political party no doubt played a significant role, the political arena was functioned primarily within the public administrative apparatus. In order to become governor, mayor, minister, or member of congress or to hold any other major political office, one had to indeed be a member of the dominant party, but more importantly one had to have experience in governmental decision-making. In other words, a political career was firmly attached to advancement within the ranks of public administrative. From 1952 to 1994 every president was educated and trained in the public administration apparatus. They had pursued a career, rising from lower positions (at the federal or state level) until becoming a minister (often, before that, serving as state governor). Thus, in order to run for the presidency (or any other major office), the traditional process became one that included first serving as a minister.

In this sense, the public administrative apparatus was the real political arena in which power was exerted. Increasingly, a successful political career was closely linked to a successful administrative career. In addition, the public administrative apparatus was the main structure in which one could develop and maintain relationships with corporations, and therefore with the constituencies of this political system. Constituencies were not necessarily citizens in the traditional sense, but individuals related to, and benefited by a specific corporation such as a union or a federation of rural organizations.

The political life of the administrative apparatus was very rich and dynamic. Over time the PRI served as a basic structure to organize the presidential decision-making in terms of the political grooming needed in order to advance in rank and hold the offices of member of congress, governor, or minister. Each president chose the next PRI presidential candidate from those three or four ministers with the strongest administrative agenda in terms of experience and rank in the existing political hierarchy.

Under these conditions, the creation of a civil service was hardly considered a political priority. The spoils systems was more or less controlled by the president and the party: high-level positions were negotiated by the president and his advisors with and within the party, and mid-level positions were granted to a mixture of people who sat high in the political hierarchy (organized as political groups called *camarillas* [Ai Camp, 2006]) and those from professional public administrators that changed rapidly from one position to another depending on which camarilla wanted their services. A camarilla was the relatively small group of persons who were close to a politician and pursuing better positions. While this is a very important variable to understand in Mexican public administration, it is not the only piece.

A large set of professional administrators, persons not necessarily attached to the camarillas, began to appear as the public administration became more and more complex during the second half of the 20th century (Dussauge, 2005, p. 765). This appearance of these positions is somewhat logical since a certain stability in decision-making was necessary due to the changes that occurred at the end of each six-year presidential term. When each new president took office, thousands of positions in public administration became available, creating in turn a temporary and potentially problematic administrative. This is why the Mexican public administration developed a large group of professional public administrators who were not attached politically to any particular camarilla, but, rather, hired by different camarillas throughout their careers. This group of professionals did not typically enjoy job stability, but they knew that after one camarilla dismissed them another would soon ask for their services (one or two months later).

This professional group of public officials became very important; they were the experts in different areas of public administration, often uniquely capable to provide a certain amount of stability. The official name of this group has been formalized in Mexico as "personal de confianza," meaning trusted or close staff, since they can be fired easily as they cannot (legally) belong to a union. They were and still are the high- to mid-level public officials (from general directors to department chiefs). By contrast, lower public officials are legally called "personal de base," meaning base staff, and are corporately unionized, making them staff members who are both legally and politically difficult to remove or fire (Arellano-Gault, 2008, p. 235).

In Mexico, even today, there is a very interesting (and Kafkanian) law known as the "bureaucratic law" (officially the Federal Law of Public Workers). This law formally requires all bureaucratic unions to belong to a larger corporation, a federation of unions (the majority of them still closely related to the PRI). For this reason, the "base staff" is a large group (approximately 1.6 million [SFP, 2010, p. 218]) with very low salaries but almost absolute job stability. This law also establishes that "personal de confianza" or trusted staff (all mid- and high-level public officials) cannot belong to a union and can be fired at will by their appointed supervisors.

But political context began to change in Mexico, specifically beginning in 1989 when an opposition party won a gubernatorial election for the first time nationwide. Since then, the slow process of democratization was constant and opposition parties won more and more offices within municipal and state governments. This continued democratization process made the possibility for an opposition party to achieve the presidency of the country a reality for the first time ever, which in turn would result in the domination of public administration by the new government, among other consequences.

Most likely the PRI perceived the risk of losing power, and thus became aware of the importance of a civil service in order to avoid having another party take over all administrative positions. Therefore, in 1999, the PRI introduced the Civil Service Law in Congress. The proposed law did not pass that year, but another one would soon succeed under a new political scenario. Early in 2000, an election year, a candidate from another party won the presidential elections for the first time in 70 years, and proposed another Civil Service Law in 2001, which was finally passed in 2003 after a series of negotiations and modifications.[3] In the next section this law is discussed in the light of the main concerns regarding one of the most notable features of Mexican political system under the PRI: unions.

MEXICAN CIVIL SERVICE: A CIVIL SERVICE WITHOUT AN ESPRIT DE CORPS

The law of 2003 seemed to have two main concerns: how to deal with the thousands of "base staff," all of them part of corporations and unions created by the PRI and legally untouchable (the bureaucratic law is still in place today, in 2012). The second concern was how to deal with trusted or close staff mainly to turn them into a solid group of public decision-makers without allowing them to become a new union or powerful political group.

The 2003 Civil Service Law takes only the trusted or close staff into consideration, and a large majority of public servants are excluded from this law. There are approximately 1,725,549 federal public officials, and of these only

---

[3]Curiously, on July 1, 2012, the PRI candidate was victorious in Mexico's presidential election.

36,028 are trusted staff who in turn are the subjects of the 2003 Civil Service Law (SHCP, 2012). The reason for this exclusion is clear: the conflict with the bureaucratic unions was out of question for the new government.

For these 36,028 public servants or trusted staff the law created a complex system of competitive hiring, constant evaluation of performance, and a relatively clear process of dismissal. The system is based on one premise: membership in the civil service is strictly a pathway for personal career development, and not a political endeavor. The system's principle function is to choose individuals, develop their capabilities, evaluate them as individuals and, if necessary, fire them based on their individual performance. The civil service is defined in terms of "professionalization" of persons as individuals as can be seen in the very name of the system, since it is officially called "professional career service").

A federal unit (the Ministry of Public Administration) is in charge of regulating the system, which is composed of three basic structures: the Selection Committees, Professionalization Committees, and Advisory Councils. The system is based on a series of exams and interviews for the case of hiring, and constant performance measurement for the case of evaluation of each person within the civil service. Designated public officials who select the candidates for a particular position form the Committees of Selection. The federal agency, which is also run by designated public officials, regulates the process. Each Ministry has its own Selection Committee.

A similar process occurs in the Professionalization Committee in charge of developing the policies and evaluative procedures for the individual positions. Again, designated officials are in charge of these committees in every ministry. Finally, the Advisory Council is composed of nearly 30 appointed officials and three citizens invited by these appointed officials to the council. The council is in charge of reviewing and analyzing the development of the system as a whole in order to propose new policies for improvement.

Two things are striking regarding this civil service, assuming that is a political institution created to avoid the spoils system, or in other words that its goal is to avoid manipulation on behalf of politicians and designated officials. First, the main political challenge of a civil service is to overcome the resistance of politicians and appointed or designated officials to be limited by a civil service in terms of the persons they would like to hire in particular public administration positions (Silberman, 1993).Despite this challenge any civil service has to deal with, in Mexico the civil service system is completely run and controlled by appointed public officials giving rise to suspicions regarding the management of the civil service.

The second striking issue is the intention to create a civil service composed of individuals pursuing careers rather than becoming the political institution that is able to avoid the spoils system. This intention is somewhat understandable given the recent political history of the country: it seems a priority to avoid the creation of a new union, one of mid-level public officials who might create a system as rigid as the one that regulates unionized public administration personnel. However, the image of this civil service is somewhat simplistic: to create a strong new public administration based on merit but not allowing it to become a political institution but essentially a sophisticated human resource system. At this point, one effect is clear: the system has had very low credibility (Arellano-Gault, 2008). There are several accounts that reveal that exams, awards, and competitions are constantly manipulated by appointed public officials in order for them to maneuver the hiring process according to their personal preferences. This is an obvious result of a system that is run by the same people the system should be controlling.

A civil service is a political institution, its basic aim is to control the spoils system, the tendency of politicians to appoint their political allies in the whole structure of public administration. It is a political institution that in any country has to fight for its existence (Silberman, 1993): politicians and parties resist its creation since it would limit their discretion to control the public administration apparatus. For several authors (Aberbach, Putnam, & Rockman, 1981; Silberman, 1993; Bekke, Perry, & Toonen, 1996) a civil service in order to survive needs to become a strong system able to defend itself since politicians and society hardly would understand its importance for a democratic governance. An esprit de corps seems necessary since a civil service need to defend itself in order to exist. As Aberbach, Putnam, and Rockman (1981, p. 224) propose, civil service bureaucrats need to become a solid political group in order to be able to execute public policy.

Some level of autonomy is indispensable in order to run public organizations and implement policy decisions. An administrative career is an important instrument to gain this autonomy. This might also explain why civil services usually become more and more rigid and procedural, over time. Once an administrative career is defined, those within the race would like to reduce uncertainties at maximum, preventing "outsiders" and "opportunist" from cheating the system. Mitigating subjectivity in decision-making becomes a priority for those within the system. Therefore, to prevent politicians and designated officials from being able to manipulate the system would become also of major importance in order to make a civil service stable, in the eyes of those aspiring to hold positions within the civil service.

If this is true, the Mexican Civil Service will change rapidly as more civil servants become certified career civil servants: they will begin to defend the system, to create its ethos. In order to see if this is happening a survey was designed in order to ask the civil servants regarding their opinion on the civil service and its current stage and evolution.

TABLE 1
Perception Regarding the Civil Service

	Did not answer	Disagree	Neutral	Agree
Being a certified Civil Service public official is more than an income category or a labor position.	19.56%	26.98%	13.41%	40.05%
I think that people belonging to the Professional Civil Service are the best persons for the administrative positions they occupy today.	19.56%	28.66%	17.38%	34.38%
I think that I have in general at least the same level of preparation and capacity than other Certified Civil Servants at similar positions.	19.56%	18.09%	14.39%	47.96%
The level of preparation of the public officials who DO NOT belong to the Civil Service is better than the Certified Civil Servants.	19.56%	47.19%	22.45%	10.79%
I observe better work conditions in my specific environment since the Law of Civil Service was passed.	19.56%	41.31%	15.97%	23.16%

Source: Martínez, 2011.

The Survey

This section uses the database produced by Martínez (2011)[4] through a survey designed to understand the esprit de corps in three Mexican Civil Services: the Federal Government, the autonomous electoral body, officially named Federal Electoral Institute (IFE, in Spanish), and the Foreign Affairs Ministry.[5] A universe of 12,328 certified public officials in these three civil services was located and an electronic questionnaire was sent to them by email. For the purposes of this article, we will concentrate just on the part of this study that deals with federal public officials. A total of 6,945 federal public servants were identified as certified public servants through use of a public email list (from the official 8,500 public servants already certified according to official data). The survey was sent to these persons getting a response rate of 31.1 percent (2,160 questionnaires were completed) or 25 percent (out of the 8,500) (Martínez, 2011, p. 41).[6]

The aim of the survey was to identify the differences in terms of esprit de corps in these three civil services. The survey intended then to observe the attitudes and concepts that civil servants have regarding their civil service system, its congruency, and the need to become more organized and open to the participation of its own members in their governance structure. The results are discussed below.[7]

Table 1 and Figure 1 summarize a set of questions designed to observe whether or not the civil service can be considered a "good system" in terms of attraction and retention of more qualified civil servants in comparison with designated officials or persons outside the civil service. The survey results presented below suggest that this may not be the case. Positions are not necessarily being held by the most suitable people for the jobs and certified public servants are not being generally perceived as better than those of other officials in government in terms of both, its preparation and capabilities. This seems to show that Certified Civil Servants do not trust the objectivity of the system, as they implicitly accept the possibility that some of them might have been hired for reasons other than merit.

The self-identification of certified civil service public officials as a group is still somewhat low. As Table 2 and Figure 2 summarize, more than 50 percent of the respondents in Martinez's survey declared that they know either "almost all" or "most" of their co-workers at the department or area level (32.48 percent and 21.80 percent, respectively), but barely know their co-workers at the organizational level as a whole (18.26 percent combined result). These results suggest that the system does not encourage civil servants to act or perceive themselves as part of a group, or necessarily to become colleagues since they are likely competing for individual positions. Nevertheless, nearly four out of ten of these public officials declared that they interact at least with few of the other certified civil service servants in their own organization.

The results presented above could also explain why as a group, the certified public servants barely hold meetings, as shown in Figure 3.

In terms of the existence of groups or associations that represent the interests of public officials in the Mexican Civil Service, the respondents correctly identified that there are

---

[4]The author acted as the director of the research Martínez developed in order to fulfill the requirements and credits for her undergraduate program.

[5]These two other Civil Services would deserve a specific study since the former is quite old and stable and the latter seems to be working pretty well in terms of creating a new esprit de corps. However, to do this is clearly out of reach for the purposes of this article.

[6]Given the short story on using surveys to study Mexican public sector after so many years of authoritarian regimes, we consider this rate of response quite encouraging. Nevertheless, our interpretation should be taken carefully given the rate of response.

[7]It is important to note the high level of "no answers" found. In Mexico the idea of answering academic surveys is still under development. Several public officials were very concerned that their identity might be known, making them open to sanctions from their bosses. This is the reason why

some of the respondents avoided answering those questions that might compromise them, regardless the constant assurances offered to them regarding the protection of their personal data.

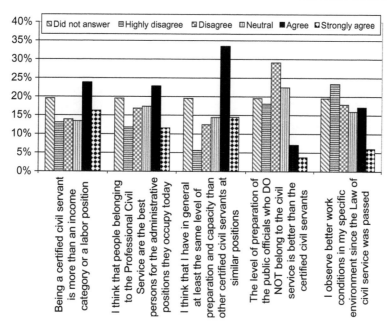

FIGURE 1   Perception regarding the Civil Service (color figure available online).
(Source: Martínez, 2011).

TABLE 2
Level of Relationship Among Members

	DID NOT ANSWER	I DO NOT KNOW ANYONE	I KNOW A FEW	I THINK I KNOW MOST OF THEM	I THINK I KNOW ALMOST EVERYBODY
Who belongs to your own organization?	34.01%	10.03%	37.71%	15.48%	2.78%
Specifically in your area or department?	20.93%	10.63%	14.17%	21.80%	32.48%

Source: Martínez, 2011.

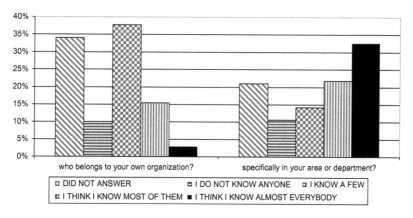

FIGURE 2   Level of relationship among members (color figure available online).
(Source: Martínez, 2011).

none. The Mexican law, intended to create a system of individuals and not groups, as stated previously, is corroborated in its effects (Figure 4).

As a group, then, federal certified civil officials are still under formation. Figure 5 summarizes several interesting results in this sense. They do not feel strongly differentiated, they do not boldly identify particular interests to defend as a group, and they do not show a general will to recommend other colleagues (to other positions, as subordinated or as a hierarchical superior) simply because they belong to

FIGURE 3   Do you have systematic reunions with other members of the Civil Service? (color figure available online).

(Source: Martínez, 2011).

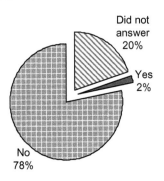

FIGURE 4   To your best knowledge, is there any organizations or association that seek to represent the specific interests of the certified Civil Service public officials? (color figure available online).

(Source: Martínez, 2011).

the civil service (Table 3). The esprit de corps is clearly still very weak.

Nevertheless, at a normative level, they feel that to be part of a civil service implies certain specific and homogenous values of public service, which are different from the values defended by other public officials (Figure 6 and Table 4).

The certified civil service public officials also identified the immaturity of the Mexican Civil Service: nearly one-third of the respondents in Martínez's survey stated that there are persons in Civil Service positions who have not followed the standard procedure of examination and selection to obtain a position (Figure 7).

When asked if certified civil service public officials should participate in the Selection Committees and the Advisory Council, almost two-thirds agreed that they should participate in these collective decision-making groups (Graphs 8 and 9).

In exploring participants' opinions regarding how to strengthen the civil service, 55.42 percent of respondents asserted that the rules of the service should be respected (by the designated public officials in charge of the system) and approximately 30 percent of them think they, as certified civil service public officials, should have representative bodies to assure that rules are followed. (Figure 10)

The results from this survey suggest that the recently developed Mexican Civil Service is still struggling to find its place within public administration. The rules and procedures

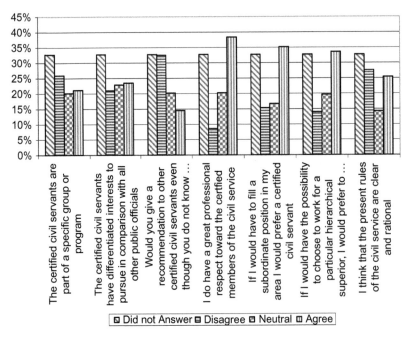

FIGURE 5   Perceptions regarding the group of certified Civil Service public officials (color figure available online).

(Source: Martínez, 2011).

TABLE 3
Perceptions Regarding the Group of Certified Civil Service Public Officials

	Did not Answer	Disagree	Neutral	Agree
The certified Civil Service public officials are part of a specific group or program.	32.75%	25.94%	20.16%	21.15%
The certified Civil Service public officials have differentiated interests to pursue in comparison with all other public officials.	32.75%	20.98%	22.83%	23.44%
Would you give a recommendation to another certified Civil Service public official even though you do not know him/her?	32.75%	32.54%	20.21%	14.50%
I do have a great professional respect for the certified members of the Civil Service.	32.75%	8.66%	20.22%	38.37%
If I would have to fill a subordinate position in my area I would prefer a certified civil servant.	32.75%	15.37%	16.68%	35.20%
If I would have the possibility to choose to work for a particular hierarchical superior, I would prefer to work for a certified Civil Service public official.	32.75%	14.01%	19.67%	33.57%
I think that the present rules of the Civil Service are clear and rational.	32.75%	27.57%	14.28%	25.40%

Source: Martínez, 2011.

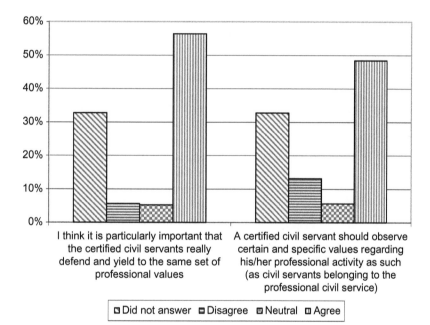

FIGURE 6   Values of the certified Civil Service public officials (color figure available online).
(Source: Martínez, 2011).

TABLE 4
Values of the Certified Civil Service Public Official

	Did not answer	Disagree	Neutral	Agree
I think it is particularly important that the certified civil servants really defend and follow the same set of professional values.	32.75%	5.61%	5.23%	56.41%
A certified civil servant should observe certain and specific values regarding his/her professional activity as such (as civil servants belonging to the professional Civil Service).	32.75%	13.18%	5.61%	48.46%

Source: Martínez, 2011.

to assure that politicians and appointed officials are not manipulating the system are still very weak. A significant share of Certified Civil Servants feel they need to develop stronger values and defend them in order to become closer as a group. Clearly, there is now a small but interesting portion of certified public officials who have begun to feel that they have to strengthen the civil service, participate in its decision-making, and develop capacities to defend its rules and procedures. This might be the seed of a new esprit de corps in the Mexican Civil Service.

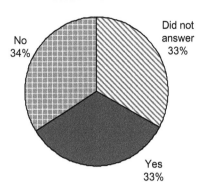

FIGURE 7 In your department or area, do you know persons that are not certified Civil Service public officials but that are occupying positions that should belong to persons that are? (color figure available online).

(Source: Martínez, 2011).

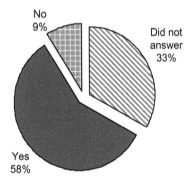

FIGURE 8 In your opinion, should the certified civil servants participate in all the selection committees? (color figure available online).

(Source: Martínez, 2011).

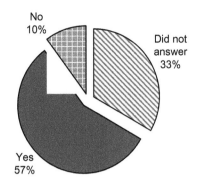

FIGURE 9 In your opinion, should certified civil servants participate in the Advisory Council for the Civil Service? (color figure available online).

(Source: Martínez, 2011).

CONCLUSION

Mexico is an interesting case to follow. Being the 14th largest economy in the world (IMF, 2012), a country of more than 112 million people, and a young democracy, the study of its civil service under construction seems important. Mexico can be viewed as a country struggling to leave behind a long and strong history of political legitimacy based on an administrative apparatus that is controlled and captured by powerful interests. Its culture is closely attached to a patrimonialist administrative structure concerned with satisfying not the citizens but the political elites. The country now conducts open and more or less fair elections and therefore the creation of a civil service has become important in the hope to transform this patrimonialist culture into a new one, closer to a public administration that has as its main objective to

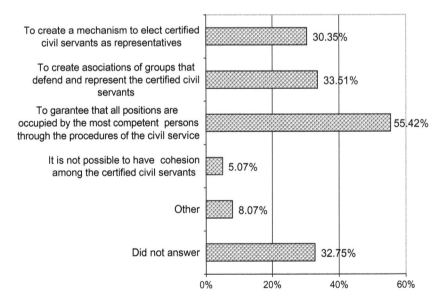

FIGURE 10 Participation in Civil Service governance (color figure available online).

(Source: Martínez, 2011).

pursue the public interest in a political context (Wamsley et al., 1990, p. 49). However, it seems as if the Mexican case is on its way to develop a civil service without taking into consideration the fact that it is also a political institution. This would be a significant mistake since there is substantial evidence that in any democracy, understanding bureaucratic politics is a critical step in order to develop a professional and strong civil service (Riggs, 1988).

Another reason for studying the Mexican case is that it is still a developing process strongly influenced by a NPM agenda. It represents a unique transition from a corporative public administration to a meritocratic system based on performance evaluation, without passing through a Weberian stage (Du Gay, 2005). It is fair to say that Mexican public administration has historically been an appendix of the political system: it used to be the most important political arena due to the domination and manipulation of political offices during the 70 years of the PRI era. Citizen satisfaction or the results obtained by public administration were not important objectives in order to obtain legitimacy. Legitimization for public administration has come basically from a political system that sees the public apparatus as the arena of power, as the arena of the main political game. Clientelism has been more important than getting quality results for the population, in general, and in the eyes of constituents, public administration has been the possession of privileged groups, looking for benefits for their political projects.

In other words, rather than developing a Weberian ethos (Goodsell, 1983, p. 143), Mexican public administration has been an instrument of political groups, not a strong structure with a strong bureaucratic ethos and a relative autonomy which enables it to run public organizations and implement public policies in a professional way. The ethos of Mexican public administration has not been based on the best characteristics of a bureaucracy (DuGay, 2005) but on one that stresses obedience to politicians and their specific interests, not those of society as a whole.

This is why a civil service is such a dilemma for the Mexican political system. The ethos of obedience is still very strong, making the idea of appointment by merit and competition still very strange and hard for politicians to accept (both in the executive and the legislative powers). Nevertheless, any civil service system becomes a "living" organization (Aberbach, Putnam, & Rockman, 1981, p. 70; Johnson & Libecap, 1994, p. 76). Certified civil service public officials logically become the most important advocates of the system. This seems to be happening in the Mexican case too.

The question, then is what ethos this Mexican civil service system will have? What kind of political nature needs to be created (as in any other civil service, Meier, 2000, p. 7)? This article argues that an esprit de corps is somewhat inevitable in time, but what would be the "essence" of the esprit de corps of the Mexican Civil Service? A particular esprit de corps, given the history of Mexican public administration,

can be somewhat undesirable, specifically the rise of a new powerful group that obtains its power through the control of public administration operation in negotiation with other powerful groups. Once again, Mexican society would become a second priority for public administration, as has been the case throughout Mexico's recent history.

In theory, a meritocratic civil service would create a group of non-politicized professionals (Hojnacki, 1996, p. 137), who are relatively free of political pressures, in order to make technical decisions, which in turn will lead to better policies in terms of their capabilities to solve public problems (Pfiffner, 2000, p. 24). If we add the arguments of NPM, civil services which have constant performance evaluations contribute to create stronger and better governments (Ingraham, 1995, p. 136).

However, as Peters (2009) more realistically argues: in practice the problem is how much politicization a civil service will live with and in what political context (Campbell & Szablowski, 1979, p. 46; Wood & Waterman, 1994, p. 16; Thomspon, 2006, p. 496). A civil service is actually a group, a collection of people who have something to defend: the rules and procedures of a civil service. These are the only things that protect them from the constant uncertainty they face due to frequent elections and changes in the political arena. New politicians in power might mean new temptations to change and weaken the rules of the civil service in order to allow more political appointments. A civil service needs to be protected, somewhat insulated from the political influence of actors outside the "administrative career" (Aberbach & Rockman, 1988). In practice, this means that a civil service is a complex system, always in the process of formation, always negotiating its path, creating routines and protecting its rules in practice (Silberman, 1993, p. 35 shows that civil services require decades to form and stabilize). How they achieve this isolation, how they develop their power space and defend it successfully, in practice, step by step, are critical questions to understand in any democracy.

What kind of esprit de corps should be developed for the Mexican Civil Service? It is something that must still be discussed. Unfortunately, the current system and law seem to be mistaken in their attempt to deny the possibility of an esprit de corps, wishing unrealistically to develop a civil service of professional individuals isolated from one another. As suggested by the survey results, the idea of avoiding the organization of people already within the system seems unrealistic; Certified Civil Servants are highly likely to organize themselves as a group, sooner rather than later. Yet, in practice, there remains another problem: a civil service that prohibits the participation of civil servants in the decision-making process. This is one of the reasons why this civil service suffers from a chronic lack of credibility: the persons with the strongest incentives to prevent the regulations of the civil service are those same individuals who are running the system.

The Mexican Civil Service is still developing, it is a fledging institution. What esprit de corps would be developed is an important question and perhaps Mexican society should debate what kind of public administration would be desirable. Do we want a strong bureaucratic ethos, a civil service with high levels of relative autonomy? Or we prefer a somewhat weak bureaucracy, strongly attached to politicians? How do we want to insulate the civil service in order to avoid its capture by powerful interests groups? How can we avoid the civil service becoming much too isolated and becoming an unaccountable political structure? These hard and complex questions need to be debated, not avoided. Leaving the civil service to the traditional history and tendencies of the Mexican political system would for sure yield again a public administration distant away from society and captured by political interests. (Hojnacki, 1996, p. 144; Uvalle, 2007, p. 88).

REFERENCES

Aberbach, J., & Rockman, B. (1988). Mandates or mandarins? Control and discretion in the modern administrative state. *Public Administration Review, 48*, 606–611.

Aberbach, J., Putnam, R., & Rockman, B. (1981). *Bureaucrats and politicians in western democracies*. Cambridge, MA: Harvard University Press.

Ai Camp, R. (2006). *Politics in Mexico: The democratic consolidation*. Oxford: Oxford University Press.

Arellano-Gault, D. (1999). Patrimonialist values and governmental organisational culture in Mexico. *International Review of Public Administration, 4*(2), 67–77.

Arellano-Gault, D. (2003). Profesionalización de la administración pública en México: ¿de un sistema autoritario a un sistema rígido? In D. Arellano-Gault, R. Egaña, O. Oszlak, and R. Pacheco (eds.) *Retos de la profesionalización de la función pública*. Caracas: CLAD.

Arellano-Gault, D. (2008). Civil Service reform: Challenges and future prospects for Mexican democracy. In J. Killian, & N. Eklund. *Handbook of administrative reform. An international perspective* (pp. 233–247). Boca Raton: CRC Press.

Bekke, H., Perry, J., & Toonen, T. Eds. (1996). *Civil service systems*. Bloomington, IN: Indiana University Press.

Campbell, C., & Szablowski, G. (1979). *The super bureaucrats*. Toronto, ON, Canada: MacMillan of Canada.

Cigler, B. (1990). Public administration and the paradox of professionalism. *Public Administration Review, 51*, 438–441.

Dussauge, M. (2005). Sobre la pertinencia del servicio profesional de Carrera en México. *Foro Internacional, 45*(4), 761–794.

Du Gay, P. (2005). *The values of bureaucracy*. Oxford: Oxford University Press.

Goodsell, C (1983). *The case for bureaucracy*. Chatham, NJ: Chatham House.

Hojnacki, W. (1996). Politicization as a civil service dilemma. In H. Bekke, Hans J. Perry, & T. Toonen (Eds), *Civil service systems* in *comparative perspective*. Bloomington, IN: University of Indiana Press.

Hummel, R. (1977). *The bureaucratic experience*. New York: St. Martin's Press.

Ingraham, P. (1995). *The foundation of merit*. Baltimore: John Hopkins University Press.

Johnson, R., & Libecap, G. (1994). *The federal civil service system and the problem of bureaucracy*. Chicago: Chicago University Press.

Klingner, D., & Arellano-Gault, D. (2006). Mexico's federal professional career service: Linked changes in public personnel management and political culture. In N. Riccucci (Ed.), *Public personnel management* (pp. 36–49). New York: Longman.

Laegrid, P. (2001). Transforming top civil servants systems. In T. Christensen & P. Laegrid. (2001). *New public management*. Aldershot, UK: Ashgate.

Martínez, A. (2011). *¿Institucionalización del servicio civil en México? Análisis comparativo del servicio profesional de carrera de la administración pública federal mexicana, el servicio electoral y el servicio exterior*. CIDE thesis.

Meier, K. (2000). *Politics and the bureaucracy*. Orlando, FL: Harcourt Brace.

Peters, G. (2009). *The politics of bureaucracy*. Oxford, UK: Routledge.

Peters, G., & Savoie, D. (1994). Civil Service reform: Misdiagnosing the patient. *Public Administration Review, 54*(5), 418–425.

Pfiffner, J. (2000). Government legitimacy and the role of civil service. In Pfiffner, J. and Brook, D. (2000). *The future of merit*. Washington, DC: The Woodrow Wilson Center Press.

Raadschelders, J., & Rutgers, M. (1996). The evolution of civil service systems. In H. Bekke, J. Perry, and T. Toonen (Eds.), *Civil service systems in comparative perspective*. Bloomington, IN: University of Indiana Press.

Reisel, W. D., Chia, S.-L., Maloles, C. M. Job insecurity spillover to key account management: Negative effects on performance, effectiveness, adaptiveness, an esprit de corps." *Journal of Business and Psychology, 19*(4), 483–503.

Riggs, F. (1988). Bureaucratic politics in the US: benchmark for comparison. *Governance: An International Journal of Policy and Administration. 1*, 347–379.

Silberman, B. (1993). *Cages of reason*. Chicago: Chicago University Press.

Uvalle, R. (2007). *Perspectiva de la administración pública contemporánea*. Toluca: IAPEM.

Wamsley, G., Bacher, R., Goodsell, C. et al. (1990). Refounding public administration. Newbury Park, CA: Sage.

Wood, D., & Waterman, R. (1994). *Bureaucratic dynamics*. Boulder, CO: Westview Press.

Documents

International Monetary Fund. (2012). *Report for Selected Countries and Subjects*. Retrieved from http://www.imf.org/external/pubs/ft/weo/2012/01/weodata

Ley Servicio Profesional de Carrera (LSPC). (2003). *Ley de servicio profesional de carrera*. Retrieved from http://www.diputados.gob.mx/LeyesBiblio/pdf/260.pdf

SHCP (Ministry of Treasury). *Federal Budget 2012*. Mexico City, Mexico: SFP.

SFP (Ministry of Public Administration). 2010. *Cuarto informe de actividades*. Mexico City, Mexico: SFP.

SFP (Ministry of Public Administration). (2011). *Quinto informe de actividades*. Mexico City, Mexico: SFP.

Performance Appraisal or Praising Performance? The Culture of Rhetoric in Performance Management in Ghana Civil Service

Justice Nyigmah Bawole

Department of Public Administration, University of Ghana Business School, Accra, Ghana

Farhad Hossain

Institute for Development Policy and Management, School of Environment and Development, University of Manchester, Manchester, United Kingdom

Kwame Ameyaw Domfeh

Department of Public Administration, University of Ghana Business School, Accra, Ghana

Hamza Zakaria Bukari

Institute for Development Policy and Management, School of Environment and Development, University of Manchester, Manchester, United Kingdom

Francis Sanyare

Department of Social, Political and Historical Studies, University for Development Studies, Wa, Ghana

This article examines the practice of performance appraisal as a critical element of administrative culture in the Ghana Civil Service (CS). It relies on three focus group discussions with senior civil servants to analyze the practice and its implications for performance of civil servants in Ghana. The article argues that: leadership seldom gives the needed attention to this administrative practice; the process lacks objectivity; it is fraught with superstition, spirituality, and fear; appraisers are rarely trained; and civil servants only become more interested in performance appraisals (PAs) during promotion-related interviews. The article therefore concludes that this process has become rhetoric rather than an important practice and that performance only gets praised rather than being appraised. The article recommends an overhaul of the PA system by integrating it into a holistic performance management program; integrating PA training into civil service mandatory training programs; and the revision and computerization of the PA system.

INTRODUCTION

Public sector performance has increasingly drawn the attention of scholars and practitioners by virtue of its role in public management, public governance, and public policy development. One wonders whether there would have been the need to be concerned about public administration at all if performance were not central to the very institutions that constitute the public sector, including the civil service. It is therefore not surprising that performance and its measurement have become an integral part of organizational life. In both private and public sector organizations, performance appraisal is inevitable in evaluating and motivating employees with reward packages that are linked to strategies of human resource management (Fletcher, 2001). Performance appraisal could also be a key aspect of an organization's performance management framework. Williams (1998), in a classification of performance management models, intimated that performance management could either be seen as a system for managing organizational performance, employee performance; or as a system that integrates both organizational performance with individual performance. In all these forms of relationships, performance appraisal is expected to play vital and varying roles in the interests of the organization (Fletcher, 2001).

In Ghana, the initiation of a post-independence national development project was supported by an administrative framework inherited from the colonial authority. While the civil service was expected to drive the formulation of government policies and programs to stimulate growth and development, a retinue of institutional obstacles later impeded this. It was obvious that the colonial administrative architecture was designed and deployed to relegate Ghanaians to low-level jobs that required minimal professional training as it served as the "formal" medium through which colonial interests were satisfied (Ohemeng & Anebo, 2012). After independence in 1957, attempts to build a national civil service saw the establishment of regional administrative institutions, parastatal agencies, quasi-government departments and state enterprises, and even though their inherent weaknesses at birth sowed the seed of sluggish administrative performance. It is therefore not surprising that recent attempts to modernize the civil service have raised several concerns over the appropriateness of organizational design, structures, financial and human resource requirements, and essential administrative competences needed for the performance of development functions (Ayee, 2001; Wunsch, 2001).

While the impact of employee performance on organizational performance has widely received attention in the literature (Antwi, Analoui, & Nana-Agyekum, 2008; Ashworth, Boyne, & Entwistle, 2010; Anderfuhren-Biget, 2012), the shortcomings of flawed appraisal systems induced by perverse administrative cultures in the civil service can be said to have received minimal discussion. This article therefore seeks to examine how PA has developed into a negative administrative cultural trait in the Ghana CS and the implication of such a practice for CS performance. The rest of the article is structured as follows: the next section gives an overview of the CS in Ghana followed by an examination of PA in Ghana CS. The conceptual framework of PA is then presented followed by the methodology. The results and discussions are presented under the contextual perspectives of PA in Ghana and ends with some concluding remarks.

THE CIVIL SERVICE (CS) IN GHANA

The public administration landscape in Ghana is dominated by a civil service made up of government ministries, departments, and agencies (MDAs) that provide a wide range of services. Prior to the establishment of the Local Government Service in 2003, the civil service spanned both central and local government levels. Owing its form and structure to the 1992 constitution, the civil service is required to drive the formulation and implementation of government policies and programs. This makes civil service performance a subject of concern as it tends to influence and reflect governments' performance.

In the early 1980s, political and economic crises that engulfed the country left the civil service in complete disarray (Ayee, 2001), opening the sluice gates for donors (e.g., World Bank, IMF) to support public sector reform programs initiated by the government (Haruna, 2001). Obviously, the institutional DNA of the civil service was infested with such administrative parasites as excessive bureaucratic processes and inhibitive rules and regulations, lack of clear policy direction, poor work ethics, low morale, and lack of professional discipline and integrity; centralization of powers, over-staffing, and the proliferation of ghost employees that stretched the governments' wage bill; and corruption and a lack of performance incentives (Owusu, 2006; Ohemeng, 2009). These led to the adoption of strategies such as retrenchment of staff (Haruna, 2003) and some minimal decentralization of authority in the civil service. At the heart of measures that sought to revitalize the transformation of public institutions into effective and efficient drivers of national development was the promotion of ideal and progressive administrative ethos (Dodoo, 1997; Ayee, 2001).

Subsequently, the promulgation of the new Civil Service Law, 1993 (Act 327), and the introduction of a Civil Service Performance Improvement Program (CSPIP) under the National Institutional Renewal Program (Ayee, 2001; Antwi et al., 2008) attempted to salvage the sinking image of the civil service. This followed the failure of the previous Civil Service Reform Program (CSRP), introduced in 1987, to restructure and review staff functions and related human resource issues. The new administrative regime (at the dawn of the 4th Republican Constitution in 1993) had a renewed focus directed towards the introduction and development of human resource capacities aimed at strengthening public management. The Office of the Head of Civil Service (OHCS) was rejuvenated to provide leadership to the civil service, overseen by a Civil Service Council and under the supervision of the Public Services Commission (PSC). Employee recruitment was made the preserve of the OHCS, whereas promotions and sanctions were supervised by the PSC. At the ministerial level under the new dispensation, the administrative machinery is headed by a Chief Director, who is the most senior civil servant and advisor to the sector minister. Chief Directors have oversight responsibility over directorates, and directors of departments as well as unit heads.

Performance Appraisal in Ghana's Civil Service

The relationship between the performance of management and employees, and how they individually or collectively influence organizational performance has been established (Debrah, 2001). Prior to the enactment of the civil service law in Ghana, staff performance was appraised using the Annual Confidential Reporting System (Haruna, 2003; Owusu, 2006; Ohemeng, 2009). Apart from being a top-down instrument, this method did not allow employee inputs into the identification of performance targets, capacity gaps, and training needs. Its disconnection from promotion decisions and other forms of motivation such as performance-based remuneration further led to doubts about its credibility as promotion and salary increases were almost always expected without hard work and results (Ayee, 2001).

Renewed attempts to modernize the civil service with the introduction of the CSRP and the CSPIP encouraged continuous assessment of individual performance with the aid of Performance Improvement Plans (PIPs) (Dodoo, 1997; Ayee, 2001). The objective was to focus on achieving institutional results that gave value for money, while giving the civil service a customer-oriented image characterized by a high sense of professionalism. A new performance reporting system was established to enable MDAs under the civil service to submit regular reports (quarterly, mid-year, and annual) about their performance to the office of the Head of Civil Service for assessment and feedback. Performance Contracts (PCs) prepared by MDAs, and signed with their supervisory agencies were linked to employee performance targets and overall organizational goals. PCs in the civil service, signed by senior bureaucrats (chief directors) and their ministers, were witnessed and approved by the OHCS while similar contracts between State Owned Enterprises (SOEs) and the Ministry Of Finance (MOF) were witnessed and supervised by the State Enterprises Commission (SEC) (Ohemeng, 2010). While PCs in the latter entailed financial indicators that gave a snapshot of SOEs' financial health, the non-profitability of the civil service focused on performance measures that reflected the contribution of different administrative levels to projected outcomes in terms of policy formulation, implementation, monitoring, and evaluation of set targets.

Under the new performance management system, routine staff appraisal was considered an entry point for implementing cultural change in the bureaucracy. The introduction of self- appraisal instruments (SAIs) under the CSPIP was seen as a mechanism for assessing the internal capacities of MDAs, and how effectively their mandates were being carried out (Ayee, 2001). While the civil service was to undergo restructuring, staffing levels and salary grades were designed to motivate and attract highly qualified professionals into the service. A survey of Regional Coordinating Councils (RCCs) and some Metropolitan, Municipal, and District Assemblies (MMDAs) involving the use of the SAI ascribed the perception of poor civil service performance to lack of financial resources and basic logistics, followed by the over-centralization of human resource decisions (Ayee, 2001). Despite optimistic arguments advanced by Dodoo (1997) that employee participation in the preparation of PIPs under the CSPIP was anticipated to lead to better outcomes, it was later revealed that government's posture and attitude as well as those of civil servants were central to the success of the program (Ayee, 2001; Owusu, 2006; Ohemeng, 2009).

It has become evident that civil servants' perceived ownership of PIPs by virtue of their participation in plan preparation was inadequate to address all the unintended consequences of performance standards and performance measurement. Ayee (2001) reminds parties involved in performance review processes to be mindful of possible controversies and vested interests in setting goals and targets for employees. Since service delivery by the civil service is evaluated differently by different stakeholders, we agree with Connolly et al. (1980) that performance appraisal should as well be varied, depending on whose performance is being assessed, how it is appraised, and under what conditions. Similarly, it is important to clarify why particular performance goals are set and how performance would be measured and how performance information will be utilized and by whom?

It is believed that the way performance information is obtained, analyzed, interpreted, and communicated influence its impact on organizational decisions and performance (Larbi, 2001; Talbot, 2008; Ashworth et al., 2010). Indeed, there seem to be some measure of consensus suggesting that reform efforts have failed to adequately deploy performance appraisal to transform attitudes of Ghanaian civil servants (Adei & Boachie-Danquah, 2003; Owusu, 2006; Ohemeng, 2009). As the civil service continues to be saddled with acute bureaucratic inertia, it will be interesting to unravel the underlying causes of such tendencies despite the implementation of performance appraisal systems. While institutional fragmentation and parallel and sometimes conflicting structures for administrative and managerial steering have been identified as impediments to the implementation of performance assessment in Ghana (Ohemeng, 2009), other studies have shown how culture affects performance appraisal (Ogbonna, 1992; Newman, 1994; O'Donnell, 1998; Riketta, 2002).

According to Debrah (2001), traditional values and customs in Ghana permeate modern administrative systems, undermining professional values of meritorious appointments and promotions, performance appraisal, and reward systems. The effect of social relations and nepotism on public sector performance cannot be underestimated (Hasty, 2005). As native custom encourages respect for the elderly, it is believed that young managers will rarely be keen on undertaking formal performance assessment of elderly staff or issue performance instructions (Debrah, 2001; Ohemeng, 2009).

In an environment where appraisal is seen as a nuisance or a necessary evil (Gomez-Mejia, 1990), the sincerity of performance feedback becomes crucial to the success of an appraisal system. Intuitively, while performance managers may avoid appraisal processes that produce negative feedback, such an attitude could stem from the absence of certain fundamental skills and conditions. Grint (1993), argues that managers' lack of interpersonal skills and staff mistrust of an appraisal system could induce perverse performance outcomes. It is believed that both appraisers and the appraised must build a certain harmonious relationship that enhances constructive feedback and the acceptance of appraisal outcomes (Gomez-Mejia, 1990). A summary of relational issues would suggest that employees and performance managers should implement their performance appraisal processes without "gaming" or allowing them to become mere cosmetic administrative exercises.

It is obvious from the review that public administration in Ghana is still evolving. Hence, understanding the Ghanaian reform experience and civil service performance requires critical re-examination, generally by evaluating the role and impact of the entire public administration landscape up to date, and particularly, by examining the commitment of civil servants to aspects of management reform such as performance appraisal. Even though motivation in the civil service apparently symbolizes the "stick and carrot" analogy, current trends in performance appraisal must go beyond emphasizing managerial skills and competence, value for money, efficiency, effectiveness, and trust in government to include such variables that seek to protect the integrity of the civil service. As many Ghanaians increasingly become more discerning, the civil service will be challenged by public concerns and demand for high professional moral standards (Haruna, 2001) backed by sincere commitment to performance and selfless, dedicated service provision.

PERFORMANCE APPRAISAL AND ADMINISTRATIVE CULTURE: A CONCEPTUAL OVERVIEW

The co-option and popularity of culture as a concept in public administration and management studies has existed for several decades, but remains a contentious subject. While tracing its origins to social anthropology, the use of culture in organizational studies has attracted widely divergent views and interpretations that are broadly attributed to theoretical hollowness and the multi-dimensionality of the construct (Ogbonna, 1992; Harris & Ogbonna, 2002). Existing literature has fully underscored prevailing conceptual, theoretical, and definitional debates as well as perspectives through

which culture is studied and understood in organizational settings (see Legge, 1994; Driscoll & Morris, 2001; Ogbonna & Harris, 2002). This would therefore not be repeated here.

Nonetheless, recurrent themes in most of the discussions of administrative culture present culture as a collection of intangible assumptions, manifested in shared values, behaviors, beliefs, artifacts, and sometimes in myths (Ogbonna, 1992; Newman, 1994; Harris & Ogbonna, 2002). If administrative culture is understood as a collection of common values, attitudes, codes, and behaviors shared by individuals, teams, and groups in organizational settings, then construing performance appraisal as a normative process would imply that some level of agreement or acceptance is reached by the parties involved. However, in practice, this might not be the case as the introduction of performance appraisal could attract negative reactions (Cleveland & Murphy, 1992; Poon, 2004). There is evidence that employee performance could be severely undermined when the appraisal instrument fails to obtain full legitimacy of the stakeholders involved (Greenberg & Tyler, 1987).

Generally, the purpose for, and the response to the introduction of appraisal is seen as the starting point for its admission into an institution's culture. Daley (1993) contends that employee appraisal could be deployed to satisfy "developmental" and "judgmental" purposes that are linked to organizational goals and standards. According to this categorization, developmental purposes are those aimed at building staff capacity and expertise through training, while judgmental purpose refers to actions such as promotions, performance-based pay increases, demotions, reinstatement, merit pay, or reassignments (Daley, 1993). While this distinction may be instrumental for an organization's performance management system, it does not illuminate the procedural features and integrity associated with the categories.

Contextualizing administrative culture as shared traits of public servants and bureaucrats within the American political system, Henderson (2004) examined the evolution of administrative culture from incipient patrician notions that made public administration a preserve for "gentlemen," through a transition period of widespread spoils that motivated public office holders to perform, to present merit-based administrative cultures. This path-dependent differentiation demonstrates how variations in administrative needs and contexts created sub-cultures that started as traditional, became inwardly self-protective, and now entrepreneurial in nature. The weakness of the above shifts in administrative culture is the failure to indicate how performance is measured under each phase. While the drive to "reinvent government" (Hood, 1991) by adopting New Public Management strategies encourages public institutions to treat citizens as "business customers," the impetus for entrenching performance appraisal in the civil service should be derived from the commitment to transform operational performance that is related, by design, to strategic objectives.

Some researchers have observed that top-down performance appraisal has become anachronistic in modern public management due to the negative performance outcomes it produces. Employee participation is thus encouraged in determining feasible performance indicators and targets (Meyer, 1991; O'Donnell, 1998; Johnsen, 2005). Since unconstructive feedback might leave employees with bad feelings that might negatively affect their performance, it is believed that many managers feel reluctant to undertake performance appraisal until considerable pressure is exerted on them to do so. Meyer (1991, p. 70) argued that performance assessment systems implemented by public sector organizations are more likely to fail than succeed because they have been reduced to bureaucratic procedure that satisfy human resource departments' annual ritual of appraisals that negligibly impact or contribute to the quality of organizational performance. There will be less hope for performance appraisal to be mainstreamed into the administrative culture of the civil service when management regard performance appraisal interviews as unpleasant exercises that must be avoided, postponed, or conducted in a hurry with minimal detail (Kopelman, 1986).

While deteriorating administrative culture may necessitate the use of performance appraisal as an instrument of control, it is still inconclusive whether appraisers and the appraisees have been able to use the appraisal process to exercise behavioral control. In order to guarantee behavior change, performance information must generate unquestionable information and feedback that is associated with desired performance outcomes (DeNisi, 2011). It is argued that employees perception of the appraisal process or their notions of "procedural justice" tend to affect both the legitimacy and acceptance of appraisal ratings (Greenberg & Tyler, 1987; Cloutier & Vilhuber, 2008). The accuracy of employee performance data has been a central focus of extensive research. The integrity of the appraisal process will thus be bolstered if the appraising authority demonstrably makes it transparent, while creating ample space for employees to express objections when they feel dissatisfied with aspects of the appraisal process (DeNisi, 2011). It has been proven that employees are more likely to accept the outcome of their assessment and will change their performance accordingly when they are convinced about the fairness of the assessment process (Johnsen, 2005; Gravina & Siers, 2011).

A critique of performance appraisal draws attention to social and contextual factors by considering affective, motivational, and political influences of the appraisal process (Poon, 2004). It is asserted that more often than not, the accuracy and outcome of an appraisal exercise is contingent on the motivation of the appraiser/performance manager (Cleveland & Murphy, 1992). It is found that appraisers may deliberately manipulate or tamper with the appraisal process to produce results that fulfill their interests (Poon, 2004). There are also reports of performance managers who deliberately inflated performance ratings of their subordinates for political reasons (Clinton, Sims, & Gioia, 1987). Some managers adjust performance scores to earn the goodwill of employees or avoid conflicts that might arise as a result of lower performance ratings (Fried & Tiegs, 1995). There is also evidence that performance managers manipulated ratings of poorly performing subordinates by giving them higher marks in order to avoid a permanent record of unacceptable performance on their personal files, while insubordinate employees were handed low marks to push them out of the organization (Clinton, et al., 1987; Poon, 2004). Indeed, when the rationale and value of performance appraisal become dubious, one wonders how employees will respond to performance ratings when they realize that their promotions or upward wage adjustments have not been fairly treated by the appraisal process?

METHODOLOGY AND DATA COLLECTION TECHNIQUES

This study is a qualitative enquiry which relies upon the results of three focus group discussions with senior level managers of local and regional government in Ghana. Participants were composed of seven district coordinating directors, two development planning officers, one regional coordinating director; and one deputy regional coordinating director. Within the local government system of Ghana, the Coordinating Director heads the administrative and permanent staffs; the planning officer heads the District Planning Coordinating Unit (DPCU), and the district structure is overseen by the Regional Coordinating Council (RCC). In this regard, the group is considered homogenous (Lehoux, Poland, & Daudelin, 2006) as all the participants are senior-level managers and work within the local government system of Ghana, albeit at different levels. This article adopted a purposive sampling regime and, specifically, the criterion sampling which samples respondents based upon their experience of the subject being investigated (Teddlie & Yu, 2007; Collingridge & Gantt, 2008; Abrams, 2010). The respondents were sampled by virtue of their privileged positions and experiences as senior civil servants.

The FGD was considered appropriate for studying the phenomenon because it allows a variety of opinions on a single subject in a single sitting. The FGD also introduces multiple and varied contextual experiences into a study. It exudes interactional spontaneity (Palmer, Larkin, de Visser, & Fadden, 2010) and social interaction (Lehoux, et al., 2006) which incites discussants into talking about nuances of the phenomenon under consideration.

The study adopted two different forms of FGD in two groups. First, participants were introduced to the topic of performance appraisal and the objective of the study explained to them (Kitzinger, 1994). After participants' consent was obtained, they were guided to discuss various aspects of the topic, followed by a comprehensive synthesis of the discussion. The second discussion was a debate (Kitzinger, 1994) between the two groups, one week after the first. One group spoke on the practical usefulness of PA and provided a justification why it should be maintained as a performance management tool in the Ghana Civil Service. The second group spoke on the practical "uselessness" of PA, highlighting the weaknesses of PA as a performance management tool and therefore tried to justify why a better system must be sought. This second approach was adopted in line with Kitzinger's (1994) advice to introduce exercises into focus discussions.

The proceedings of the discussions were tape recorded and transcribed. The transcripts were reviewed by the researchers to generate, organize, and interpret common themes and ideas that emerged from the data (Thomas, 2006). In the end, six themes were identified which are discussed in the next section.

EXAMINING THE CONTEXT: EMPIRICAL PERSPECTIVES ON PA IN GHANA'S CIVIL SERVICE

The findings of the study were distilled into six themes representing aspects of PA in the CS. These themes are the mechanical aspects of PA; superstition, spirituality, and the fear factors; victimization and intimidation of subordinates; correlation between the PA system and organizational objectives; objectivity in PA; and outcomes and purposes of PA. These themes are discussed below.

The Mechanical Aspects of PA in Ghana's Civil Service

Several elements were identified with the PA system in Ghana CS. The first is that the PA forms are not easily accessible as employees need to buy them from the Government Printer, the Ghana Publishing house in Accra. The second element is the concern that the forms are not user-friendly. The forms are said to be too detailed, demanding information on both developmental and evaluative aspects of PA (Boswell & Boudreau, 2002), making it very technical and time-consuming to complete. The arguments are that the process requires so much information, some of which is difficult to obtain at the end of year. This results in a situation where managers ask their subordinates to complete forms for their endorsement. In other words, employees actually appraise themselves. "Managers ask their subordinates to complete the forms so that they will just vet and endorse. What use is this process if we can't assure ourselves that it is done fairly by the people who are required to conduct PA? This way, the subordinates will praise themselves rather than being appraised."

It appears that managers do not perceive PA as a process aimed at positive organizational cultural change. Acquisition and utilization of appropriate data in the performance appraisal process is considered a critical factor with consequential effect on the outcomes and eventual usefulness of the process (Harris, 1994). With the current state of affairs, the usefulness of performance appraisals in the Ghana Civil Service is compromised. This is consistent with Meyer's (1991) assertion that the existence of the process only fulfills the paper requirements rather than serving useful purposes.

Other issues that relate to the mechanical aspect of the PA are the arbitrary and subjective nature of PA. In the Ghana Civil Service, there are no guidelines on scoring and assessing candidates and superiors are seldom given any training on how to score and appraise their subordinates. Also, until recently when attempts have been made to revise the forms, the PA forms in use had been in existence for almost four decades. As a result of these challenges, PA is only sought after when employees are due for promotion interviews.

Superstition, Spirituality, and the Fear Factors

The focus discussion revealed that there are elements of fear, superstition, and spirituality in PA administration in the Ghana Civil Service. Some supervisors are said to be chronically guilty of poor performance and so do not have the moral courage to realistically appraise their subordinates. The second elements were superstition and spirituality and that supervisors are sometimes fearful that subordinates would invoke spiritual curses against them if they rated them poorly. It was reported that some subordinates are known to send superiors to pastors, mallams, and shrines for curses or to be "worked" upon for preventing these employees from getting promoted. It is a common occurrence in most churches, especially charismatic and Pentecostal churches, to hear pastors ordering prayers against supervisors who are determined to negatively influence their members' promotion. This has the effect of putting considerable social pressure on appraisers. Subordinates are able to invoke spirituality to pressure appraisers for favorable appraisals because religion is at the heart of Ghanaian society.

A participant shared a story of how he found charms and amulets under his seat in his new office the first day he reported to a new station:

> I found black powder and some charms under my chair and this scared me. I feared for my life and thought initially of asking for reposting but decided against the idea. I prayed and asked for the items to be removed. This really affected the way I did many things including how I appraised my subordinates because, I didn't know who or what the purpose of these were.

The consensus was that if appraisals are done in fear, their objectivity and usefulness is certainly in doubt. In other words, the social (Levy & Williams, 2004; Ferris & Treadway, 2008) and religious contexts of appraisals have significantly influenced their outcome, quality, and use.

Victimization and Intimidation of Subordinates

Aside from the above pressures, both appraisers and those being appraised appropriate both intrinsic and extrinsic rewards from the PA systems of the Ghana Civil Service. We identified that in the least, managers are accused of using and continue to use PA practice as a mechanism to intimidate and pressure subordinates into submission. This is probably a reflection of managers' use of the PA system as a source of additional positional power. Subordinates who are not in the good graces of their superiors are said to have been appraised very negatively. This potentially affects interpersonal relationships and can negatively affect the self-esteem of those being appraised which could result in low performance. Subordinates have sometimes been reminded by their supervisors that PA will come up so you better "behave" or you have yourself to blame (Monyatsi, Steyn, & Kamper, 2006). This is said to be responsible for the ability of some superiors to use their subordinates for unofficial activities as employees need to cultivate the favor of their superiors. A participant laments: "In fact, PA is an effective tool. If someone wants to get you out of the system, PA is an effective tool to do so especially that we don't have good appeal systems in place and the fact that superiors tend to support each other in the event of appeals."

Male managers are said to use PA as a tool to sexually exploit their female subordinates. An example of this allegation was cited using a case that received extensive media reportage in Ghana. A male director of the National Disaster Management Organization (NADMO) in Kpando District was said to have sexually harassed a female employee who got transferred when she refused the sexual demands.

In the local government service, Chief Executives (CEs) (political heads) are required to appraise the Coordinating Directors (CDs) (the Administrative heads). This was considered problematic as some CEs take advantage of PAs to punish un-cooperating CDs. CDs who insist on professionalism rather than political patronage to the advantage of the CE and his political party have often suffered as they have been transferred very frequently. This is said to be referred to as "stubborn cat back-passing" in apparent reference to the fact that such CDs are hardly accepted by any CE and hence get transferred from place to place. A participant intimated: "CDs do not want to be appraised by CEs simply because, they fear political victimization especially if you are not seen to belong to their side of the political divide."

It is therefore imperative to be mindful of political and social dynamics that significantly influence PA processes in the CS (Ferris & Treadway, 2008; Levy & Williams, 2004). Another participant, in proving the point that the PA system is laden with victimization, recounted his experience as follows:

I personally had a problem in one of the districts I worked in. I was rated average during PA because I had insisted on rendering a task in a way I considered professionally reasonable. When I went before a panel for promotion, they enquired whether I had a problem with my boss as they considered his comments detestable. I had to explain the incident to convince them that I was not to blame.

These comments are in line with findings of Monyatsi et al. (2006, p. 223) that PAs are used to "oppress . . . , reprimand . . . and punish . . ." subordinates who do not "conform" to dictates of superiors and to favor the "boot lickers." For those affected by the victimization and intimidation, the appeals system that is supposed to offer such victims the opportunity to seek redress is also quite faulty and rather slow. This casts a negative light on the accountability systems which are supposed to be built into any rigorous performance appraisal process meant for developmental and evaluative purposes.

Correlation Between the PA System and Organizational Objectives

Some of the tenets of the PA system are said to be at variance with CS organizational objectives. To effectively appraise performance requires regular updates of job analysis information outlining job descriptions and specification. This way individual job description will tie into organizational objectives and provide the bases for PA. The Ghana Civil Service was said to have some jobs that do not have updated job analysis results. Also, outcomes in the civil service are considered remote from action. Consequently, at best, outputs serve as measuring standards which may not necessarily feed into the overall objective of the organization. These culminate in arbitrary objective-setting. There is also often no correlation between what the organization's objectives are and the standards required of appraisees. One participant observed: "I often set targets for my subordinates based upon what I think they should do for the year. For instance, all reports for a quarter should be submitted by the 15 of the ensuing month and I appraise them based upon such targets."

The extent to which both task and context responsibilities are assessed vis-a-vis their implications for the attainment of organizational goals are often not clarified (Ferris & Treadway, 2008). Beyond these, performance appraisal in the Ghana Civil Service is considered a system of praise singing and an instrument for gaining promotion. It is not considered as part of a holistic performance management strategy. Some civil servants therefore get offended when PAs do not conform to their expectations that they will enable them to get promoted.

Objectivity in PA

Objectivity in PA was questioned by participants of the FGDs who observed that several elements in the PA system do not facilitate objectivity of appraisals. Several elements in the Ghana Civil Service work against the attainment of objectivity in PA. One of such elements is the outdated PA form. Until recently when efforts were made to revise the PA forms, the forms had been in use for almost four decades and had outlived their relevance. Also, the absence of guidelines and standard criteria (DeNisi, 2011) leads the process to conjecturing according to appraisers' whims and caprices. A participant wants to know how to interpret a score of "above average" from two separate raters within the same or similar organizations.

There is also no training on the conduct of PA and supervisors rely on their personal understanding and idiosyncrasies to rate employees. In addition, the face-to-face contact was also said to make it difficult to score objectively (Levy & Williams, 2004) during PAs. The comments from one participant summed up the objectivity dilemma of appraisers in Ghana Civil Service:

> You work with everybody, you are nice to everybody, and so you can't look into a face and say, you haven't worked [satisfactorily] so I will rate you low. You see, the person has worked for three years and normal or natural process demands that the person should be promoted. Then between you and that person you try to rate that person low or say you haven't done well. This is very difficult to do. It is very difficult to be objective.

The implication is that, if everybody was nice to you, then everybody is likely to get a high score even if they did not merit the score. This could be problematic and may obfuscate the essence of PA.

Outcomes and Purposes of PA

PAs are meant to identify training needs of employees (Babiak, Neumann, & Hare, 2010), be the basis for rewards and promotions (Aguinis & Pierce, 2008), and be a source of information for employees on their performance to motivate them to give their best (DeNisi, 2011). However, in the Ghana Civil Service, PAs hardly serve these purposes. Selection of employees for training is hugely political, especially if the training programs come with some financial benefits (e.g., per diems, etc.) and even more so when the training program takes place outside Ghana. A number of factors such as affinity with the boss, perceived political affiliation, and ethnic backgrounds may influence employee selection for training. In the same way, rewards and promotion are to some degree not dependent on PA results. There is no wonder PA does not receive the kind of attention it deserves in the Ghana Civil Service.

PA remains one of the key ways to measure employee performance. Participants observed that PA remains a critical part of managing employees' performance. They argued that although the practice may have some challenges, it is very useful in assessing employees' performance on the job. It generates vital information not only on how employees are performing now, but also on how to make them better

performers in future. In other words, PA has a developmental purpose, aimed at helping to develop the capacities of employees (Daley, 1993).

PA also contributes to building a relationship between employees and their supervisors. The process demands that supervisors engage their subordinates in open discussions about their performance. Subordinates are also provided the opportunity to review the assessment of their supervisors and to express their opinions on how they have been assessed. This platform acts as a check against arbitrariness and opulent victimization.

One organizational cultural element that makes PA an important practice is the esprit de corps in the civil service. The esprit de corps has the tendency to encourage supervisors to feel a sense of responsibility towards subordinates and their development. Trust, confidence, and cohesion ensues as a result.

PA measures performance and helps to address performance shortfalls and skills deficiencies. This way, the Civil Service is able to predict its future skills needs and make provision to address these.

CONCLUSION

Culture is said to die hard, and as a result PA as a cultural element of the Civil Service in Ghana may continue for a long time. Since organizations are hesitant to let go of PA (Masterson & Taylor, 1996), this article proposes that PA be examined within the larger context of performance management. As it stands now PA is taken out of context and considered an isolated theme. This way, it may continue to cause negative feelings among civil servants. It should therefore be linked to the overall performance management strategies of the organizations which should focus on the roles of individual employees within them.

Since civil servants in Ghana are required to undergo a certificate and diploma training in public administration, the curriculum of this training should include not only how to conduct PA but a detailed discussion of its essence for continual employee development and organizational performance. It should include how to set and evaluate objectives using the job analysis outputs. In this sense, it is worthwhile to indicate that job analysis should be regularly conducted and periodically updated. The Public Services Commission should be required to take charge of this function of the conduct of job analysis at regular intervals.

The civil service cultural trait of bureaucratic paper pushing should be reworked to ensure that PA is computerized. An overall strategy will be to progress towards the development of software for PA. This way, standards, guidelines, and frameworks for analysis could be integrated into the software.

Performance contracts should be revisited in the Ghana Civil Service to exact accountability from service directors and heads. These will ensure that supervisors become wary of the kind of scores they assign to subordinates as the performance of these subordinates will influence their ability to meet the performance target of their ministries, departments, and agencies.

Performance of employees in the Ghana Civil Service (CS) has been described as abysmal and has received significant attention and reform efforts have been undertaken aimed at correcting these performance deficits. As an important administrative cultural element, PA can play a crucial role in enhancing the performance of Ghanaian civil servants. However, the attitude towards this administrative cultural trait leaves much to be desired. This article establishes that the leadership in the Ghana Civil Service seldom gives the needed attention to this administrative practice. Appraisers are seldom trained to perform this important function and have often done it haphazardly. Civil servants only consider the practice as a tool for promotion and not a mechanism for performance improvement. The letter of PA is pursued rather than its spirit. The practice has become rhetoric rather than a substantive cultural element meant to make any impact on the behavior of civil servants.

We recommend an overhaul of the PA system by integrating it into a holistic performance management program, integrating PA training into civil service mandatory training programs, and reintroducing performance contracts to ensure that leadership takes PA seriously. A revision and computerization of the PA system is also necessary. In addition, we suggest further research into the role of superstition and spirituality in promotion in the Ghana Civil Service.

REFERENCES

Abrams, L. S. (2010). Sampling 'Hard to reach' populations in qualitative research. *Qualitative Social Work, 9*(4), 536–550.

Adei, S., & Boachie-Danquah, Y. (2003). The Civil Service Performance Improvement Program (CSPIP) in Ghana Lessons of experience. *African Journal of Public Administration and Management, 14*(1 & 2), 10–23.

Aguinis, H., & Pierce, C. A. (2008). Enhancing the relevance of organizational behavior by embracing performance management research. *Journal of Organizational Behavior, 29*(1), 139–145.

Anderfuhren-Biget, S. (2012). Profiles of public service-motivated civil servants: Evidence from a multicultural country. *International Journal of Public Administration, 35*(1), 5–18.

Antwi, K. B., Analoui, F., & Nana-Agyekum, D. (2008). Public sector reform in Sub-Saharan Africa: What can be learnt from the civil service performance improvement program in Ghana? *Public Administration and Development, 28*(4), 253–264.

Ashworth, R., Boyne, G., & Entwistle, T. (Eds.). (2010). *Public service improvement: Theories and evidence.* Oxford: Oxford University Press.

Ayee, J. R. A. (2001). Civil service reform in Ghana: A case study of contemporary reform problems in Africa. *African Journal of Political Science, 6*(1), 1–41.

Babiak, P., Neumann, C. S., & Hare, R. D. (2010). Corporate psychopathy: Talking the walk. *Behavioral Sciences & the Law, 28*(2), 174–193.

Boswell, W. R., & Boudreau, J. W. (2002). Separating the developmental and evaluative performance appraisal uses. *Journal of Business and Psychology, 16*(3), 391–412.

Cleveland, J. N., & Murphy, K. R. (1992). Analyzing performance appraisal as goal-directed behavior. *Research in Personnel and Human Resources Management, 10*, 121–185.

Clinton, O. L., Sims, H. P., Jr., & Gioia, D. A. (1987). Behind the mask: The politics of employee appraisal. *The Academy of Management Executive (1987–1989), 1*(3), 183–193.

Cloutier, J., & Vilhuber, L. (2008). Procedural justice criteria in salary determination. *Journal of Managerial Psychology, 23*(6), 713–740.

Collingridge, D. S., & Gantt, E. E. (2008). The quality of qualitative research. *American Journal of Medical Quality, 23*(5), 389–395.

Connolly, T., Conlon, E. J., & Deutsch, S. J. (1980). Organizational effectiveness: A multiple-constituency approach. *The Academy of Management Review, 5*(2), 211–217.

Daley, D. M. (1993). Performance appraisal as an aid in personnel decisions: Linkages between techniques and purposes in North Carolina municipalities. *The American Review of Public Administration, 23*(3), 201–213.

Debrah, Y. (Ed.). (2001). *Human resources management in Ghana.* London: Routledge.

DeNisi, A. S. (2011). Managing performance to change behavior. *Journal of Organizational Behavior Management, 31*(4), 262–276.

Dodoo, R. (1997). Performance standards and measuring performance in Ghana. *Public Administration and Development, 17*(1), 115–121.

Driscoll, A., & Morris, J. (2001). Stepping out: Rhetorical devices and culture change management in the UK civil service. *Public Administration, 79*(4), 803–824.

Ferris, R. G., & Treadway, C. D. (2008). Culture diversity and performance appraisal systems. In L. D. Stone & F. E. Stone-Romero (Eds.), *The Influence of culture on human resource management processes and practices.* New York, London: Taylor & Francis Group, LLC.

Fletcher, C. (2001). Performance appraisal and management: The developing research agenda. *Journal of Occupational and Organizational Psychology, 74*(4), 473–487.

Fried, Y., & Tiegs, R. B. (1995). Supervisors' role conflict and role ambiguity differential relations with performance ratings of subordinates and the moderating effect of screening

Gomez-Mejia, L. R. (1990). Increasing productivity: Performance appraisal and reward systems. *Personnel Review, 19*(2), 21–26.

Gravina, N. E., & Siers, B. P. (2011). Square pegs and round holes: Ruminations on the relationship between performance appraisal and performance management. *Journal of Organizational Behavior Management, 31*(4), 277–287.

Greenberg, J., & Tyler, T. R. (1987). Why procedural justice in organizations? *Social Justice Research, 1*(2), 127–142.

Grint, K. (1993). What's wrong with performance appraisals? A critique and a suggestion. *Human Resource Management Journal, 3*(3), 61–77.

Harris, L. C., & Ogbonna, E. (2002). The unintended consequences of culture interventions: A study of unexpected outcomes. *British Journal of Management, 13*(1), 31–49.

Haruna, P. F. (2001). Reflective public administration reform: Building relationships, bridging gaps in Ghana. *African Studies Review, 44*(1), 37–57.

Haruna, P. F. (2003). Reforming Ghana's public service: Issues and experiences in comparative perspective. *Public Administration Review, 63*(3), 343–354.

Hasty, J. (2005). The pleasures of corruption: Desire and discipline in Ghanaian political culture. *Cultural Anthropology, 20*(2), 271–301.

Henderson, K. M. (2004). Characterizing American public administration: The concept of administrative culture. *International Journal of Public Sector Management, 17*(3), 234–250.

Hood, C. (1991). A public management for all seasons. *Public Administration, 69*(1), 3–19.

Johnsen, Å. (2005). What does 25 years of experience tell us about the state of performance measurement in public policy and management? *Public Money & Management, 25*(1), 9–17.

Kitzinger, J. (1994). The methodology of focus groups: The importance of interaction between research participants. *Sociology of Health & Illness, 16*(1), 103–121.

Kopelman, R. E. (1986). *Managing productivity in organizations: A practical, people-oriented perspective.* New York: McGraw-Hill.

Larbi, G. (2001). Performance contracting in practice: Experience and lessons from the water sector in Ghana. *Public Management Review, 3*(3), 305–324.

Legge, K. (1994). *Managing culture: Fact or fiction* (Volumes. 397–433). Oxford: Blackwell.

Lehoux, P., Poland, B., & Daudelin, G. (2006). Focus group research and "the patient's view." *Social Science & Medicine, 63*(8), 2091–2104.

Levy, P. E., & Williams, J. R. (2004). The social context of performance appraisal: A review and framework for the future. *Journal of Management, 30*(6), 881–905.

Masterson, S. S., & Taylor, M. S. (1996). Total quality management and performance appraisal: An integrative perspective. *Journal of Quality Management, 1*(1), 67–89.

Meyer, H. H. (1991). A solution to the performance appraisal feedback enigma. *The Executive, 5*(1), 68–76.

Monyatsi, P., Steyn, T., & Kamper, G. (2006). Teacher appraisal in Botswana secondary schools: A critical analysis. *South African Journal of Education, 26*(2), 215–228.

Newman, J. (1994). Beyond the vision: Cultural change in the public sector. *Public Money & Management, 14*(2), 59–64.

O'Donnell, M. (1998). Creating a performance culture? Performance-based pay in the Australian public service. *Australian Journal of Public Administration, 57*(3), 28–40.

Ogbonna, E. (1992). Managing organisational culture: Fantasy or reality? *Human Resource Management Journal, 3*(2), 42–54.

Ogbonna, E., & Harris, L. C. (2002). Managing organisational culture: Insights from the hospitality industry. *Human Resource Management Journal, 12*(1), 33–53.

Ohemeng, F. L. K. (2009). Constraints in the implementation of performance management systems in developing countries. *International Journal of Cross Cultural Management, 9*(1), 109–132.

Ohemeng, F. L. K. (2010). The new Charter System in Ghana: The 'holy grail' of public service delivery? *International Review of Administrative Sciences, 76*(1), 115–136.

Ohemeng, F. K., & Anebo, F. K. (2012). The politics of administrative reforms in Ghana: Perspectives from path dependency and punctuated equilibrium theories. *International Journal of Public Administration, 35*(3), 161–176.

Owusu, F. (2006). Differences in the performance of public organisations in Ghana: Implications for public-sector reform policy. *Development Policy Review, 24*(6), 693–705.

Palmer, M., Larkin, M., de Visser, R., & Fadden, G. (2010). Developing an interpretative phenomenological approach to focus group data. *Qualitative Research in Psychology, 7*(2), 99–121.

Poon, J. M. L. (2004). Effects of performance appraisal politics on job satisfaction and turnover intention. *Personnel Review, 33*(3), 322–334.

Riketta, M. (2002). Attitudinal organizational commitment and job performance: A meta-analysis. *Journal of Organizational Behavior, 23*(3), 257–266.

Talbot, C. (2008). Performance regimes—The institutional context of performance policies. *International Journal of Public Administration, 31*(14), 1569–1591.

Teddlie, C., & Yu, F. (2007). Mixed methods sampling. *Journal of Mixed Methods Research, 1*(1), 77–100.

Thomas, D. R. (2006). A general inductive approach for analyzing qualitative evaluation data. *American Journal of Evaluation, 27*(2), 237–246.

Williams, R. (1998). *Performance management.* London: International Thomson Business Press (Essential Business Psychology Series).

Wunsch, J. S. (2001). Decentralization, local governance and 'recentralization' in Africa. *Public Administration and Development, 21*(4), 277–288.

Administrative Culture in Bulgaria: Sources, Foundations, and Transitions

Deyana Marcheva

Independent Researcher, Sofia, Bulgaria

The article examines how the unique historical experience of Bulgarian society has shaped administrative culture in Bulgaria. The sources, foundations, and transitions of Bulgarian administrative culture reveal continuous tensions between political and social values, between ideology and practices. The concept of administrative culture provides an insight into the "empty shell" issue in the process of Europeanization of Bulgaria and has further policy implications.

INTRODUCTION

The purpose of this article is to examine how the unique historical experience of Bulgarian society has shaped administrative culture in Bulgaria.

First, the article sketches some social and political patterns, psychological orientations, and arrangements in a historical perspective and provides an interpretive profile of the sources of Bulgarian administrative culture. Second, it explores the tension between traditional and modern structural drivers in the re-established Bulgarian state at the end of the 19th and the beginning of 20th century. Thirdly, the article demonstrates that the socio-political transitions in Bulgaria have reinforced duality at the core of the national administrative culture. Understanding this specific imprint has policy implications and it is crucial for the success of the administrative reforms in Bulgaria as a newly acceded member of the European Union.

The concept of administrative culture has been overshadowed by two related concepts, "organizational culture" and "political culture." Besides its legal and organizational structure public administration is marked also by values, orientations, and perceptions. In the last two decades an expanding field of research in administrative culture has proved its relevance as "a mode of understanding public administration across cultures" (Jamil, 1994). Book-length research of administrative culture has been published for Israel (Caiden, 1970), Canada (Dwivedi & Gow, 1999), India (Sharma, 2000), and Bangladesh (Jamil, 2007). The concept of administrative culture is applied to national and regional cases mostly to characterize and identify the administrative system of a nation state (Dwivedi, 2005, p. 20). It is also used as an explanatory construct to understand differences and similarities between countries or unions (Henderson, 2011, p. 4). The culture component is also essential for successful cooperation between different institutions (Thedieck, 2007).

The notion of administrative culture has hardly had any explanatory role for understanding public administration in Bulgaria. As far as throwing any light on the subject, the accounts have reduced it to the concept of organizational culture (Sotirova & Davidkov, 2004). And yet the analysis of Bulgarian administrative culture provides an insight into the "empty shell" issue in the process of Europeanization of Bulgaria and has further policy implications.

SOURCES OF ADMINISTRATIVE CULTURE IN BULGARIA

The unique historical experience of Bulgaria has been determined by its location between Europe and Asia, at the junction of trade routes and strategic military positions. The story of the Bulgarian state's formation begins in the 6th and 7th centuries with the Slavic incursions into the Balkan Peninsula at the borderline of the Byzantine Empire (Runciman, 1938, p. 26). The name Bulgaria comes from the

Bulgars, tribes composed of skilled, warlike horsemen who, in the mid-7th century, migrated from the steppes to the north of the Black Sea towards the south of the Danube River.

In 681 Byzantium recognized by treaty the Bulgar control of the region between the Balkans and the Danube and this is considered to be the starting point of the Bulgarian state (Zlatarski, 1918, p. 204) Subsequently the 8th and 9th centuries saw a process of consolidation of a common culture between the Slavic and Bulgar tribes. That process has been facilitated by the conversion from tribal paganism to Orthodox Christianity, accepted as the official religion of Bulgarian state at the end of the 9th century (Zlatarski, 1927, p. 54). The spread of Christianity was sped up by the work of Saints Cyril and Methodius, who invented an alphabet for writing the Slavic language, known as Old Church Slavonic or Old Bulgarian. On that basis a distinct Slavic culture was consolidated and subsequently passed through periods of both expansionist independence (in the High Middle Ages) and subordination to outside political systems (Byzantine Empire and Ottoman Empire).

From the 9th until the 14th century Bulgaria competed with the Byzantine Empire for regional domination in the Balkans. During this period, Bulgaria was strongly influenced by the Byzantine political and administrative patterns:

- *Absolute conception of monarchical authority*— The authority of the Byzantine Emperor (Basileus) extended both to the state and to the Church, and he made laws in both civil and religious matters. (Diehl, 1923, p. 726). In Bulgaria Simeon I the Great (893–927), who received his theological education in the University of Constantinople, reproduced the same political model. He nominated the bishops to be elected and conferred investiture on them. He convoked their councils and interfered in theological disputes.
- *Outward appearances and external forms of imperial majesty* (Diehl, 1923, p. 727)—Endless processions and the splendor of imperial trappings were designed to present Basileus as an emanation of the divine. The emperor turned the new Bulgarian capital Preslav into a magnificent religious and cultural centre, intended more as a display of his realm's heyday than as a military fortress.
- *Two-fold hierarchy of rank and office*—the Historical sources recorded the details of a two-fold hierarchy, at the beginning of the 10th century, that determined the rank of all those who had anything to do with the court (dignitaries) or with public administration (high officials) in Byzantium. Eighteen dignitaries, whose titles were derived from the civil or military services of the palace, formed the grades of a kind of *administrative aristocracy*. These personages were also the 60 holders of the offices of public administration, occupying the posts of central government and the high military

or administrative commands. Every official had two titles, one honorary, marking his rank in the administrative nobility, the other indicating the actual office with which he had been invested. Both dignity and office, and advancement in either, depended entirely on the goodwill of the Emperor, who and dismissed officials at his pleasure. (Diehl, 1923, p. 730). These conceptions and model of the Byzantine Empire were spread in the Bulgarian state and administration in the High Middle Ages (Biliarski, 1998), although the latter has never been as complicated and sophisticated as the former.

Bulgarian cultural specificity was determined by the social characteristics of the southern Slav peoples that have always been known as being "neither dishonorable nor spiteful, but *simple in their ways*" (Bartford, 2001, p. 59). The most prominent presentation of the Slavic culture has been made by Procopius:

For these nations, the Sclaveni and the Antae, are not ruled by one man, but *they have lived from of old under a democracy*, and consequently everything which involves their welfare, whether for good or for ill, is referred to the people. It is also true that in all other matters, practically speaking, these two barbarian peoples have had from ancient times the same institutions and customs . . . as a general thing, every man is constantly changing his place of abode . . . I suppose, living apart one man from another, they inhabit their country in a sporadic fashion . . . . (Dewing, 1924, pp. 269–274)

Some researchers have argued that "democracy" is derisively applied by Procopius (Benedicty, 1963, p. 46). Others point out that Procopius could not distinguish between acephalous societies and "primitive democracies" (Evans, 1989, p. 63). In any case Procopius uses the term democracy to explain what was seen as the opposite of Byzantine absolute monarchy. Further, the anonymous author of the *Strategikon* described Sclavenes as "both independent, absolutely refusing to be enslaved or governed, least of all in their own land" (XI 4.1). While Sclavenes might unite to attack or repel an enemy at one time, at another they would fragment into feuding factions, quarreling over land.

By reference to the fact that Slavs were unable to fight a battle at very short range many historians have pointed out the "lack of strategy," "lack of government," and "ill feeling toward one another" (Zasterova, 1971, pp. 51–52) as primary features of the Slavic "segmentary society" (Nystazopoulou-Pelekidou, 1986, p. 354). In such a system, very close to what Evans-Pritchard called an "ordered anarchy" (Fortes & Evans-Pritchard, 1940, p. 296), the functions of maintaining cohesion and social control can be performed simply by the "opposition" and "balancing" of constituent groups.

Hence, the very cultural characteristics of the Slavs have always represented a strong resistance to the impact and assimilation strategies of the Byzantine Empire. Any administrative culture in medieval Bulgaria was to develop in the heart of the inevitable collision between the values of Byzantine political culture and the values of Slavic social culture. Within this tension was generated very early on a specific modal pattern of Bulgarian culture of denial of state and administration.

At the end of the 14th century, both the Byzantine and the Bulgarian cultural and political institutions fell under the Rule of the Ottoman Turks for nearly five centuries. Certain patterns of the Ottoman-Turkish political culture have inevitably penetrated into the social life of Bulgarian people.

The Ottoman Empire developed as a highly advanced organization of an absolute monarchical state based on a dual system of military ("Central Government") and civil administration ("Provincial System"). It was a fundamental rule of the Ottoman Empire to exclude its subjects (the reaya) from the privileges of the military (Inalcik, 1964, p. 44), namely officers of court and army, civil servants, and Muslim scholars. The military were a special class to whom the Sultan had delegated religious or executive power through an imperial decree.

The lineaments of patrimonial bureaucracy emerged as the most typical characteristics of Ottoman polity (Mardin, 1969, p. 259). The basic premise of the patrimonial system, that the ruler is personally responsible for the welfare of his subjects, remained deeply rooted in the psychological orientations of Bulgarian people. Even today the successful approach of any high governmental official in Bulgaria would be to play the role of a patrimonial bureaucrat. At the same time the view of the people toward the administrators and bureaucrats is not as servants, but as rulers.

This could be explained with yet another characteristic of the Ottoman social culture—the lack of those "intermediate" structures representative of the towns in the West that formed the institutional base of civil society and that have been regarded by the cultural historians as constituting the difference between Western feudalism and Eastern despotism.

The fear of any disintegrative influences was the leitmotif of Ottoman statesmanship for a long time (Mardin, 1969, p. 271). It was impossible for autonomous structures to develop in the Ottoman society because any such drive for independence would have been nipped in the bud by forced uprooting and resettling of people. In the Ottoman Empire the Bulgarian ethnic group developed as inherently cellular, self-contained, and readily reproducible units isolated from other cultures. This cultural isolation became the main hindrance to the formation of civil self-awareness and solidarity in Bulgarian society (Genchev, 1988).

The rigid status order prevailing in the Ottoman society was at the root of a dichotomous cultural structure cleaved between political top dogs and underdogs, representing two fundamentally estranged ways of life. The first can be termed the culture of the palace, the second one that of the provinces (Mardin, 1969, p. 270). The "great" culture was associated with such features as war and administration, as life-time occupations, freedom from taxation, etc. On the other side, the rural Turks and the other conquered peoples in the Balkans used various vernaculars, engaged in agriculture or trade and were subject to many taxes and duties, all of those representing the "little" culture. The concept of civilization was the core of the self-image of the Ottoman elite, while the "Turk" was used in a pejorative sense because it meant being "tribal." The clash between the "great" and the "little" culture was inevitable and it could be interpreted as an aspect of the key historical conflict between the military and the kinship society (Jenks, 1908, p. 308). This clash turned into a source for associating administrative culture in Bulgaria with something separate and outside the culture of the nation, something beyond of the reach and control of the ordinary people.

For Bulgarians the Ottoman bureaucracy has symbolized the conqueror, oppressor, and enslaver for almost five centuries. This symbol predetermined Bulgarian denial of the very idea of bureaucracy, because it was indispensably identified with domination and slavery. One might say that the old pattern "people against the state" was historically reinforced and extended to the pattern *people hate and fear the state.*

At the same time the fear of extermination strengthened the *psychology of the "bent head,"* briefly explained by the Bulgarian proverb: "the sword will not cut the bent head" (having its English equivalents in the phrases: "bend your knee and save your head," "a bent head turns away wrath"). Over centuries "the bent head" has turned into an irreversible archetypal response of Bulgarians towards any kind of oppression and injustice, including that by the administration. Some aspects of the culture of denial of state and bureaucracy were reproduced following the National Liberation in 1878 after the Russo-Turkish War (1877–1878).

FOUNDATIONS OF ADMINISTRATIVE CULTURE IN MODERN BULGARIA

Most of the values and beliefs that laid down the foundations of administrative culture in Bulgaria have been formed and developed in the years of Bulgarian state re-establishment at the end of 19th century and the beginning of 20th century.

It is possible to identify two basic layers in the foundations of Bulgarian administrative culture. One of those layers reproduces the past experiences of national social patterns in Bulgaria and might be called archetypal responses to the state and administration. The other layer—institutional drivers of modernization, represents the process by which the administrative values and practices of Western Europe have been instilled into the re-established Bulgarian nation state at the beginning of the 20th century. The tension between those two has determined most of the characteristics and aspects of development of administrative culture in Bulgaria.

Bulgaria's first steps of as an autonomous principality (including the set-up of government and administration) were made under the supervision of a Russian Emperor's Commissar. At the same time the first Bulgarian constitution on April 16, 1879, known as the Tarnovo Constitution, reproduced the models of Western constitutional monarchies. Bulgarian government and administrative culture has emerged under the influence of two opposite drives—on one side, the pursuit of modernization, associated with the political values and practices of the nation states in Europe; and on other side, the persistence of traditional inclinations in favor of Eastern patrimonial values.

Although the first Bulgarian constitution was based on the *separation of powers* doctrine and on the *rule of law* principle, Bulgarian administrators and officials could not get rid of the well-known patrimonial attitudes and orientations. Equality before law was guaranteed by a general opportunity to rise in the state service system. The constitution specifically underlined the importance of the "Service to State and Society" and introduced the requirement that officials should have Bulgarian nationality (exception to this rule possible only through a resolution of the Parliament). Constitutional provisions covered also the oath of allegiance to the King and the constitution sworn by each official, the principle of accountability of each official for his service, and the right to a pension of each official appointed to government service.

At the end of the 19th century and the beginning of the 20th Bulgarian administration building was focused on the strengthening of statehood and development of public legal thinking. Within the official structures, rules and norms were connected with family, debts of gratitude, and mutual favoritismamong members of the political elite. Bulgarian officials were traditionally chosen according to their loyalty to the governing political party. Local administration developed in the absence of a strong town culture in Bulgaria. The merchant class was too weak to generate an emancipated circle of intellectuals capable of development of civil service as a profession.

The first Bulgarian constitution never used the term "public servants." The only form of connotation of any service was in the total depersonalization of "Service to State and Society." Neither the constitution, nor the laws in the newly re-established Bulgarian state introduced the concept of "civil service" with its guarantees for political and partisan neutrality of the administration. People working in the administration were named "officials." They were seen as people holding office and power rather than serving the public. Hence, administrative culture in Bulgaria was developed as a *culture of officials*. And it is not a stretch for it to be assumed to be a culture of misfeasance and malfeasance. Many works in Bulgarian literature and popular culture in the

beginning of 20th century were harshly critical of the patterns of behavior of the "officials" and "clerks." They were mostly criticized for being incompetent, dishonest, and corrupt.

The social image of the Bulgarian clerk was identified with an "eloquent guest on the table of the State," a phrase borrowed from the title of a famous story written by "the patriarch of Bulgarian literature" Ivan Vazov (1850–1921). The monologue of the clerk in that story reveals his mixed feelings and self-image:

> . . . Do not seek character in the local clerks, those "solid screws in the governmental machine" as they are sometimes called, they are in the opinion they are told to be, and they pay homage to the god they are instructed to pay. In order to save their cushy job they are ready to sacrifice all that constitutes their human face . . . There are hundreds of such political chameleons to whom it is a shame to hold out your hand, do you understand? And now these are big fish, powerful officials and they made their houses and arranged their welfare . . . .

The servile mentality inherited from the Ottoman slavery could not be disguised under any new official uniform in the re-established Bulgarian state. Although the administrator's self-image does not mirror that of the harshest critics, the negative social attitudes unlock a variety of psychological defense mechanisms—denial, rationalization, suppression and repression, displacement, and others. These strategies reduce the officials' flexibility to respond to change and interfere with their capacity to connect with the others and result in an administrative culture of isolation from the public.

All these could be easily identified with vestiges from the past but could not provide us with an account of modernization trends in the re-established Bulgarian state. This account usually sticks to the idea of under-development of Bulgarian society and the non-unilinear nature of its modernization (Stokes, 1997). It also renders the widely shared interpretive view of the Balkans in terms of East-West dichotomy. While the development in the Western culture was seen as moved by a self-generated dynamics of social transformation, the societies in the East were seen as non-dynamic and moved mostly by forces from the outside world. In this paradigm of the under-developed society the political superstructure was assigned with a creative and revolutionary role for the purposes of social transformation. The political institutions were expected to compensate for the missing conditions for Western-type dynamism (Mishkova, 1994, p. 3). This explains to a certain extent why most changes in Bulgarian administration were usually a result of crucial political impact and pressure for reforms from the outside.

However, understanding the nature of nation-building and administrative culture in Bulgaria is impossible if it is restricted only to the paradigm of Western modernity denying the backward societies any autonomous capacity for progressive development. It is too exaggerated to attribute a "deficiency" of self-transformation energy to Bulgarian social culture, especially by imposing external social views and patterns. If we take this route we may even deny the cultural specificity of self-transformation in different societies. Scholars, analyzing in the context of the East-West dichotomy, see political modernization in the Balkans as superficial Westernization (Stokes, 1997). In this perspective the modern state building is interpreted as a smoke screen for the unchanged structures of persisting traditional culture. The dependency theory adds yet another aspect to this phenomenon—a blind emulation of Western political and administrative institutions in the under-developed countries (Stokes, 1980).

The adoption of modern liberal ideas and parliamentary institutions in the first constitution proved to be premature for the pre-industrial society in Bulgaria. The constitution alone could not produce a democratic liberal administrative culture. Rather it turned into a facade behind which continued to exist traditional, status-based, and patrimonial cultural structures.

The institutions of constitutionalism did not function in Bulgaria as they did in Western Europe but it does not mean that their role was merely decorative. The early introduction of political liberties and broad franchise in Bulgaria provided for involvement of much broader social strata in politics and administration. Many political and administrative practices in Bulgaria were incongruous with the formal constitutional framework of liberalism and corresponded much more to the patterns of patrimonial rule and bureaucracy. Nevertheless, the ideological role of the first constitution for the formation of political and legal values in Bulgaria remains indisputable.

In the beginning of the 20th century Bulgarian politicians and administrators believed that their primary role was to catch up with the modern West. In this context they developed a sense of inferiority and a tendency toward political subservience. They sought to prove their own worth through nationalist ideology that served to legitimize the authority of the bureaucracy, but did not assist it in solving social and economic problems (Stokes, 1980, pp. 64–66). The national energy was concentrated on formalistic institutional building and turned away from serving the public. This resulted in purposeful imitation of some administrative patterns of the European nation states by taking shortcuts through the formal techniques of legislation and institutions. The latter were supposed to compensate for the lack of authentic administrative practices and traditions in Bulgarian society resulting from the five-century Ottoman rule.

The duality of Eastern versus Western values is found at the core of Bulgarian administrative culture. It has reflected the ways of responding to the structural and conjunctural circumstances and challenges brought by the history of the nation state. Bulgarian history in the 20th century is the story of alternating transitions of the political system—the transition from constitutional monarchy to communism after World War II and the transition to democracy after the fall of communism in 1989. In both transition cases the modal patterns of Bulgarian administrative culture evolved within *the continuous tension between ideology and practice.*

COMMUNIST ADMINISTRATIVE CULTURE: BETWEEN IDEOLOGY AND PRACTICE

The foundations of the communist state in Bulgaria were built upon the ideas of Lenin (1870–1924) and in accordance with the model of the Soviet Union. It was widely proclaimed that in the first stage of the communist society all people became employees of the state and the whole society became one office, where there was equality in pay and work. In short, in the communist state "society becomes administration" (Heusala, 2005, p. 117).

After the capitalist bureaucracy has been renounced it was necessary to justify its very existence in the communist state. Ideologically the administration did not exist separately from the state and the very concept of state was in itself transitional. It was seen as process advancing apparatus, which would die away in its old forms and generate radically new types of administrative relationships.

It was envisaged that the power of ideology would penetrate every segment of society and would make any administration useless. Ultimately bureaucracy would be replaced by the rotated simple control and accounting habits of the people (Lenin, 1972, p. 315). Thus, administrative tasks would eventually cease to be special tasks. After the administrative tasks are simplified to the tasks of accounting and control by the people themselves, the state ceases to be a political formation and the public functions loose their political nature by becoming mere bureaucratic actions.

At the end of this evolution, the idealized communist state would have meant a situation in which people use internalized traditions and guidelines on a voluntary basis without coercion. In this sense the line between state and society was to be abolished, and the two were to become one. Accordingly, there was no place for free civil society in this formation. Hence, the administration was not supposed to exist as a separate unit in the chain of power centers but as a means for the overall organization of the new state where there was a fusion of structures and social system.

All people, including officials, were ideologically identified with servants of the proletarian system and executioners of orders. As such they were expected to be responsible, modestly salaried, replaceable, and easily dismissed. The status which used to be attached to such positions and the remnants of the capitalist "leadership" role of administrator were expected to be wiped out. (Heusala, 2005, p. 120). After all people started to be viewed as "servants of the state" the old division between officials and citizens was transformed into a division between members and non-members of the Communist Party. Party membership required that party members followed the orders of the local communist party office. This type of control was the most intense and gave the party an ideological upper hand in case of administrative dysfunctions. The smallest daily issue required approval from the above or from the communist party (Galligan, Langan II, & Nicandrou, 1998, p. 19). Hence, the administrative process was marked by slowness and delays. At the same time the official communist discourse in the press criticized the administration for being "bureaucratic" and for lack of initiative and waste of resources and, thus, stalling the development of communist society. For these deficiencies in the administration the communist party was, of course, never at fault.

State servants were virtually executioners of the orders and decrees, issued within the uniform command structures for policy implementation and centrally guided by the communist party. The main foundations of daily legal authority were the instructions and decrees of the Central Committee of the Bulgarian Communist Party. The party instructions were, in this manner, sub-laws of the state and many of them were non-public and access to them depended on the position occupied by the administrator. Actual laws which the Parliament passed were of minor importance or merely decorative.

The system required iron discipline and loyalty to the communist party and to the party functionaries. No values of difference have been tolerated. Any kind of detour, insubordination or non-conformity was swiftly sanctioned (Vezenkov, 2008). Any career as an administrator was dependent on membership in the communist party. And despite the "antibureaucratic" attitudes in communist ideology, in practices the Communist Party turned into a typical bureaucratic machine exercising totalitarian control over everyone and everything. Communist ideology and practices actually reinforced the uttermost servile dispositions in Bulgarian administrative culture. They were further overbuilt with slandering and calumniation practices encouraged by the party functionaries and by the communist State Security.

The informal practices and the patterns of corruptions were significantly intensified in the communist administrative culture. Corruption was morally justified as a form of assistance and mutual cooperation between people. Moreover, such type of behavior was seen as habitual, even "innocent." For instance, an unofficial role in the arbitration of goods and services in the planned economy was played by the secretaries of the party organizations and all those individuals who possessed knowledge of what people to use in different situations to achieve a goal. Such knowledge was consciously learned by the party functionaries as a set of social skills that allowed them to maintain and better their positions.

The growing discrepancy between the ideological discourse and the factual reality, presented a widening double-standard and generated the administrative culture of "mimicry." Most of the actions and decisions of the administration were justified with the communist ideology through the instrument of mimicry. It was clear to everyone that most of the tasks were completed for practical, and not for ideological reasons, but it was necessary to give each one a communist label. Later on the communist ideology was interpreted to be so vague that it could be used to legitimatize any decision, even opposite. Hence, decision-making in the administration usually waited for instructions from above. The reasoning process was nothing but using the same clichés for the opposite decisions.

As a result, the public view of administration became even more cynical in Bulgaria. Anecdotes and funny stories about the communist party functionaries flourished. The administrative culture in communist Bulgaria developed between servility and calumny between the mimicking to communist imperatives and the informal practices, between the total fear of and the derision of the party functionaries.

BULGARIAN ADMINISTRATIVE CULTURE IN THE TRANSITION TO DEMOCRACY

After the fall of communism in 1989 Bulgarian society committed to the values of democracy, the rule of law, and human rights. Bulgarian transition to democracy developed in three basic dimensions:

1. Transformation was supposed to be achieved through total denial of any legacy of communism, including ideas, myths, experiences, structures, and patterns. At a certain point, anything that had to be rejected or denied without rational argumentation could be easily disqualified only by putting the label "communist," "legacy of communism" on it.
2. Democratic values were supposed to permeate Bulgarian culture in the process of adopting the new Constitution in 1991 and a whole bunch of new substantive and procedural laws establishing the institutional framework of democracy, rule of law, market economy, restitution, and so on. The successful transition to democracy was conceptualized through revival of the values of the Tarnovo Constitution 1879.
3. Bulgarian transition to democracy at the end of the 20th century was interwoven with the chief strategic goal of Bulgaria to become a member of the European Union (EU). The EU turned into the new ideology for Bulgarian society and occupied the place of denounced communist ideology.

Those basic dimensions of Bulgarian transition to democracy were inevitably reproduced in the administrative culture. They predetermined the way in which all types of survival techniques—servility, denial, displacement, and so on, have been developed in response to the new social and political realities.

Some of those responses could hardly be seen as unique for Bulgarian administrative culture as they could be seen in any society in transition. All these could be grouped in two categories—resistance and adjustment. They are both a result of the inevitable conflict between the new and the old values and practices in the administrative culture, but represent two opposite reactions to that conflict.

In Bulgarian post-communist administrative culture these opposite trends are best reflected in the post-communist development of the science of administrative law. If one compares the administrative law textbooks and articles from the communist period (1960–1990) and the post-communist period (1990s) one could hardly find any difference in structure, language, and ideas. The totalitarian conception of "state government" continued to be the first theme in the course syllabus of administrative law even a decade after the fall of the Berlin Wall. Even after the term "executive branch of the government" succeeded in breaking through the old conceptual framework, it was only an adjustment to the language of the new democratic constitution. It could hardly touch the core of the totalitarian bureaucratic ideas.

Moreover, there is still the ongoing resistance of Bulgarian administrative doctrine to admit the proper place and role of the concepts of "public service" and "administrative contract," as well as most of the terms and ideas of New Public Management (Barzelay, 2000; Politt & Bouckaert, 2000). The law students in Bulgaria may never even hear about the clash between traditional bureaucracy and New Public Management, let alone try to get deeper into the ideas of reinventing the public sector.

Even today Bulgarian administrative legal doctrine's use of the concept "public administration continues to decline." That's why in Bulgaria most of the philosophical and political departments in the universities have appropriated the study of public administration and separated it from the study of administrative law. At the same time, in the state standards for legal education in Bulgaria the Master's degree in law is granted within three types of specializations "Justice," "Public Administration," and "International Law." Evidently Public Administration can be used as a title of a legal specialization (as an "adjustment" modal pattern), but continues to be ignored in the curriculum of the law faculty (as a "resistance" modal pattern). Hence, the law students may choose to specialize in Public Administration but will never be introduced to even the concept of public administration, let alone any theories, methods, and the like.

This discrepancy between form and substance continues to be an essential feature not only of administrative studies, but also of all the aspects of Bulgarian administrative culture. In the post-communist period the upper-level administration proved to be much more flexible, receptive, and open-minded than the administrative scholars regarding the introduction and implementation of new concepts and ideas. This phenomenon is indisputably attributed to the negotiations for accession of Bulgaria into the EU, in which the upper-level administration played a key role. Thus, most of the transformative energy in the democratic administrative culture in Bulgaria at the end of the 20th century and the beginning of the 21st was mobilized not by democratic theories and ideas, but by the pressure imposed from Brussels. Bulgarian administrators actually learned a lot in the interaction with the EU administration. The high level administrators, not the scholars, introduced the promises of New Public Management to Bulgarian society.

There is disagreement as to what extent the values of New Public Management have infiltrated Bulgarian administrative culture. Some of the patterns of New Public Management, including the orientation towards outcomes and efficiency, found a way into Bulgarian administrative culture in the process of gaining EU membership. Indicative of this fact is the well-known career strategy of most youngsters in Bulgaria of gaining three to five years of experience in the public administration and then seeking jobs in the private sector.

This trend also demonstrates the lack of devotion and attachment to the public service as an important characteristic of contemporary administrative culture in Bulgaria. Public service is not seen as an end to itself, but as a means to something else. This basic attitude is to a certain extent determined by the archetypal Bulgarian denial of state and administration. However, it has been reinforced by the multiple corruption practices in Bulgarian post-communist administration that seem to have strengthened the common conception of public service as a temporary job or as a means to personal enrichment. And it is hardly a surprise for anyone given the general cultural matrix of survival techniques that have turned into personal success strategies.

In Bulgaria nowadays three typical administrative subcultures are easily identified: traditional, entrepreneurial, and political (Henderson, 1998). There are no hard and fast lines among these. All elements may be included in any group or structure in the administration, but for heuristic purposes one should accept that the dominant mode determines the category.

The vast majority of Bulgarian administrators share the *traditional administrative culture*, with emphasis on the separation of politics from administration and on the adherence to legal mandates and procedures. The specific Bulgarian imprint on this type of sub-culture is the enduring tension between ideology and practice. It never bothered the traditionalists and they were masters of the survival techniques.

The *entrepreneurial administrative culture* was born in the last decade in those agencies or groupings within the administration that were responsive to the New Public Management models. The emphasis upon innovation, market competition, adaptability, and proactivity mobilized new modal patterns in the administration that were the very opposite of the traditional ones. At the end of the day what the entrepreneurs actually shared with the traditionalists was their total disregard of the public service as a value in itself.

The orthodox administrative doctrine in Bulgaria would immediately denounce even the idea of a *political administrative culture* mostly for fear of being identified with communist ideology. The truth is, however, that most high-level administrative operations at state and municipal levels are closely tied to partisan politics. Their emphasis upon sophisticated maneuvering for advantage, much like the usual patterns of behaviour among elected politicians, could be described in no other terms but political administrative culture.

The administrative culture of specific agencies in Bulgaria has been marked by an emphasis upon a "we versus them" mentality, and cautiousness in dealing with the public, because of the possibility of criticism and unfavourable publicity. Though it could be seen as a resistance to the new positive values of transparency and publicity, such administrative culture could only be a result of these very same values. Only after the administrators start to operate in the public eye do they become wary of bad publicity. Hence, any such "cautious" administrative culture might be interpreted as a step forward toward democracy.

The new administrative procedural code, adopted in 2006 in Bulgaria, has set "dispassion and objectivity" as basic principles of administration. Nevertheless, Bulgarian administrative culture has a long way to go to be truly identified with these values. Usually administrators credit themselves with adherence to rules and regulations without distortion by particularistic criteria. This is sometimes inconsistent with necessary flexibility and responsiveness but its focus is avoidance of favouritism, nepotism, cronyism, and any kind of partisan bias.

The culture of Bulgarian public administration has not yet encompassed a real concern for competence and merit in administration, as well as for ethical behaviour of all public servants. One typical example in this regard is the failure of the conflict of interests' law in Bulgaria. Although a special statute has been adopted to specify the obligations of all public servants whenever any private interest might affect their dispassionate and objective decision-making, the court has distorted the very idea of conflict of interests by the reduction of the private interest to an "illegal benefit." That interpretation actually blocked the effectiveness of the law and made it virtually impossible to apply adequate standards to the conflict of interest in the administration.

The major gap in the present Bulgarian administrative culture is the lack of accountability. Corruption in all branches of government in Bulgaria, and especially in the sphere of justice, is the reason for the ongoing EU legal monitoring mechanism intended to ensure that reforms take place. It is commonplace in Bulgaria that none of the administrators are held accountable for their actions. None of the administrators ever considers the consequences of any legal action because

its effects will only reach the institution and will never reach the person behind the administrative decision.

In Resolution 1787 (2011) on the implementation of the Court's judgments, adopted on January 26, 2011, the Parliamentary Assembly of the Council of Europe noted "with grave concern" the continuing existence of "major systemic deficiencies which cause large numbers of repetitive findings of violations of the Convention and which seriously undermine the rule of law" [*Dimitrov and Hamanov v. Bulgaria* (Application nos. 48059/06 and 2708/09), *Finger v. Bulgaria* (Application no. 37346/05), May 10, 2011, ECHR]. In May 2011, after a long dealing with large groups of identical cases stemming from the same underlying problem, the European Court of Human Rights (ECHR) issued the first "pilot judgment" against Bulgaria, ECHR urging Bulgaria to address its "systemic deficiencies" in the justice system, as well as to introduce compensatory remedies for the victims of protracted civil, administrative, and criminal proceedings.

The systemic deficiencies and the "empty shell" seem to be reproduced in the new institutions developing in Bulgaria in the process of EU membership. The problem "formal structure without substance" (Bugaric, 2006) has been widely discussed in the Europeanization literature that deals with the national implementation of EU legislation (Featherstone & Radaelli, 2003; Grabbe, 2006). Researchers have not been optimistic about the real impact of the adopted formal rules and have suggested that most of the new EU legislation would exist only on paper (Dimitrova, 2010, p. 142).

The European Union continues to exert pressure on the Bulgarian administration to change, modernize, and become proactive. It is a common belief in Bulgaria that the country's administrators and public servants may never become accountable to the Bulgarian public, but they will certainly become accountable to Brussels, Luxembourg, and Strasbourg. The external drivers of the EU, the ECHR, and of globalization in general, proved to be the most powerful forces for transformation of the Bulgarian administration.

The "empty shell" issue (Dimitrova, 2010) in the Europeanization process is actually the new modus operandi of the old tension between ideology and practice in post-communist Bulgaria. No structural reforms have the potential to resolve this problem as they inevitably reproduce it over and over again. Policy on a different plane could be the key to the empty shell issue in Bulgaria. Closer relationship, partnership, and intensive interaction among government and civil society would make it possible to foster democratic practices and to overcome the culture of denial of state and administration. That would reduce the gap between the actual performance of public administration and the citizens' perceptions and expectations in Bulgaria and would make it possible for the passive and surviving administrator to be replaced by a proactive and devoted one.

CONCLUSION

Bulgarian administrators have started to seek a lifelong career in the EU administration. This may be the first step to appreciating public service in Bulgaria as a value in itself. In the new digitalized era the patterns of public administration are changing at such a speed that one can hardly trace all the patterns of immersion and acculturation and all the continuities and discontinuities in the administrative culture. The transitions in Bulgaria, however, have clearly demonstrated that externally driven reforms cannot reach to the core of administrative culture. Policy-making in reducing the distrust gap in Bulgarian society may work a change in the attitudes, beliefs, and values of both people and administrators in Bulgaria.

REFERENCES

Barzelay, M. (2000). *The new public management*. Berkeley: University of California Press.

Benedicty, R. (1963). Die auf die frühslawische Gesellschaftsbezügliche byzantinische Terminologie. In *Actes du XII-e Congrès international d'études byzantines* (Vol. 2), (pp. 45–55). Belgrade: Comité yougoslav des études byzantines.

Biliarsky, I. (1998). *Institutions of medieval Bulgaria. Second Bulgarian Kingdom XII–XIV century*. Sofia: Universitetsko izdatelstvo "Sveti Kliment Ohridski."

Bugaric, B. (2006). The Europeanisation of national administration in Central and Eastern Europe: Creating formal structures without substance? In W. Sadurski, J. Ziller, & K. Żurek (Eds.). *Après enlargement. Legal and political responses in Central and Eastern Europe* (pp. 201–230). Florence: European University Institute.

Caiden, G. (1970). *Israel's administrative culture*. Berkeley: Institute of Governmental Studies, University of California.

Dewing, H.B. (1924). Translation from *Procopius in seven volumes* (Vol. 4). London/New York

Diehl, C. (1923). The government and administration of the Byzantine Empire. In J.B. Bury, *The Cambridge medieval history, Vol. IV, The Eastern Roman Empire (717–1453)* (chap. 23). Cambridge: Cambridge University Press

Dimitrova, A.L. (2010). The new member states of the EU in the aftermath of enlargement: Do new European rules remain empty shells? *Journal of European Public Policy, 17*(1), 137–148.

Dwivedi, O. P. (2005). Administrative culture and values: Approaches. In J.G. Jabbra & O.P. Dwivedi (Eds.) *Administrative culture in a global context* (pp.19–36). Ontario, Canada: De Sitter Publications

Dwivedi, O. P., & Gow, J. (1999). *From bureaucracy to public management: The administrative culture of the government of Canada*. Peterborough, ON, Canada: Broadview Press.

Evans, H.M.A. (1989). *The early medieval archaeology of Croatia A.D. 600–900*. Oxford: BAR International Series 539.

Featherstone, K. & C. Radaelli (2003). *The politics of Europeanization*. Oxford: Oxford University Press.

Fortes, M., & Evans-Pritchard, E. (1940). *African political systems*. Oxford, UK: Oxford University Press.

Galligan, D., Langan II, H., & Nicandrou, C. (1998). (Eds.) *Administrative justice in the new European democracies*. Oxford: Open Society Institute, COLPI, and the Center of Socio-Legal Studies.

Genchev, N. (1988). *Bulgarian culture in the 15th–19th century*. Sofia: Universitetsko izdatelstvo "Sveti Kliment Ohridski."

Grabbe, H. (2006). The EU's transformative power: Europeanization through conditionality in Central and Eastern Europe. Basingstoke: Palgrave Macmillan.

Henderson, K. (1998). Continuity and change in American administrative culture. *Africanus, 28*(2), 8–18.

Henderson, K. (2011). *Comparing administrative cultures: United States and the European Union*. 7th Transatlantic Dialogue, Strategic Management in Public Organizations, Newark, NJ.

Heusala, A. (2005). *The transitions of local administration culture in Russia*. Academic dissertation, University of Helsinki.

Inalcik, H. (1964). The nature of traditional society. Turkey. In R.Ward & D. Rustow (Eds.). *Political modernization in Japan and Turkey*. Princeton, NJ: Princeton University Press.

Jamil, I. (1994). Administrative culture. A mode of understanding public administration across cultures. In C. Coyle (ed.) *Research in Urban Policy* (Vol. 5). London, England: JAI Press.

Jamil, I. (2007). *Administrative culture in Bangladesh: Tensions between traditions and modernity*. Dhaka: A.H. Development Publishing House.

Jenks, E. (1908). *Law and politics in the Middle Ages*. New York: Henry Holt.

Lenin, V. (1972). *Collected works* (4th English edition) (Vol. 27, pp. 314–317), R. Daglish (Ed.), C. Dutt (trans.). Moscow: Progress Publishers.

Mardin, S. (1969). Power, civil society and culture in the Ottoman Empire. *Comparative Studies in Society and History, 11*(3), 258–281.

Mishkova, D. (1994). *Modernization and political elites in the Balkans, 1870–1914*. University of Sofia Working Paper 94–1.

Nystazopoulou-Pelekidou, M. (1986). *Les Slaves dans l'Empire byzantin*. In The 17th International Byzantine Congress, Major Papers (pp. 345–367), Washington, DC.

Runciman, S. (1930). *A history of the First Bulgarian Empire*. London, England: G. Bell and Sons.

Sharma, R.D. (2000). *Administrative culture in India*. New Delhi: Anamika Publishers & Distributors.

Sotirova, D., & Davidkov, C. (2004). Administrative culture: Towards effective management strategies and practices. Sofia: EON-2000.

Stokes, G. (1980). Dependency and the rise of nationalism in Southeast Europe. *International Journal of Turkish Studies, 1*, 54–67.

Stokes, G. (1997). *Three eras of political change in Eastern Europe*. New York: Oxford University Press.

Thedieck, F. (2007). *Foundations of administrative culture in Europe*. Baden-Baden: The Congress of Local and Regional Authorities of the Council of Europe, Nomos Publishers.

Vezenkov, A. (2008), *Power Structures in Bulgarian Communist Party. 1944–1989*. Sofia: Institute for Research in the Recent Past, (in Bulgarian).

Zasterová, B. (1971). *Les Avares et les Slaves dans la Tactique de Maurice*. Prague: Academia.

Zlatarski, V. (1918). *Medieval History of Bulgarian State, Vol. I, History of First Bulgarian Kingdom. Part I. Age of Hunn-Bulgar Domination (679–852)*. Sofia: Academichno Izdatelstvo "Prof. Marin Drinov."

Zlatarski, V. (1927). *Medieval History of Bulgarian State, Vol. I, History of First Bulgarian Kingdom. Part II. From Slavianisation to the fall of First Bulgarian Kingdom (852–1018)*. Sofia: Academichno Izdatelstvo "Prof. Marin Drinov."

Implementation of Strategic Organizational Change: The Case of King Abdul Aziz University in Saudi Arabia

Abdulrahaman Ali Alhazemi, Christopher Rees,
and Farhad Hossain

*Institute for Development Policy and Management, University of Manchester,
Manchester, United Kingdom*

The aim of this research is to examine the role of leadership, culture and learning in the implementation of strategic organizational change in the public sector of Saudi Arabia. In order to address this aim, a case study was conducted in King Abdul Aziz University (KAU). The case study methodology involved interviews with senior employees of the organization. The findings reveal that Arab culture was found to influence the change process as the drivers of the strategic change attempted to turn the university into a modern institution with some values drawn from western culture; learning and training featured prominently in the findings as staff and students were required to learn various skills in order to adopt new systems of education and management; and leadership was found to be crucial as it emerged that the strategic change at KAU was linked to broader aspects of strategic change pioneered by the Ministry of Higher Education. The study also identified various barriers to effective implementation of strategic change such as adherence to the status quo by some groups within Saudi society, the antagonism of some actors towards standard human resource processes, and signs of the inflexibility of management and leadership.

INTRODUCTION

Strategic change has become an important area of study within the field of change management as researchers have realized that organizational change could be potentially more important when it is strategic in nature (Senior, 2006). Many researchers consider change as a common phenomenon in any organizational setting. They have defined change as a sort of variation in the internal environment of the organization. This variation from the existing state may be triggered purposefully by the organization itself or may be imposed on the organization by the changes in the external environment.

Change has also been defined as a disruption as change necessarily implies a disruption of the present conditions prevailing in the external and internal environment (Cannon & McGee, 2008). The disruption could be positive or negative. Even though change has been stated to be a commonly and frequently observed phenomenon in any organizational setting, not all changes are of equal magnitude or importance. Researchers have observed that some changes have more far reaching consequences for the organization than the other changes (Fountain, 2001; Mills et al., 2009). Thus, strategic changes are carefully separated from other changes on the basis of frequency, magnitude, importance, and consequences. Very few researchers have defined strategic change as a response to a stimulus from within the organization (Rowland, 2007). Rowland (2007), who presents a different perspective, argues that strategic change may originate even from within the organization and not necessarily from outside.

The aim of this research is to examine the role of leadership, culture, and learning in the implementation of organizational change in the public sector of Saudi Arabia. In order to address this aim and the research questions presented below, the study examines leadership, culture, and learning using a case study of strategic change in King Abdul Aziz

University (KAU). Currently the university is undergoing a massive strategic change in order to transform itself into a modern world-class educational institution (KAU, 2010). The specific questions this research addresses are:

1. What roles are played by leadership in the implementation of strategic change?
2. What aspects of Saudi culture exert a major impact the implementation of change?
3. How important are learning and training in the process of change management?

Even though strategic change literature has been rich in theoretical and empirical research, most of these studies have focused on the developed West. Very few researchers have explored strategic change management in the developing Middle East (Rees et al., 2007). In contrast, by means of the case study of KAU, this research broadly attempts to study the nature and factors of strategic organizational change management in Saudi Arabia.

The article is structured as follows: the next section sets out a theoretical overview of the field of strategic organizational change management. Following this discussion, the next section presents the research context and the methodology employed to address the research questions stated above. Following the presentation of the findings, the concluding section of the article summarizes the key lessons and areas for further research.

STRATEGIC ORGANIZATIONAL CHANGE MANAGEMENT: A THEORETICAL OVERVIEW

There are a number of factors that have been identified by various researchers to determine the extent to which strategic change initiatives could be introduced successful in organizations. This section attempts to analyzekey strategic change factors as they relate to the theoretical scope of this article.

The capacity of an organization to implement change has been found to be a crucial factor determining the results of strategic management initiatives (Coda, 2002; Christensen & Raynor, 2003; Epstein et al., 2004; Tushman & Smith, 2004; Yang & Yang, 2008). Prior to examining a number of key factors which are seen to impact on organizations' capacity to change, there are numerous factors which have been linked to the effectiveness of change processes (Rees, 2008a). For example, Mazzola (2003) states that the planning that precedes strategic change implementation is the most important factor or process that determines the results of the strategic change. Mazzola (2003) found that those organizations that tend to spend time researching the situation and also in studying the environment while incorporating these changes carefully into their plans tend to be more effective in their strategic decision making than those organizations that appear to be less prepared and planned for their strategic

change initiatives. Thus, preparation and planning are found to be crucial factors in strategic change management.

Rebora and Minelli (2007) offer a different perspective when they argue that the nature of the change itself is an important factor in determining the extent of success that the organization is likely to enjoy. The researchers state that organizations are likely to enjoy far greater successes with changes that are less radical and more along the mainstream than those changes that are completely radical in nature. Another factor that has been emphasized by the researchers is the degree of relationship between firm and the environment. Yet another perspective is offered by Aaker (2001) who proposes that those organizations that have the tendency to stay very close to the external environment typically enjoy greater success with their strategic change initiatives because they tend to be in lock-step with the changes in the environment and so are less likely to be compelled to introduce radical organizational change in a reactive way. On the other hand, those organizations that have a tendency not to align themselves with the environment are typically compelled to implement major strategic changes periodically, thus increasing the risk of failure of the change implementation and management processes (Ansoff, 2006).

In recognizing the wide range of perspectives on change that seek to explain successful strategic management, the current study explores the factors of leadership, culture, and learning and training. The rationale for examining these particular factors is centered around three considerations. First, these factors feature prominently in established change management literature (Egan, 2002; Rees, 2008b; Cummings & Worley, 2009). Second, the very nature of these factors suggests that they will exert an over-arching influence on the types of factors and issues, such as planning, the nature of the change, and engagement with the external environment, which have been discussed previously. For example, effective leaders are likely to engage in planning, understand the nature of the change, and seek to engage with the external environment. Third, study explores strategic change management in the relatively under-researched non-Western context of Saudi Arabia; as such, the authors considered it to be appropriate to examine factors such as leadership, culture, and training and development which were likely, at a general level, to offer insights into strategic change management in this context. The next sections of the article discuss each of these factors.

Role of Leadership in Strategic Change Management

Leadership is one of the widely cited factors that have been identified as playing a critical role in determining the results of change management programs. Palmer and Dunford (2002) attempt to answer one of the most discussed questions in change management literature—whether change can be managed. They developed a model that incorporates two different images about change management: management as controlling and management as shaping. Palmer and Dunford (2002) also identify three different images of outcomes of change management; intended, partially intended and unintended. Using the combination of these two different sets of images, the authors present six different views of managing change; directing, navigating, caretaking, coaching, interpreting, and nurturing. On the basis of their findings, the authors argue that it is possible to manage change to a significant extent. From this conclusion it can be observed that leadership plays a very crucial role in strategic change management.

Furthermore, changing the style of management and leadership could lead to variations in the results of the change management programs. Pitt (2005) attempts to develop a dynamic change management model which is capable of explaining change management processes in a growth-oriented organization. According to Pitt (2005) the most important factors are "the size of the firm and how habituated its routines have become, its levels of demographic diversity, internal conflict, and staff morale, the change propensity of its top management team (TMT) and the availability of interpretive skills and extent of strategic issue diagnosis." Top management's propensity for change has been cited one of the most important factors determining change.

In attempting to emphasize the association between leadership and effective change management, Carnall (1986, p. 105) presents an integrated approach to strategic change management. He states "leadership is central because to achieve effective organizational change requires us to elevate analysis over consensus. Easy options are in short supply! Implementing major organizational change demands the combination of action and analysis into a new managerial synthesis." According to Carnall (1986), there are three very important functions of leaders in the context of organizational change—Leaders are expected to: manage the transition from old set up to the new system in an effective manner; deal with organizational cultures and the issues that arise from clash of cultures; and are expected to manage the organizational politics in a manner that it would not hinder the progress in change management. More importantly, achieving organizational change and learning are outcomes of effective leadership.

Role of Culture in Strategic Decision-Making and Change Implementation

Culture has been found to be play important and pivotal roles in organizational decision-making and so has been found to be a factor in strategic change management and implementation. Many researchers have found aspects of culture, both national and organizational, play deterministic roles in long-term strategic decisions. Schneider and Meyer (2006) conduct a survey among the bank managers in the United States about the case of deregulation of banking sector in the country. They identify that the managers of the

European banks are more likely to interpret the condition as a threat or a crisis than are the managers of American banks. Schneider and Meyer (2006, p. 307) state "national culture was found to influence interpretation and responses . . . This study indicates that different cultures are likely to interpret and respond to the same strategic issue in different ways."

Since the organizational response to the change in environment is dependent upon on the nature of interpretation of the change, the culture, which is found to influence the interpretation of the change, may also be considered an important factor determining the nature of response that the organization may generate towards the environmental changes. Shane (2006) studies the case of the choice between licensing and direct foreign investment decisions by organizations in order to understand the influence of culture upon on the crucial strategic decisions made at the organizational level. Shane (2006) notes that national culture affects the degree of trust managers have in their own decision-making and so concludes that national culture is an important determinant of strategic change.

A number of researchers have also identified corporate culture as an important determinant of strategic decision-making processes and initiatives in organizations. Camerer and Vepsalainen (2007, p. 115) state that "corporate culture is a set of broad, tacitly understood rules which tell employees what to do under a wide variety of unimaginable circumstances." Sayles and Wright (2007) argue that it is imperative for the top management of the organization to ensure that the organizational culture matches the requirements of organizational strategic change contemplated by management. The authors argue that when the organization fails to have a culture that is conducive to change then it is likely that the change initiatives would fail or would be less effective than intended.

Role of Learning and Training in Strategic Change Implementation

The previous section of this article critically analyzed a cross-section of research to identify a host of factors that could determine the degree of success an organization may enjoy in implementing strategic changes. However, this research also examines the role of learning and training as important factors in strategic change management. This section analyses literature that has examined the learning and training abilities of organizations.

Sarin et al. (2010, p. 143) critically explore the role of training in determining the effectiveness of strategic change in organizational contexts. The authors use the case of training to sales personnel to implement online sales channels, which the authors consider "a strategic change" in organizations. It is found that "formality of training has a positive effect and voluntariness has a negative effect on the perceived effectiveness of training in a change implementation context." The authors find that there are two crucial factors involved—training effectiveness and learning orientation. The process of training is found to be of significant value to the organization when there is a very high degree of training effectiveness and learning orientation. On the other hand, when the learning orientation of the employees is weak, it is found that the strategic change implementation is not as effective as it otherwise would have been. Thus the authors emphasize learning and training as very important factors in strategic change decisions and implementation.

Garcia-Morales et al. (2007) studied the role of personal knowledge and organization learning in strategic change context in organizational environment. They found that personal mastery is an important factor that influences the organization change initiatives through direct and indirect influences upon the degree of innovation in the organization. They also found that organization learning and organizational performance are positively correlated and organizational innovation influences the organizational performance positively to a significant extent. Thus, Garcia-Morales et al. (2007) related organizational learning directly and indirectly to the organizational performance. The indirect impact of organizational learning on organization performance is through the process of innovation.

The preceding discussion has highlighted the extent to which factors such as leadership, culture, training, and learning are, in general terms, considered to be critical factors in the successful implementation of strategic organizational change. However, there is evidence that the impact of these factors in certain geographical regions has not been investigated in any real depth. For example, Rees et al. (2012) have highlighted the lack of research on organizational change in the Middle East. As revealed by the research questions presented in the introduction section, the current study is centered upon aspects of organizational change in Saudi Arabia.

Saudi Arabia falls along a spectrum of cultural characteristics of many Arab countries. It is distinctly tribal, conservative in its adherence to Islam, and influenced by significant exposure to the West (Dadfar et al., 2003; Baker et al., 2007; Rees & Althakhri, 2008). The relationship between religious leaders in Saudi government and the ruler dates back to King Abdul Aziz who founded Saudi Arabia. King Abdul Aziz consolidated more than half the Arabian Peninsula and the tribes that crisscrossed its terrain in the course of a few decades. However, all the kings since him have had to balance this important relationship. In addition, Islam has exerted a major on all aspects of life in Saudi Arabia (Common, 2008).

In formulating the scope of the current study, it was noted that strategic change management should take into account the critical changes in the external environment as well as the external stakeholders who could also determine the extent of success of the strategic change process. Given that this study is centered upon change management in the higher education sector in Saudi Arabia, it is important to clarify the extent to which this sector has experienced major change over recent years.

National Context of the Study: Higher Education in Saudi Arabia

One of the most noteworthy aspects of government policy relating to higher education in Saudi Arabia is that the Ministry of Higher Education in Saudi Arabia has ushered in a strategic change process which has major implications for the whole sector. The 8th Development Strategic Plan (2005–2009) attempts to expand significantly the capacity of the existing education institutions as well as to improve radically the quality of education provided by these institutions. Some of the most important objectives of the plan are to expand admission capacities in universities, to concentrate on research and development, to increase the number of scholarships to students, to implement accreditation programs for colleges and to develop collaboration between higher education and the private sector. In the 2010 budget, the Saudi Arabian government expanded the budget for education and training by 13 percent; this constitutes over 25 percent of the total budget (Kingdom of Saudi Arabia, 2009). Thus, the Ministry of Higher Education in the country actually plays a key leadership role in the strategic change implementation processes within the higher education sector in Saudi Arabia.

When examining the impact of government policy on the higher education sector in Saudi Arabia, one of the most important developments has been the rapid increase in the number of universities and other forms of higher education institutions (see Figure 1). In the year 2006, there were only 7 universities providing higher education to the students in the country. However, in the year 2010 there were 24 government universities and 8 private higher education institutions (Ministry of Higher Education, 2009a, 2009b).

The data contained in Figure 1 also provide an indication of the increasing degree of competition in the higher education sector in Saudi Arabia. This emergence of competition is a key change that has occurred in this sector. The private education institutions, in particular, have adopted some western style educational practices and these have become popular among students (Prokop, 2003). Before the advent of these modern universities, the students had to travel to the United States or Europe to acquire the higher degrees that would increase their opportunity to land a suitable job within multinational companies in the country (Altbach & Knight, 2007). The private higher education institutions are also bringing in new departments and courses into the country.

Another element of the picture of change in the higher education system in Saudi Arabia has been the increasing participation of women (see Table 1). In fact, the most recent figures available from the Ministry of Education in Saudi Arabia indicate that there are now more women than men enrolled in higher education (see Table 1).

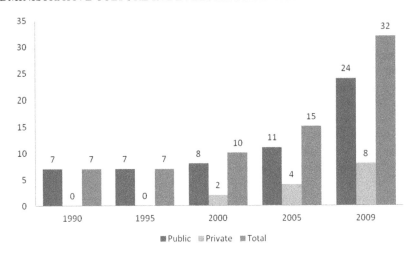

FIGURE 1   Number of higher education institutions in Saudi Arabia.
Source: Ministry of Higher Education (2010).

TABLE 1
Rates of Women's Participation in Higher Education in Saudi Arabia

Year	Faculty Members			Enrolled Students		
	Total	Male	Female	Total	Male	Female
1990	10,186	7,509	2,677	132,827	71,934	60,893
1995	13,301	9,400	3,901	218,878	115,942	102,936
2000	18,295	12,483	6,442	404,094	178,099	225,995
2005	26,566	17,813	8,753	603,767	253,551	350,216
2009	29,708	18,283	11,421	728,867	315,974	412,893
Growth rate	192%	143%	327%	448.7%	339.2%	578%

Source: Ministry of Higher Education (2010).

In summary, the review of literature confirms that factors such as leadership, culture, learning, and training should be considered critical to the successful implementation of strategic organizational change. However, there is a scarcity of research that has examined the impact of these factors on strategic organizational change initiatives in contexts such as the Middle East. Hence, having clarified, in general terms, the topical nature of these factors in relation to change management processes, the decision was taken to explore the impact of these factors in a defined organizational context within a Middle Eastern setting, namely a higher education establishment in Saudi Arabia. A background review of the existing policies of the Ministry of Higher Education in Saudi Arabia (see above) revealed the extent to which the entire higher education system in Saudi Arabia is undergoing a major government-driven strategic change. This led the researchers to examine the research questions using a case-study analysis from the higher education sector in Saudi Arabia. Thus, through this approach, the study addresses the research questions stated above in the introductory section. Further information about the context and methodology used to address the research questions is presented below.

METHODOLOGY

The organization selected as the case study for the study is King Abdul Aziz University (KAU). KAU was founded in Jeddah in 1967, and was originally a private university that was established and run by several businessmen. KAU is one of the largest universities in the country with 80,000 students and approximately 5,000 academic and administrative staff. In 1971, the university was converted into a state university. In reflecting the cultural norms of Saudi Arabia, KAU has two campuses; one for male students and one for female students. This research was based within the male-only campus. As part of the public sector reform in Saudi Arabia, in recent years KAU has been going through a strategic change process. In order to study the roles played by leadership, culture, and learning and training on the change implementation in KAU this study is based upon interviews with senior employees of the organization.

Primary research often requires appropriate data to be collected from a suitable sample (Marshall & Rossman, 2006) drawn from a population. Given the research questions of this study, the decision was taken to involve only respondents with senior managerial roles as they were likely to be able to offer informed views about the defined aspects of the strategic issues relating to KAU. Hence, a complete list of staff members occupying senior management positions such as deans, heads of academic departments, and heads of functional departments was obtained from the administration department of the university. A sample of 16 prospective respondents was randomly selected; these senior people were invited to participate in the interviews and all accepted. In initial discussions surrounding the administration of the interviews, some of the respondents specifically asked the researchers not to use any kind of electronic recording equipment that could identify their voices and identities.

Therefore, in all cases, the interview responses were noted down on paper for future analysis.

A structured interview format was developed. This format was centered upon 10 key interview questions derived from the research questions of the study. The interview questions are presented below.

1. What is the most important strategic change that has been implemented in KAU?
2. What is the role of Arab culture and social practices in determining the course of change management?
3. Who are the most important players in implementing the change?
4. What are the factors that play important roles in determining the course of change?
5. What are the biggest challenges faced by the university in implementing the strategic change?
6. What is the role of learning and training in aiding implementation of strategic change?
7. Is the university successful in the process of strategic change implementation?
8. What is your take on the competition among higher education institutions in Saudi Arabia? Do you think that the present strategic change at KAU is influenced by the competition?
9. Is the strategic change at KAU guided by the leadership at the Ministry of Higher Education, Saudi Arabia? If yes, to what extent?
10. What are your suggestions for better management of strategic changes?

The 16 interview respondents included deans of various departments as well as other senior academic and administration staff. These senior management personnel are responsible for bridging the gap between the management and the staff to ensure that there are no conflicts between the two levels. While the senior managers are responsible for planning, designing, and controlling the plans and procedures, the administration staff are concerned with implementation of the tasks (Scheider & Meyer, 2006). Table 2 shows the breakdown of the sample used for this research.

In terms of biographical information, the sample of interviewees was made up of 16 men. The average age of the respondents was 41 years, and their average length of service at the university was 16 years. All of the interviewees were graduates and 30 percent of the interviewees were holders of

TABLE 2
Interview Sample

Deans	6
Senior Academic Managers	5
Senior Administration Staff	5
Total	16

Source: Authors' construct.

a post-graduate degree. The interviews were conducted over a period of 8 weeks. In accordance with the social norms of the context, the male interviewees were interviewed by the first-named author who is a male. The interviews were conducted in Arabic.

RESEARCH FINDINGS AND ANALYSIS

Cultural Considerations

The respondents unanimously agreed that cultural considerations had played a very important role in determining the nature and course of the strategic change process in KAU. For example, one respondent pointed out that: "KAU is one of the oldest universities in the country and is run by the Ministry of Higher Education as it is classified as a 'government university,' Therefore the university is expected to comply with the cultural and social norms, which are common in the country, as the country itself is known for its Islamic way of life." Nevertheless, there was some recognition among the respondent group that the culture of Saudi Arabia was not a static entity. For example, one respondent pointed out that: "the culture in Saudi itself is undergoing tremendous change including the infusion of western education methods, growing importance to women and modernization." He stated that the strategic change in university reflects the modern side of the culture of Saudi Arabia rather than the age-old traditions. He also noted that some people believe that this could dilute the cultural values of the country.

Another respondent emphasized that the strategic change designed to enable KAU to become a world class modern university: "may require some very important points such as employment of women teachers in large numbers, adoption of western education practices and allowing free interaction between male and female students in the college." However, he insisted that these factors do not necessarily mean that the cultural values are compromised. Another respondent stated that: "there are some powerful people in the ministry who have managed to block some aspects of strategic change plan by citing that those changes would compromise the cultural values, which Saudi stands for."

Some of the respondents extended this discussion and identified that the biggest challenge facing the strategic change process has been the apparent contradiction between a modern outlook and, in the words of one respondent: "the age-old traditions in the Saudi society," The majority of the respondents highlighted that Saudi society is based on the religion of Islam, which also governs every single aspect of human life in the country, including education. Traditionally, this resulted in a culture which insisted that education is only for men and that this male-dominated education must be based on the values preached by the Koran, the Holy book of Islam.

The clash between the values underpinning this traditional perspective and the more western-based beliefs about education was explicitly recognized by a number of the respondents. For example, one respondent highlighted his perception that Western-based education: "states that the best way to learn is through questioning" while traditional Saudi values are: "based on believing without questioning." This contradiction between modern values and traditional cultural values was identified as the biggest problem in the change management process by most of the respondents.

Yet even within this group of respondents, another perspective emerged. In the words of one respondent: "You can discover when you read each chapters of our holy Koran how it encourage us to think carefully and observe everything around and make them as a questions to answer those questions by many way. Positive thinking has positive effects not only on the person himself but also on the others." Similarly, another respondent pointed out that:

> As I understand from our religion, when we begin to discover the essence of humanity within and become knowledgeable of the essence of self, a doorway to understanding Allah and that may lead us into different classes constituting among ourselves. That may help us to answer questions that about change in general and specifically in our humanity. Therefore, the Islamic values are based on believing with deep questioning, as well as the modern values are based precisely on questioning.

These responses clearly show that there have been some contentious decisions made by the management of the university during the course of its strategic change implementation as some aspects of the change process may have been seen by some to violate certain aspects of the traditional cultural values of the country as a whole. This finding provides evidence that cultural values and Arab traditions have played a significant role in determining the course of the strategic change process and arguably engendering a degree of resistance to it. The interviews revealed that cultural considerations have exerted a significant impact on the strategic change management process. This impact was evident in the responses provided by the 16 respondents and, arguably, was particularly significant because of the context of the study. Taking the interview responses together, the influence of Arab culture and the Islamic way of life were considered relevant to the change management process because KAU and its senior staff were, to a degree, expected to conform to traditional customs and norms rather than effecting changes which may challenge these customs and norms.

Leaders and Influencers of Organizational Change

There was significant consensus that the university's mission to be transformed into a world-class university constituted the most significant change in recent times. These sentiments are expressed in the words of two of the respondents who stated that the strategic change process would: ". . . redefine the education paradigm in the entire country," and ". . . change the future of the university forever." However, others thought that the change would be slow. In the words of one participant, real change would: "take many years before the effect could be realized."

The respondents were asked to identify some of the most important leaders who were involved in the process of implementing the change. The overwhelming majority of the respondents stated that both the senior management of the university and the officials from the Ministry of Higher Education were actively engaged in providing leadership for the strategic change process. In addition, several respondents stated that the faculty members had formed a vital part of the leadership of the strategic change underway as most of the parts of the change plan affect some part of the teaching practice directly and indirectly.

Several of the respondents identified students as some of the most influential stakeholders who were, in an indirect way, exerting a major influence on the strategic change process. For example, one respondent stated:

> We can say that the faculty and management are the most important in the strategic change process; however according to me, the most important are the students. If they do not understand and appreciate the change and its potential positive impact on their careers then all these efforts would not bear fruits. Therefore I think students form the most important group in the strategic change process.

The respondents were also asked to identify the factors that they considered important in determining the course of the strategic change that is underway at KAU. Eight out of sixteen respondents instantly stated that the leadership of the university and the Ministry of Higher Education in the country was the most important guiding force for the strategic change. For example, one of the respondents stated: "the strategic change in the university is not a stand-alone happening; it is part of the major over-hauling of the education system undertaken by the ministry in accordance with the vision of the supreme leadership of the country at the highest levels." Similarly, another respondent stated: "modernization of such an old university which represents the culture of the country is not an easy task to accomplish without the active involvement of the leadership of the country and the ministry." Another said: "Arab culture itself is undergoing some massive changes and modernization; and said that he considered the strategic change at KAU: "as a manifestation of the underlying changes in the social fabric of the country as a whole." These views were echoed by another respondent:

> Do you think only our university is becoming modern? Look around, the entire society is getting modernized. There is the advent of internet and media which has changed everything here. I have been living in this country for the past 43 years

and I have not seen anything of such a large scale before. The modernization of university is just a small part of the overall changes taking place in our culture and social values. So the change is determined and guided by the change outside.

The respondents were also asked to provide some suggestions for better management of the strategic change process. One of the most common response was that the senior management of the university should take into account the interests and opinions of the faculty members during the course of change implementation and should not make autocratic decisions. For example, one respondent said:

> We are totally aware of the decision-making process and we appreciate our leadership and have trust in our leaders. However since we are one of the biggest groups that would be involved in implementing these change plans, it would be better if the management takes into account our ideas as well. We might be able to add value from the perspective of faculty members as we are the ones who actually interact with our students.

On this theme of involvement and participation, another respondent stated that: "the students should be better informed of the changes and their benefits." Another respondent remarked: "the university needed to increase the number of professors as the change, which is underway, lays great emphasis on knowledge building research and so the present professors may have to spend significant time in research apart from teaching." Other respondents were less willing or able to make specific suggestions about how the change process could be better managed though, at the same time, these respondents acknowledged the existence of some resistance to change among the staff. For example, one respondent, while not making a specific suggestion, stated: "there are some frictions between the decision-makers and the lower level staff and so the senior management should function efficiently to ensure that such frictions do not cause problems in effective implementation of strategic changes."

Learning and Training

As a group, the respondents placed learning and training issues at the center of the strategic process though there tended to be some variations in their responses. For example, five respondents addressed the issue of learning and training specifically from a macro perspective. That is, they expressed the view that the changing nature of learning and training in the country was a major driving force behind the strategic change process implemented within KAU. One respondent summarized his views:

> The companies in Saudi want highly trained professionals to be employed. If we do not supply them with adequate manpower they will not be able to implement our Saudization

policies.[1] The students are also coming forward to study higher education as they are seeing that educated professionals are experiencing rapid development in their careers in multinational companies. So this change is actually caused by the changing landscape in corporate environment in Saudi. The businesses want modern youth with western educations. So we have to bring western education to our country; otherwise our good students will find their demand met by colleges in the US and UK.

Twelve out of sixteen respondents stated that learning and training are the biggest factors that have aided strategic change management in the university. For example, in the words of one respondent:

> The essence of the change into world-class university is knowledge-based. We want to ensure that our students would get access to better knowledge and better means of getting it. This is the purpose of this change. So everything here is based on training and learning. The faculty have been trained in various aspects of modern teaching. For example, we have conducted training in computers for over 4000 faculties over the past 3 years. They have learned the various methods of encouraging the students to strike interesting and intellectual discussions in the classrooms. They have been trained to use case studies, as universities like Harvard in US use. The students have been trained to use the modern library catalogue system; the administration staff has been trained to use the modern computer-based administration packages. Another respondent went as far as to state: So everything about this modernization of university has been learning and training.

CONCLUSION

This research studied the important factors that have played very crucial roles in the implementation of strategic change in KAU in the university's attempt to become a world-class institution. The most important factors that have been observed to play major roles in strategic change implementation are culture, leadership, and learning and training. Even though the country's higher education system continues to be dominated by the government universities, in recent years private educational institutions have started to play increasingly important roles in enhancing the nature and quality of human resources in the country.

Specifically, private universities, armed with their own funds have ushered in a revolution in terms of the research activity and number of departments and the thrust to provide women education and employment. Besides, the private universities have also started attracting students who otherwise may have travelled abroad for a western education. These students have been impressed by the education system in

---

[1] i.e., Saudi Government policies initiated in 2005 with a motive to encourage Saudi nationals to take local jobs.

the private universities, which is designed to reflect closely styles of education and teaching that are more prevalent in the western education system.

Our empirical observations suggest that it is concluded that the factors of leadership, culture, and training and education, were all considered by the respondents to be vital in the strategic change management process operating within the case-study organization. For example, Arab culture was seen to play an important role in the change management process because the university itself was subject to wider cultural influences. Thus, even though the strategic change at the university was welcomed and adopted by most of the participants, some respondents expressed concern that the nature of change could move the university away from a learning and education system which was predominantly shaped by Islamic and other local tribal value systems to a more western-based un-Islamic system of education. It is concluded that national culture does exert a very strong but varying influence on the acceptance and implementation of strategic change within the Middle Eastern context that has been explored in this study.

A conclusion of this study is that certain aspects of leadership represented crucial considerations when examining the implementation and management of the change management process. For example, the scale of the hierarchical approach to decision-making emerged from the interview responses; it was observed that the respondents, as senior managers themselves, were of the view that all of the important decision-making powers at the university were concentrated at the top of the organization; further, these powers were exercised in an autocratic manner. Yet the study also found the respondents acknowledged the existence of resistance to change within the case-study organization. The respondents reported that this resistance manifested itself in different ways, for example, strict adherence to very old Arab traditions, an unwillingness to adopt modern work systems, continued and excessive dependence of state universities upon the ministry for their funding and other resources, and the lack of willingness on the part of the senior management to pay heed to the suggestions and preferences of the operational staff.

The respondents also highlighted that learning and training issues were crucial to the implementation of the strategic change within the chosen context in Saudi Arabia. For example, the findings indicate that both the teachers as well as the students in this setting have been exposed to significant learning and training during the process of strategic change implementation. Specifically, it is observed that strategic change of this nature involves the acquisition of knowledge of the modern education system from the West. Therefore the success of the strategic change depends to a significant extent on the ability of the participants to learn and use the modern tools and techniques of learning and training, given the fact that the university is in the business of imparting high-quality education to its students through its faculty. It is concluded on the basis of the observations made from primary research that, in this specific Middle Eastern context, learning and training are important factors in strategic change management processes.

Finally, this research draws its observations and conclusions on the basis of a relatively small sample of senior employees of a public sector organization in Saudi Arabia. Further studies are needed to widen the sample base of organizations and respondents. For example, future studies on strategic change management in educational establishments in the Middle East could extend knowledge in this subject area by including respondents based in national policy-making organizations (such as Ministries of Education) and also students and their parents in order to acquire contrasting perspectives. Similarly, although the current study has yielded some useful data and insights, no assumptions should be made about the generalizability of the findings to other contexts. Nevertheless, given the difficulties associated with gaining access to senior people in organizations in Saudi Arabia and the corresponding lack of literature on strategic change management which has emanated from this country, the current study has offered some useful insights into strategic change management in this context.

REFERENCES

Aaker, D. A. (2001). *Strategic market management*. New York: Wiley.

Altbach, P. G., & Knight, J. (2007). The internationalization of higher education: Motivations and realities. *Journal of Studies in International Education*, *11*(3–4), 290–305.

Ansoff, H. I. (2006). Strategic issue management. *Strategic Management Journal*, *1*(2), 131–148.

Camerer, C., & Vepsalainen, A. (2007). The economic efficiency of corporate culture. *Strategic Management Journal*, *9*(51), 115–126.

Cannon, J. A., & McGee, R. (2008). *Organizational development and change, CIPD toolkit*. London: Chartered Institute of Personnel and Development.

Carnall, C. A. (1986). Managing strategic change: An integrated approach. *Long Range Planning*, *19*(6), 105–115.

Christensen, C. M., & Raynor, M. E. (2003). *The innovator's solution: Creating and sustaining growth*. Cambridge, MA: Harvard Business School Press.

Coda, V. (2002). Le determinati del successo aziendale negli studi di strategia. *ISEA*, 1–12.

Common, R. (2008). Administrative change in the Gulf: Modernization in Bahrain and Oman. *International Review of Administrative Sciences*, *74*: 177–193.

Cummings, T.G., & Worley, C.G. (2009). *Organization development and change* (9th edition). Mason, OH: South-Western Cengage Learning.

Dobson, A. (2005). *How to conduct effective interviews*. London, UK: Jaico Publishing House.

Egan, T.M. (2002). Organization development: an examination of definitions and dependent variables. *Organization Development Journal*, *20*(2), 59–69.

Epstein, M. J., Davila, T., & Matsuik, S. (2004). Innovation strategy and the use of performance measures. *Advances in Management Accounting*, *13*, 27–58.

Garcia-Morales, V. J., Liorens-Montes, F. J., & Verdu-Jover, A. J. (2007). Influence of personal mastery on organizational performance through organizational learning and innovation in large firms and SMEs. *Technovation*, *27*(9), 547–568.

King Abdulaziz University (KAU). (2010). *Transformation toward a world-class university: Actions and prospectives in the case of King Abdulaziz University (KAU)*. Retrieved April. 7, 2010, from http://www.kau.edu.sa/Show_Res.aspx?Site_ID=351&LNG=AR&RN=54585

Kingdom of Saudi Arabia. (2009). *Highlights of fiscal years 2009 & 2010 and recent economic developments*. Retrieved Aug. 11, 2010, from http://www.sec.gov.sa/News/المالية وزارة من بيان.aspx?lang=en-US

Marshall, C., & Rossman, G. B. (2006). *Designing qualitative research*. London, UK: Sage Publications.

Mazzola, L. (2003). Commercializing nanotechnology. *Nature Biotechnology*, *21*(10), 1137–1143.

Mills, J. H., Dye, K., & Mills, A. J. (2009). *Understanding organizational change*. Abingdon, UK: Routledge.

Ministry of Higher Education. (2009a). *Universities statistics*. Retrieved Aug. 3, 2010, from http://wwww.mohe.gov.sa/en/studyinside/universitiesStatistics/Pages/default.aspx.

Ministry of Higher Education. (2009b). *Private higher education universities*. Retrieved Aug. 3, 2010, from http://wwww.mohe.gov.sa/en/studyinside/privateedu/Pages/listphe.aspx.

Ministry of Higher Education. (2010). *Higher education in the Kingdom of Saudi Arabia Indicators and international comparisons*. Riyadh, Saudi Arabia: Observatory of Higher Education.

Palmer, I., & Dunford, R. (2002). Who says change can be managed? Positions, perspectives and problematics. *Strategic Change*, *11*(5), 243–251.

Pitt, M. (2005). A dynamic model of strategic change in growth-oriented firms. *Strategic Change*, *14*(6), 307–326.

Prokop, M. (2003). Saudi Arabia: The politics of education. *International Affairs*, *79*(1), 77–89.

Rebora, G., & Minelli, E. (2007). *Change management*. Milan: ETAS.

Rees, C.J. (2008a). Guest editorial: Organizational change and development—Perspectives on theory and practice. *Journal of Business Economics and Management*, *9*(2), 87–89.

Rees, C.J. (2008b). Organization development in the 21st century. In C. Wankel (Ed.), *21st century management: A reference handbook* (pp. 435–443). CA: Sage.

Rees, C.J., & Althakhri, R. (2008). Organizational change strategies in the Arab region: A review of critical strategies. *Journal of Business Economics and Management*, *9*(2), 123–132.

Rees, C.J., Althakhri, R., & Mamman, A. (2012). Leadership and organizational change in the Middle East. In B. Metcalfe & F. Mimouni (Eds.) *Leadership development in the Middle East* (pp. 129–149). Cheltenham, UK: Edward Elgar.

Rees, C.J., Mamman, A,. & Bin Braik, A. (2007). Emiratisation as a strategic HRM change initiative. *International Journal of Human Resource Management*, *18*(1), 33–53.

Rowland, H. (2007). Organizational development: The new buzz word. *Strategic Direction*, *23*(1), 3–4.

Sarin, S., Sego, T., Kohli, A. K., & Challagalla, G. (2010). Characteristics that enhance training effectiveness in implementing technological change in sales strategy: A field-based exploratory study. *Journal of Personal Selling and Sales Management*, *30*(2), 143–156.

Sayles, L. R., & Wright, R. V. L. (2007). The use of culture in strategic management. *Leadership in Action*, *5*(4), 1–9.

Scheider, S. C., & Meyer, A. D. (2006). Interpreting and responding to strategic issues: The impact of national culture. *Strategic Management Journal*, *12*(4), 307–320.

Senior, B. (2006). *Organizational change*. Harlow, UK: Pearson Education.

Shane, S. (2006). The effect of national culture on the choice between licensing and direct foreign investment. *Strategic Management Journal*, *15*(8), 627–642.

Tushman, M. L., & Smith, W. K. (2004). Innovation streams, organization designs and organizational evolution, In M. L. Tushman & P. Anderson (Eds.). (2004). *Managing strategic innovation and change*. (2nd edition). New York: Oxford University Press.

Public Sector Reforms in Fiji: Examining Policy Implementation Setting and Administrative Culture

Mohammad Habibur Rahman

Public Policy and Administration, University Brunei Darussalam, Gadong, Brunei Darussalam

Rafia Naz

School of Management and Public Administration, The University of the South Pacific, Suva, Fiji

Alka Nand

Department of Management and Marketing, University of Melbourne, Melbourne, Australia

For many years, public management reform has been an evolving concept. New Public Management (NPM) and Good Governance have been the two ground–breaking ideas, generating colossal discourse over the past three decades. Inspired by NPM-led policy changes in the developed world, many developing countries have lately joined the reform bandwagon but achieved limited success. Policy analysts observe that the policy planners in the developing world seem to have spent more resources in policymaking than addressing the policy implementation challenges. Also, the policy transfer effort ignored the issue of administrative culture. Focusing on Fiji, this article examines how the country's recent public sector reform initiatives have largely failed to bring about expected results. Based on the case studies of two organizations, it explains that the success and failure of policy change occurs in several ways, manifesting multiple challenges including a lack of well-prepared implementation framework and culture change.

INTRODUCTION

The nature and focus of public sector reforms have undergone significant changes over the years. With the advent of the Weberian approach, which introduced the strength of hierarchy, rule-based administration, and neutrality, public administration was geared towards a more hierarchical, merit-based, centrally controlled state apparatus during the prolonged colonial era. The post-colonial states, embarking on a journey of continuous reform, embraced various approaches including "development administration" of the 1950s–60s, "structural adjustment" during the next two decades, "New Public Management" (NPM) in the 1980s–90s, and the "good governance" agenda in the new millennium.

In the context of the current global economic downturn, following the adverse effects of *laissez-faire* economy and big public sector spending policies of some European states on the one hand and numerous corporate corruption and declining ethics on the other, the post-good governance era is witnessing a potential discussion of the merits of the Weberian model of bureaucracy. Some argue that as an alternative to NPM and good governance, the Weberian approach can justifiably be reclaimed as a model that emphasizes impartiality, rule-following, expertise and hierarchy rather than manipulation of incentive structures and market competition. Evidently, public sector reform/restructuring has altered with time, and no single approach is universally applicable.

This article reviews public sector reforms of the mid-1990s in selected countries of the South Pacific in general and Fiji in particular, with the backdrop of successful NPM-led reforms in their wealthier neighbours New Zealand and Australia. For analytical purposes, various factors such as the policy implementation conditions and administrative culture were taken into account, as they influenced the reform in Fiji, implying that Fiji is unique in its policy landscape, administrative history, and culture, which are different from that of New Zealand and Australia, therefore modeling reform approaches from these countries needs to be undertaken cautiously.

After a brief theoretical revisit of NPM, policy implementation framework, and administrative culture, the article attempts to explain why the NPM-led public sector reforms in New Zealand and Australia were a success. The focal thrust of the article then goes on to assessing the impact of administrative reforms in Fiji. With case studies support, the article highlights how good policy implementation and administrative culture facilitated reform success in some Fijian public organizations and vice versa.

CONCEPTUALIZING POLICY IMPLEMENTATION FRAMEWORK AND ADMINISTRATIVE CULTURE AS KEY DETERMINANTS FOR REFORM

The public sector reform agenda that has been at the core of policy discourse in many developing countries in the recent past requires an understanding of not only policy planning and design but also its implementation. As the study of public policy developed over the past few decades, the focus of experts has been more on planning and design than on implementation of policies. Policy implementation came to the forefront when policy makers and experts tried to explain why "policy fails" in the developing world in particular. Likewise, it is also important to acknowledge the importance of the specific administrative culture of a society/organization to measure the results of reform adopted there. Hence, the conceptual focus of this article is to examine the implementation challenges and administrative culture vis-à-vis NPM-led public sector reform.

Revisiting New Public Management

The concept of New Public Management (NPM) surfaced as a response to continual weaknesses observed in the bureaucratic model resulting from the dynamic environmental changes (Appana, 2011). The management and organization

ideas contained in NPM can be traced back to earlier debates in public administration (Savoie, 1995; Thomas, 1998). The theoretical roots of NPM goes all the way to the Chicago (Friedman, 1953) and Austrian (Hayek, 1978) schools of political economy, with their links to the New Right, in conjunction with the new institutional economics of Arrow (1963) and Niskanen, Jr. And Niskanen (2007). Additionally, NPM is said to be a combination of economic organization theory and management theory (Aucoin, 1990; Hood, 1991). It was presented as framework of general applicability or a "public management for all seasons" (Hood, 1991, p. 8).

Basically NPM edges around the views of freedom to choose and freedom to manage thereby proposing achievement of results through accountability. It endeavours to compare levels of performance achieved to expected performance thereby giving more importance to the end results (Lodhia & Burritt, 2004 Appana, 2011). The NPM approach stresses the need for a private sector approach towards public sector management and sees the role of government officials as accountable managers who are empowered with a particular responsibility (Hood, 1995; Parker & Gould, 1999).

Understanding Policy Implementation Challenges

First and of utmost importance in implementing public policies is the role of leadership. Leaders are important because they focus their attention on three areas:

1. spearheading participatory development of a vision for public sector reform;
2. motivating and bringing out the best in staff; and
3. encouraging more direct involvement of stakeholders in the implementation of reform and thereby promoting greater responsiveness and accountability of public servants to the needs and concerns of citizens and clients in society.

Doig and Hargrove (1990) argue that one of the keys to successful entrepreneurial leadership in government is to develop and nourish external constituencies who support new programs and goals and to neutralize opposition to the leader's decisions and initiatives.

It is generally acknowledged that an important element in successful leadership of reform is vision. The vision, however, cannot be the product of one person, where the leader "pens" a vision for all to adopt. Rather, it needs to be developed in partnership with staff and key stakeholders who are involved in the reform. A shared vision must build on the individual visions of staff in the organization. This requires that employees have a clear view of the bigger picture both in terms of the challenges facing the organization and where it is heading. Thus, what characterizes a leader is the ability to facilitate the development of a common vision that expresses the aspirations of both staff and key stakeholders with regard to where the organization wants to be in the future.

The second challenge is capacity building. It is a central success factor to policy reform, making government capable in partnering with the private sector, creating an efficient market economy, and delivering goods and services to citizens. A major part of capacity-building is aided by mobilizing resources. Mobilization of resources includes both ". . . planning and doing. This includes preparation of concrete action plans; clarification of performance targets and standards; and conduct of those activities." Managing this implementation task calls for a collegial and collaborative management style and negotiation and conflict resolution (Brinkerhoff & Crosby, 2002, p. 29). Understanding the nature of the existing and obtainable resources that policy makers can deploy is critical to countering challenges to carrying out reforms.

The next challenge comes in coordinating policies. The primary role of coordination is to ensure that any particular policy initiative is broadly aligned with the explicit and implicit objectives of the government (Stewart & Ayres, 1998, p. 26).

The fourth challenge is monitoring progress and impact of policy change. As many policy reforms are long-term, monitoring in the form of process indicators is important. Monitoring policy change requires mechanisms both for periodic review and evaluation and for tracking policies across multiple agencies. Among the most common problems in the policy implementation process is setting targets or time frames for achieving certain policy outcomes (Brinkerhoff & Crosby, 2002).

Participation/consultation is another salient challenge that affects legitimization, constituency building, resource mobilization and allocation, and policy monitoring. Consultation brings key stakeholders together for policy dialogue and problem solving and increases the sustainability of policy. Periodic consultation between implementers and beneficiaries also increases efficiency by generating timely inputs and greater cooperation so that delays are reduced (Alesina, 1994). Stewart and Ayres (1998, p. 26) say that "there is no single greater cause of policy break-down than failure to consult key interests." These key interests include civil society, citizens, and private sector.

The sixth challenge in policy implementation has to do with policy legitimization. According to Brinkerhoff and Crosby (2002), it is necessary to have a political champion who must assert that the proposed policy reform is necessary and vital. The authors highlight that policy legitimization should be done early in the implementation process so that there is some degree of ownership for change.

The seventh challenge is constituency building. Brinkerhoff and Crosby (2002) view that any policy needs to be marketed and promoted and an adequate constituency for the policy be developed. Constituency is defined by Brinkerhoff and Crosby (2002, p. 26) as "those who will benefit by the change . . . They maybe consumers of the service provided, providers of inputs, or officials within the implementing agency who find their position or status enhanced by the change." Brinkerhoff and Crosby further mention that constituency building complements and amplifies the legitimization process. Gillespie et al. (1996) say that support for policy change must be of sufficient importance to overcome or at least neutralize the forces opposing implementation.

The next challenge is resource accumulation. Ames (1987) says that resource accumulation means securing both initial funding and assuring the policy a place in the governments' budget allocation process. To implement a new policy, human, technical, material, and financial resources are needed (Mazmanian & Sabatier, 1989; Grindle & Thomas, 1991).

The last challenge is organizational design and modification. Significant policy changes affect an agency in terms of its internal arrangements and of its relations with its operating environment. This may call for new structures and procedures. This issue of organizational design poses several problems. The most crucial is to do with inertia of the bureaucracy (Brinkerhoff & Crosby, 2002).

The following framework (Figure 1) depicts the aforementioned set of measures that serve as the theoretical framework for this article in assessing the empirical evidence on why policy implementation fails. The framework will also serve as a guideline for assessing the good and bad cases in the sections that will follow.

Administrative Cultural Norms and Values

The administrative culture of any part of the globe reflects the distinctiveness and complexity of the various regional, national, and local realities; their unique historical experiences; their forms of insertion (subordination or domination) into the system of regional and global relations; and their levels of development and fragmentation (Dwivedi). Just like all cultures, administrative culture has the potential to change over time. Some of the agents that influence changes include the political culture and values along with subcultures of departments and agencies and professional subcultures (such as accountants, lawyers, etc.). So in a way the administrative culture is an amalgamation of all these influences. When applied to new public management reforms, administrative culture may be characteristic of the following: democratic capitalist values, a corporate culture of some sort, management by results, excellence, best practice, etc. (Dwivedi).

POLICY IMPLEMENTATION IN THE SOUTH PACIFIC: REVIEW OF SUCCESSES AND FAILURES

The need for public sector reforms in the Pacific Island countries (PICs) are as compelling today as they were

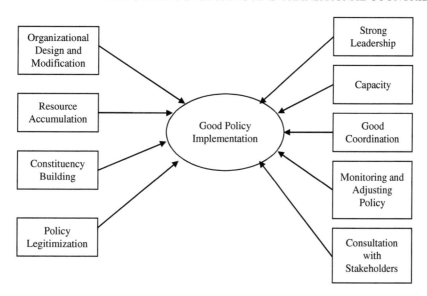

FIGURE 1   Policy implementation challenges: Theoretical framework.

in the mid-1990s, with major agendas such as macroeconomic stability, public sector efficiency, and private sector development.

The Recent New Zealand and Australian Experience

Australia and New Zealand often seen as the trailblazers of new public management have now adopted a more collaborative type of public management better known as the "whole of government" (Christensen & Lægreid, 2007).

The "whole of government" approach

The "whole of government" approach seeks to apply a more holistic strategy by applying insights from the other social sciences rather than just economics (Bogdanor, 2005). According to Perry (2005) cited in (Christensen & Lægreid, 2007, p. 1059), reform efforts under this approach reflect a combination of path dependency and negative feedback thereby promoting coordination and integration. This terminology can be traced to the reign of Tony Blair in 1997. He introduced this concept "joined-up government" with the aim to better grasp issues spanning the boundaries of public sector organizations, administrative levels, and policy areas (Richards & Smith, 2006). This term in a nutshell tries to facilitate horizontal and vertical coordination in order to eliminate situations where different policies undermine each other (Christensen & Lægreid, 2007). It allows for greater efficiency of scarce resources, creates synergies by bringing stakeholders together, and offers the public a more flawless rather than disjointed access to services (Pollitt, 2003). The "whole of government" concept can best be seen as an umbrella term describing a group of responses to the problem of increased fragmentation of the public sector and

public services and a wish to increase integration, coordination, and capacity (Ling, 2002; Christensen & Lægreid, 2007).

Reasons for this new adoption

The first and more obvious reason for adopting this approach has to do with overcoming the issues pertaining to the "pillarization" of the public sector under the new public management reforms (Gregory, 2006). The second reason relates to the dynamic changes taking place worldwide. For instance, insecurity from terrorism has had some serious repercussions for public sector reforms in Australia (Halligan & Adams, 2004) and for New Zealand bio-security has become a critical issue (Gregory, 2006). On a more universal note, natural disasters, disease outbreaks, and pandemics are on the rise and have led to a tightening of government which Australians refer to as the "thinking up and out" strategy, which embraces "whole of government" measures (Christensen & Lægreid, 2007).

With this approach, an option is to hierarchically strengthen and reassert the centre which in the case of New Zealand and Australia can be seen by a strong (politically and administratively) prime minister's office (Halligan & Adams, 2004; Christensen & Lægreid, 2007). There is also a focus in bringing back specialised agencies under greater central control. Another example is the development of organisational units in these two countries. These units include new cabinet committees, interministerial, or interagency collaborative units, intergovernmental councils, lead agency approaches, circuit breaker teams, super networks, task forces, cross-sectoral programs, or projects with the main purpose of getting government units to work better together (Gregory, 2006; Christensen & Lægreid, 2007). The year 2003 saw a new cabinet Implementation Unit established in Australia to assist with "whole of government" activities.

In addition, the Australian government made efforts in 2002 to promote and facilitate coordination to areas such as national security, demographics, science, education, sustainable environment, energy, rural and regional development, transportation, and work and family life (Halligan & Adams, 2004). Hierarchical efforts undertaken in Australia include creating coordinative structures inside existing central structures, increasing the strategic leadership role of the cabinet, and focusing more on following up central decisions. These efforts have been undertaken with the intention to put pressure on the sectoral authorities so as to compel them to collaborate and coordinate better (Halligan, 2006; Christensen & Lægreid, 2007).

Procedural efforts have also been initiated. In New Zealand, more importance has been placed on effectiveness, broader long-term "ownership" interests, and greater outcome focus, in contrast to the more short-term and narrower "purchaser" efficiency and output focus that was typical of the new public management reforms (Boston & Eichbaum, 2005).

The idea is to work in a smarter and pragmatic manner. Australia demonstrates this sort of collaboration via one-stop shops that aspire to deliver a seamless service (Halligan, 2006). Similarly, in New Zealand service delivery organisations are being guided by network governance to furnish the principles of the "whole of government" approach (Considine & Lewis, 2003).

Administrative culture: Australia and New Zealand

While the "whole of government" approach seems to be the preferred practice just like the new public management reform, it too requires culture change. With the "whole of government" approach, a more cohesive culture grounded on common ethics is critical. This doesn't come so easily given the fact that the new public management reforms along with the post-reforms focused on a sense of values,

trust, value-based management, team building, participation, self-development, and other factors. Changes in approach may confuse the public sector and potentially corrode loyalty and increase trust issues (Christensen & Lægreid, 2007). The report "Connecting Government: Whole of Government Responses to Australia's Priority Challenges" (Management Advisory Committee, 2004), underlined the need to build a supportive Australian public sector culture that encourages whole-of-government solutions by formulating value guidelines and codes of conduct under the slogan "working together."

While this seems to be the practice undertaken in these two countries, there are also discussions on rhetoric and skepticism about the whole approach. For instance, in Australia it can be viewed as a fashion that suits political and administrative leaders who desire to be seen as thinking about big ideas. Among examples supporting this notion is the concept of "value-based government," something that was brought into the country and spread as a fad but has now become more formalized. Another example is the accrual output-based budgeting system (Carlin & Guthrie, 2003). Similar to the case of New Zealand, Gregory (2006) observed a gap between what was preached and what was practiced.

Reiterating earlier discussions, the whole-of-government approach has difficulties and challenges of unintended risks, ambitious agendas, and uncontrolled consequences and therefore demands greater balance (Ryan & Walsh, 2004). Effective implementation requires changed accountability system, dominant cultures, and structural arrangements (Christensen & Lægreid, 2007). As Figure 1 indicates, political will and influences coupled with organizational and professional culture shapes administrative culture through historical evolution in a geographic space. But Pollitt argues that just like new public management, administrative culture may not be a universal solution to problems everywhere always and may not be appropriate in all circumstances (Pollitt, 2003). It needs a cooperative effort by those involved in lower-level politics and people on the ground.

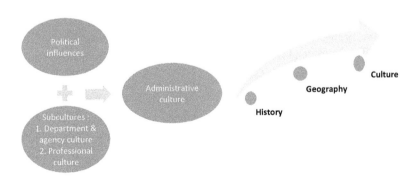

FIGURE 2   Administrative culture and performance (color figure available online).

NEW ZEALAND: REFORM MOTIVATOR FOR PACIFIC ISLAND COUNTRIES

Two factors have considerably influences the PICs to initiate policy change towards public sector reform:

1. globalization, and
2. successful reform in New Zealand in the contemporary time.

Over the last decade or so, New Zealand has gone through many reform programs of the social and economic policies and of the public sector. New Zealand witnessed in mid-1984 an economic crisis as a result of a decade of worsening trade balances which manifested in a decline of approximately 30 percent in the country's terms of trade.[1] The country's deficit was 9 percent of Gross Domestic Product (GDP) and public debt stood at 60 percent of GDP.

The situation worsened when accompanied by high levels of inflation and slow economic growth, which tremendously reduced per capita income (OECD, 1983, 1984). Following a mid-1984 election campaign dominated by economic issues, the Muldoon government was defeated resoundingly at the polls and a Labor-led government took power.(Bale & Dale, 1998).The new government put in place reforms to correct the core problems of design, implementation, and outcome of the reform program (OECD, 1990–94). The objective of the new government was to create an "efficient public sector that was also responsive to the strategic policy direction of the government" (Bale & Dale, 1998, pp. 103–104).

The following are the good practices evident in New Zealand reforms:

1. The public service is more efficient and also smaller. One reflection of efficiency is that, in three years, without adjustment to their budgets to reflect price increases, departments have shown little evidence of a decline in the volume or quality of output. (Scott, 1994).
2. The smaller public sector is beginning to show clear improvements in operating efficiency and in responsiveness to clients. It costs the government less than it did ten years ago, and is no longer a regulatory impediment to ideas and productive energies in the wider economy and community. (Scott, 1994)
3. Three key aspects of the reforms are seen as highly successful: (1) transparency in the activities and processes of the state; (2) the liberation of managers from central input controls; and (3) the new financial management and accounting systems are revolutionizing the ways in which departments and officials work (Scott, 1994)

[1] Terms of trade refers to the quantity of exports that have to be sold to pay for a particular level of imports.

The success of New Zealand reforms demonstrate that leaders can "anchor" as an integral whole for the parts of reform process to be tied together. This implies taking a more holistic and integrated approach to reforms. Coherence and consistency of New Zealand reforms is remarkable and can only be sustained through "indigenous ownership" and "political will." It is also clear that leadership sets the course for shared vision, achievable objectives, and support from stakeholders.

Overall Ranking in the PICs

The Asian Development Bank (ADB) (2004) highlights key achievements in the PICs. In its 2004 report "Governance in the Pacific: Focus for Action," ADB ranks Samoa as the top performer in public sector reform. Samoa has been able to display strong local ownership, where the reform program is clearly focused and appropriately sequenced. There has been significant progress in strengthening the regulatory framework of the financial sector (which is the target of the reform program), and there is tangible development of financial markets with the lifting of interest rate and credit control.

Vanuatu may be classified as the next most successful program to date. Bipartisan ownership and public support continues for the reform program. The number of ministries has been reduced from 34 to 9; a new value-added tax has been successfully introduced; the public service has been restructured, and professional and performance accountability initiated. A new legislative framework for good governance has been introduced and tangible benefits are evident in greater transparency in government decisions. The Development Bank of Vanuatu has been closed and its assets and portfolio taken over by the successfully rehabilitated National Bank of Vanuatu. The regulatory frameworks governing private sector investment have been liberalized.

The case of the Solomon Islands, achieving the third position in the ranking, best demonstrates how a determined reformist government, in spite of huge obstacles, is still able to take a country successfully down the reform path. Despite political uncertainties and human resource constraints, the government has stabilized the economy, brought recurrent expenditure under control, restructured public debt, reduced public service expenditure by 8 percent, and introduced a professional and performance orientation in its public service.

Next in the performance ranking is the Cook Islands, where a comprehensive reform program was supported by the ADB. A huge cut has taken place in the public service (57 percent of staff separated over 1996–98), but the number of ministries at 22 is still too numerous for a small economy. While progress is being made towards fiscal balance, the situation is still fragile. The passage of legislation establishing principles of fiscal responsibility, improved accountability, and transparency has been a significant development. The introduction of a performance orientation in public expenditure management is an achievement, though the durability of the recently introduced output-based budgeting and accrual accounting systems is in doubt due to constraints in local capacity.

In the Federated States of Micronesia (FSM), the reform program was also one of the first supported by the Bank in the Pacific. The focus has been substantially on fiscal reform, and extensive public service downsizing has been achieved. This has strengthened state finances and has left them better placed to adjust to any future reduction in external grants. Achievements have also included privatization and contracting out of some departmental activities and the transfer of power, water, and sanitation to public utility authorities. However, national and state leadership did not gain the complete commitment of some state legislatures to the reform process. The process of downsizing of the public sector could have been handled better in terms of how payouts were made, transition-preparation for those separated from service, and monitoring of the process.[2]

Key Challenges for PICs

According to the same ADB (2004) report a number of key challenges have been highlighted. ADB stresses that serious weaknesses exist in government policy development and in decision-making capacity which explains the lack of sustainability of reform initiatives in several PICs. Weaknesses in policy formulation, it stresses, are evident in all PICs, but inadequate policy implementation skills are of even more concern, as these often lead to inconsistent applications of approved policies. It stresses that "stop/start, piecemeal approach to initial reform initiatives" is due mainly to a lack of policy formulation and analysis skills in central agencies and sector departments. It is generally recognized that skills and resource constraints in all PICs are making reforms difficult. ADB says that the main reasons why implementation fails is due to the following : (1) the short-term nature of aid providers' funding programs; (2) the absence of a government-driven statement of priorities; (3) the lack of comprehensive, properly sequenced, and realistic implementation plans; and (4) inadequate emphasis on capacity building in the design and monitoring of projects.

The most important issue that the ADB report highlighted is that the key reason for the difficulties PICs had with sustaining the reform initiatives was because politicians and public officials perceived that the reforms were being "imposed" by aid providers, not only in the timing and prioritization of policies, but also in the scope and content of the reforms. Moreover, another issue raised in the report says that coordination between aid providers and recipient PICs is inadequate. The recipient countries must *themselves* be in the driver's seat for aid coordination. Samoa is an example of how a country can reap the benefits of better aid coordination: the government knows its priorities and where the needs are, and works with aid providers to direct assistance to specific projects and programs.

PUBLIC SECTOR REFORMS IN FIJI

In Fiji, public enterprise reforms were first mentioned in the late 1980s with the actual reform process commencing in 1985 (Appana, 2003). Consequently, as part of government policy, reforms were first introduced in 1992 during the government's 1993 budget address to Parliament (Ministry of Finance and National Planning, 2001, p. 69; Appana, 2003). To justify reforms the Rabuka Government claimed that public enterprises were not operating at high levels to achieve efficiency and effectiveness.

Apart from this internal pressure to reform, external pressure also had its share of influences. Globalization, and the success elsewhere in New Zealand and Australia prompted Fiji to bring in "reforms." Donor agencies, particularly the ADB, the International Monetary Fund (IMF), and the World Bank (WB) also insisted on reforms (Duncan & Bollard, 1992; Prasad & Reddy, 2002). These reports highlighted not only positive aspects but also the disappointing economic performance experienced despite significant aid levels received along with favourable external environments. According to the World Bank, much of the sluggish performance exhibited by the Pacific member countries was attributed to the inability to stimulate private investment in productive sectors due to lack of a supportive policy environment and absence of dynamic growth strategies (Sutherland, 2000). This assessment was also recognised and identified by the ADB and other donors in various reports (Hook, 2007). Other critics also agree that the internal and external factors are both responsible for driving reforms in Fiji (Reddy, 1997).

In its decade-long reform journey, Fiji embarked on two key reform strategies: privatization of public enterprises and civil service reform with the introduction of performance management and change leadership (the introduction of Chief Executive Officer [CEO] replacing the Permanent Secretary designation). The early start at reform was confused as there was not adequate preparation in terms of legislation for the different stages of reform or the development of financial and governance framework and a lack of experienced staff at public sector reform (Hook, 2007).

The progress of reforms in Fiji has been slow, ineffective, and far from complete (Reddy et al., 2004). Reddy et al.'s (2004) study shows that political instability, bad governance, improper timing of reforms, lack of stakeholder involvement, lack of institutional capacity, and lack of resources (human, financial, technical, material) are the major weaknesses in the reform process. Political instability has created

---

[2] See: http://www.adb.org/Documents/Books/Reforms_Pacific/chap1.pdf.

a major loss of human and financial capital resource base, and in face of economic decline in the country there had been a lack of "ownership" of reforms as well as in wastage of resources. Hence, less funds were available to support reforms. The general lack of consensus and cooperation among the key political players and among trade unions and business communities also posed a great challenge. Realizing the predicament because governments are formed by weak coalitions, political leaders pushing for reforms have lost some of their enthusiasm, as seen in Fiji.[3] In Fiji, the change and uncertainty associated with regime and vested interests has further complicated the reform program as well as created policy changes. The change in political leadership with various governments coming in and out has brought with it different policies towards reforms. Unlike the SVT [Soqosoqo ni Vakavulewa] and the SDL [Soqosoqo ni Duavata ni Lewenivanua], the People's Coalition government [Fiji Labor Party], due to its adherence to general labor principles, had been clearly populist, left-leaning, and sympathetic to workers (Reddy et al., 2004).

Reddy (1997) comments that the greatest challenge is to always keep in mind that change in corporate culture will take time. The point he elucidates is that individuals become complacent and create their own "comfort zones" throughout their working lives. To disrupt this and make them move in a completely new direction, especially towards reforms, is definitely not an overnight possibility. If and when it does go through the reform process, the most prudent factor—the staff's attitude will be the greatest challenge in implementation. Reforms in Fiji were further hindered by lack of institutional capacity (Reddy et al., 2004). Reddy's research brings to light the fact that the institutions in Fiji are inappropriate and under-performing. Further, this study stresses that Fiji needs to focus on building sound socio-economic and political institutions/processes to improve governance (in both the private and public sectors); increase transparency and accountability; install legal, regulatory; and supervisory frameworks; be sensitive to societal needs; and have ownership and legitimacy.

Despite the critique presented above, the Fiji Government press release highlighted that the Qarase Government was trying to set good leadership examples through creating awareness of reforms. representatives from the civil service were involved in this campaign. It was aimed at providing information to government ministries and departments about the status, objectives, and benefits of reforms (financial management and public enterprise reform program). The Chief Executive Officer (CEO) of Public Enterprises Ministry, Parmesh Chand, said that "once government officials at divisional and district levels are better informed about reforms, they will accordingly outreach to the broader community"

(Press Releases, Fiji Government: Awareness on Reforms to Target Divisions, February 17, 2006). He added, "we need to take reforms ultimately to the people so that they can assess for themselves what it all means to them in terms of benefits and improvements in livelihoods" (Press Releases, Fiji Government: Awareness on Reforms to Target Divisions, February 17, 2006).

Nonetheless, numerous reforms were initiated and executed with mixed results. In the following section, two case studies are presented to demonstrate this.

Good Reform: The Fiji Police Force

The Fiji Police were established after the British colonized Fiji on October 10, 1874. During the colonial days, the officers cadre within the force consisted mainly of expatriates from the United Kingdom. After independence in 1970, the surge towards development and modernization encouraged urban drift. An economically conscious Fijian society created a lot of expectations from its government and police service. While changes were evident in the society, the Fiji Police Force (FPF) maintained the old way of doing things.

In 1987 the first military coup took place after the Indian-dominated Labor party won the election. The military, led by the then Commander Major General Sitiveni Rabuka, took over the government and nullified the constitution. Rabuka later declared Fiji to be a Republic. In 2000 another takeover occurred, led by George Speight with the help of a unit from the Military Counter Revolution Warfare (CRW). These events greatly affected the country socially, economically, and morally.

It was during the event of 2000 that the integrity of FPF was very much doubted. Public confidence and trust in police faded away and gaps between police and the people increased. This was because of the alleged involvement of the former Commissioner of Police and some senior police officers in the coup event. During the political turbulence of 2000, the Deputy Commissioner of Police, Moses Driver steered the organization to at least gain some respectability from the people. A man of wisdom and foresight, and also very selfless in his efforts to increase the integrity of the police, he recommended that Fiji needed an expatriate as Commissioner of Police to bring back the confidence and trust of the people to the organization.

This saw the appointment of Andrew Hughes, a career officer from the Australia Federal Police. He has worked at the community, divisional, national, and international levels of policing, specializing in investigations and investigation management. Appointed on July 15, 2003, he inherited all sorts of problems: a militaristic hierarchy; lack of resources; internal bickering; nepotism; poor working conditions; lack of transparency and accountability, and low morale.

Administrative culture is all about the values/norms and practices that public servants pledge to follow and think should be done which also reflects on what actually

---

[3]Retrieved from http://lnweb18.worldbank.org/eap/eap.nsf/Attach ments/RER+2002/$File/RER_Gray+Cover.pdf#search='how%20success ful%20have%20reforms%20been%20in%20pacific'.

is displayed as their actual behavior. The Administrative Culture of the FPF was coercive, unethical, and non-transparent. The FPF operated as a closed system where input from the stakeholders was not sought, the processes and approaches were non-transparent, and the actual service delivery element (output) to the citizens was slow and unresponsive due to not only low morale and nepotism but also because of the bureaucratic rigidness and lack of expertise to tackle the upcoming changes. They basically lacked vision and foresight.

Hughes slowly took up the challenges by employing a consultative process that involved discussions with his chief officers, members of FPF, and also with members of the public. Based on his consultations and input from the key stakeholder groups, he developed his new policing direction to meet the needs of current Fiji citizens. a good element in the successful implementation of the reform process. He created a broad-based constituency of support in and outside the FPF that recognized the need for change in the delivery of services to the public.

The Commissioner embarked on good governance in setting a Strategic Plan for the organization such as the change of police uniform to let the community know and see that the organization was a professional body; and developing high-level policies to ensure that the organization's service delivery was aligned to its mission, vision, and values. The vision of FPF is to be a well-respected and effective contributor to Fiji's law and justice sector, and other policing agencies as innovative and effective in crime prevention and enhancing community safety with the values of serving with integrity, building personal capacity, expending community partnership, and looking after our people so that all can have harmonious working relations. To achieve the vision, mission, and values; the Commissioner developed policies on training development, investigative development, community policing, and reforming HRM practices including overseas and local training by the university and physical fitness.

Obongo (2007, as cited in Marwa and Zairi, 2009) says that the competence of the civil servants is an important determinant in facilitating improvements in quality and timely delivery of services. The entire purpose of setting up training of and development opportunities for police officers was to enhance their leadership and management capabilities and capacity. Hughes displayed the qualities of an effective leader and drove the change programs by having a strategic vision and the changes were directed towards ensuring a better police force that was ethical and professional in its conduct with citizens. Hughes, as an outside expert was able to understand the cultural values of the Fijian society; that they are based on communalism and collectivism. So he tried to involve everyone in the process to achieve the best for the FPF. He reoriented the administrative culture.

These changes took FPF to a new shift in culture and application of contemporary policing practices. On culture change the commissioner emphasized good behavior and professional approach to policing activities. On accountability and transparency the police force has its code of ethics which outlines the core tasks and behaviors in the performance of policing activities.

The initiatives resulted in the upgrading of the force working condition, e.g., increase in salary by 30 percent; CID allowances increased by 100 percent; and detective and plain clothes allowances increased by 100 percent, while human resources increased by 816. In the same vein, the purchase of more patrol cars increased the mobility of force to respond rapidly to crimes. Also introduced was award night where hard-working officers are rewarded for outstanding service.

These reform initiatives have led to substantial improvement in Fiji policing work with increase in detection rate to 50 percent and establishment of a National Intelligence Service under the government's Strategic Development Plan for Fiji. The new reforms in the police also featured the introduction of modern management practices (an internal Board of Management as an accountable peak decision making body) and major review of community policing as well as widespread consultation with key stakeholders and partners, that has resulted in the development of a specific model better suited Fiji's local culture and environment.

Poor Practice: Public Service Commission

The Public Service Commission (PSC) in Fiji experimented with a short-lived performance management system that ended as a failure. The beginning of the 21st century has witnessed the enhanced role of PSC in initiating civil service reforms in Fiji. Of this the most famous and talked about was the Performance Management System (PMS), which was introduced in January 2004 to motivate and develop a professional productive workforce along with extensive training programs.[4] In order to bring about the performance-based pay system through the implementation of PMS, CEOs were required to establish a performance improvement program. The Public Service Commission states that the aim of this program is to provide the means to foster a higher performance culture and a method for deciding on merit pay, as well as provide an effective mechanism for managing poor performance.

It was envisioned that these administrative cultural values/norms (which at that point in time they thought should be done) would provide a link between the broadest aims of each Ministry or Department. According to PSC, the PMS awareness training programs commenced and the "PSC

---

[4]The Graduate Certificate in Public Sector Management is offered as an on-the-job education program aimed at improving the management capacity of Fiji civil servants. It provides an understanding of governance and public sector management concepts vis-à-vis their practical implications in Fiji and the South Pacific.

and Ministries/Departments will be jointly responsible for the conduct of training programs."[5]

At the end of 2005 saw that the government was not sure what to do with regard to PMS due to huge implementation difficulties and financial implications. Therefore the government finally returned to the Cost of Living Adjustment (COLA) approach and provided a 3 percent COLA payment for the year 2004 on December 22, 2005.[6] This payment was designed to maintain the purchasing power of the existing wages of all civil servants in the case of inflation[7] (safety valve rather than a reward for all public servants). But the PMS was a system to act both as a reward and a compensation for inflation.

Although the PMS system was implemented for a good reason, it had its fair share of criticisms. There were several disputes regarding PMS and a tribunal hearing was held starting on May 16, 2005, and ending on July 15, 2005. At the end of the hearing, reports were submitted to the tribunal for an official decision. The tribunal pointed out a number of discrepancies within the PMS policy. These included:

1. PMS was thought to help maintain the purchasing power of the existing wages of all public servants but apparently this has not been the case;
2. there were a number of shortfalls such as a lack of objectivity, difficulty in measuring performance, and excessive and confusing paperwork;
3. it was questioned on its efficiency;
4. the tribunal believed that the PMS did not promote equity in pay determination;
5. the PMS was not sustainable in terms of its cost; and
6. it did not ensure that the commission would necessarily achieve their objective of reduced operation costs.

Administrative practices are one of the reasons for the suspension and failure of PMS. The PSC suspended this as it was not agreed to by the public service unions. It was the government that had strongly pressed for PMS which was criticized by the unions and condemned as unworkable in a World Bank review.[8] The administrative cultural practices of the Fijian society based on the premise of collective bargaining has contributed to the bottleneck.

The cultural values/norms of the workers itself (public servants) added to the difficulty. The Fijian society is generally reserved and arrogant when it's about assessing their performance. So the western administrative cultural values which the NZ model advocated were not welcomed.

PSC was not competent enough in employing the right formula for PMS. The unions wanted a cost-of-living-adjustment (COLA) and government wanted PMS and PSC was the arm of government responsible for moving forward with this initiative. When the arbitration ruled in favour of unions, then PMS as a change management strategy seemed expensive for the government. This reflects on the poor planning on the part of the government and PSC. The administrative values are very laid back and inactive. There seems to be no proactive strategies in place.

The administrative practices demonstrates that PSC in particular did not have the "Right Commitment." They were pushed into this initiative by the government. That is why PSC did not analyze the application and implementation issues related to PMS. It did not know how feasible it was.

The administration had low morale, unions did not accept this change management, and the cooperation from other stakeholders was not forthcoming. How the ministries and CEOs coordinated the efforts is not clear. The PSC did not have the capability to facilitate the reform (PMS).

SOME OBSERVATIONS

The government probably embarked on the PMS a bit too soon to follow the footsteps of Australia and New Zealand. This is a major problem associated with policy transfer. The government was the one pressing for this transfer. The Fijian cultural context has been such that there has always been a strong preference for uncertainty avoidance (Chand & White, 2006). Given this, it can be clearly seen that as they have a greater tendency to stick to rules and regulations, and not indulge in risk-taking initiatives or in introducing changes, the policy transfer of employing Australian and NZ models failed.

Also, before embarking on this PMS policy, continuous training and awareness of PMS for all public servants should have been considered. The capacity to initiate change should have been developed. For instance, the CEOs themselves lacked interpersonal skills. The public servants' input was not solicited in the PMS design as it was a transplant of the model, done without considering the contextual and administrative cultural factors that negatively impacted the implementation.

PMS was a model successful in Australia and New Zealand, so the government thought this will work in Fiji. The PMS policy in these two countries is outcome-based, while Fiji is still in its infancy, with an input-based level. There was no sign of Strength Weakness Opportunity and Threat (SWOT) analysis and diagnosis of the applicability of this model to Fiji. The NZ-inspired model was adopted because it focuses on western administrative cultural values that support risk-taking, empowerment, customer-orientation, "right-sizing," and merit-based performance.

[5]http://www.fiji.gov.fj/cgi-bin/cms/exec/view.cgi/15/1849.

[6]Fiji Government Press Release for December 22, 2005.

[7]Fiji Government Press Release for October 21, 2005.

[8]Retrieved from http://www.rnzi.com/pages/news.php?op=read&id=25335.

It was mentioned by the general secretary of the Fiji Public Service Association, Rajeshwar Singh, that they will be working with the government to devise a new system of assessing public servants' performance.[9] There is no mention of how the public servants themselves will be involved in developing indicators to measure performance or of them having knowledge on how they will be assessed. Before the performance measures are designed, it is critical to evaluate and analyse the job descriptions. Nothing on this has ever been indicated.

Leadership is a crucial element of achieving successful policy transfer and its implementation. It is the leader's responsibility to create a vision that must be aligned with the objectives. The PMS policy should have been appropriately aligned with implicit and explicit goals of the government. This alignment was lacking, because the Tribunals report noted "lack of objectivity" as one of the shortfalls.

The government was ill-prepared for the disruptive symptoms of PMS and they did not realize that assessing the thousands of civil servants in the state workforce would be a nightmare. The inertia of bureaucracy and expectation of a life-long job and benefits of the civil servants in Fiji led to problems of morale. Changing staff morale requires a "political champion" to be able to actively induce changes and reduce resistance to PMS.

The government pushed PMS to PSC. For a policy transfer to succeed, it is vital that not only top mangers be involved in consultation, but also operational managers and staff to be affected by the new policy. Due to lack of participation and consultation, followed by lack of legitimization and constituency building, PMS failed as "ownership of PMS was lacking."

The tribunal report raised that another shortfall was in measuring performance. This clearly shows that when the PMS was implemented, performance measures were not adequately designed. And when performance indicators are not in place, benchmarking becoming difficult. This is also reflective of "policy complexity." In this case, the complex nature of PMS made it even harder to set performance measures.

In the Pacific there are many aspects that have shaped local cultural attitudes. Some of the indigenous cultural approach to neo-liberal reform might be traced to traditional economic systems. Schika (2005), cited in (Hook, 2007), explains that the production of root crops (common among the Pacific islands) created a different sort of economic system from cultures that are dependent on rice or wheat. The local cultivation of root crops has led to local villages being self-sufficient in food but that it could often not be stored and this reduced the opportunity to produce and build up surpluses or to undertake trade. There also developed a collective-based culture that emphasized working together and not praising individual effort. The collectivist culture is important in the Pacific lifestyle historically (Hook, 2007). Furthermore, the idea of critique and individualism is not promoted (in the context of village settings).

When one thinks about NPM, it is centred on freedom of choice and management (Appana, 2011) and is "an ongoing change effort to alter administrative process and culture that in turn takes place within a larger economic, social, and political reform context" (Klingner, 2000, p. 369). By focusing on performance management, single-purpose organizations, and structural devolution, new public management has the tendency to ignore the problems of horizontal coordination (Fimreite & Lægreid, 2005). Such issues create fragmented, self-centered authorities and generally lack cooperation and coordination which eventually affects effectiveness and efficiency (Boston & Eichbaum, 2005). A combination of these questions the integrity of accountability and capacity (Christensen & Lægreid, 2001).

While NPM is a commendable approach to undertaking and seeing through reforms, it needs to be realigned with the Fijian context. According to Appana (2011), the NPM model contains a number of internal tensions and contextual weaknesses especially in traditional contexts like Fiji when viewed in terms of the fact that NPM has "no clear overall understanding of democracy and the role of the bureaucracy in the political system" (Christensen & Lægreid, 2009, p. 5). There is very little in the NPM model that acknowledges the peculiarities of the Fiji context. It is largely for these reasons that public sector reforms in general and public enterprise restructuring in particular are likely to have mixed results in Fiji (Appana, 2003).

POSTSCRIPT: THE POST-COUP SCENARIO IN FIJI

Fiji experienced yet another coup on December 5, 2006. The coup came about as a result of conflict between the then Laisenia Qarase Government and the military. The general unrest was attributed largely to one of the three bills (the Reconciliation Tolerance and Unity Bill, Qoliqoli Bill, and the Land Tribunal Bill) that were to be discussed and considered in Parliament (Lal, 2007). The bill that generated more debate across the spectrum was the Reconciliation Tolerance and Unity Bill, one that intended to offer pardons to some of the people who had participated in the 2000 coup. It is imperative to note that crime such as rape, homicide, and desecration of Hindu temples had been on the rise ever since the disputed bill was introduced (Wikipedia, 2008). Consequently, on December 5, 2006, the military moved into the capital city Suva, and a state of emergency was declared by Commodore Frank Bainimarama. In a Fiji Government Press Release (January 11, 2006) Commodore Frank Bainimarama stated that "The primary objective of the

---

[9]Retrieved from http://www.rnzi.com/pages/news.php?op=read&id=25335.

Interim Military Government is to take the country towards good governance, rid us of corruption and bad practices and at the same time promote the well-being of Fiji and its people at the earliest possible opportunity."

As emphasized by the Interim Prime Minister Frank Bainimarama in many of his speeches, his administration has mounted a "clean up corruption" campaign (Duncan, 2007). The interim administration has a plan to move forward and the genesis of the plan is the president's mandate which seeks to "remedy the abuse, mismanagement and bad governance which was brought about by SDL-led Government under leadership of Mr. Qarase in the last six years". Their policies are non racial and are not dictated by race or religion as were those of the former government (*Fiji Times*, 2007).

The Reconciliation Bill has now been put aside as the interim administration focuses on building a better way forward for Fiji. The new government has taken the following efforts to improve public sector management in order to create social harmony in Fiji:

1. It has set up the Fiji Independent Commission Against Corruption (FICAC) as a practical means of ridding all sectors of the economy of corruption.
2. The government has reviewed the affirmative action policies and has directed government assistance to many disadvantaged children and communities regardless of race. Other efforts include change in the relevant regulation, mainstreaming of government assistance, encouraging multiculturalism in schools, and evaluation of the impact of Fijian Affirmative Action projects, school review policy, and classification of schools.
3. It has engaged its efforts in accelerating a number of reforms in the various government ministries and departments. One critical plan is to reform the public sector. The Minister for Public Service, Public Enterprise, and Public Sector Reforms has been given charge to reduce the size and cost of the civil service and at the same time bring about efficiency, quality and timely service.

The military-backed government in Fiji is enjoying a mixed reception by Fijians. As described by Lal (2007), earlier the churches (particularly the Methodist church), the non-governmental organizations (NGOs), Great Council of Chiefs, and the National Federation Party have all demanded that democracy be restored in the country at the earliest as they do not approve of a military-ruled country. On the other hand, groups and organizations such as the Fiji Kisan Sangh and the Human Rights Commission remain supportive of the interim administration's policies and anti-corruption efforts.

Among the donor countries, the Australian and the New Zealand governments and their media openly condemned the coup (Wikipedia, 2007) with New Zealand threatening sanctions against Fiji and travel bans on members of the interim administration (Lal, 2007). New Zealand, apart from sanctions and bans, tightened travel restrictions on military personnel and civil servants appointed by the interim administration, froze the new Seasonal Employer Scheme that would have allowed Fijian citizens to acquire temporary visas to work in New Zealand, cancelled training for Fiji soldiers, stopped new development assistance schemes and suspended training programs for Fiji's public sector under the regional governance programs (*Fiji Sun*, 2006; Lal, 2007). The United States' immediate reaction was to suspend $2.5 million dollars in aid money pending a review of the situation. The Commonwealth of which Fiji is a member suspended all membership on December 8, stating that the coup was an infringement of the Commonwealth principles.

LESSONS LEARNED

In this article, "policy failures," which become accentuated as a result of problems in implementation, have been identified. To ensure success and sustainability of policy implementation in the long run, the following preconditions are proposed:

1. In Schiavo-Campo's view, long-term sustainability requires tackling issues of power head on with "a clear and public mandate, unquestioned political support and the material and human resources necessary to carry out its function" (Schiavo-Campo, 1994, p. 9). To this can be added the need to embed the strategy in founding legislation and to ensure that key central agencies are fully committed to the changes. The inertia of bureaucracy and old-age bureaucratic culture circumvents policy implementation. However, even under these circumstances policies can be at risk with the loss of someone to champion them. Here, Sabatier and Mazmanian (1980) call this persona "fixer," someone who can step in to implementation processes with the power to stop them from going off the rails (Sabatier & Mazmanian, 198, p. 24).
2. Effectiveness of policy implementation depends on establishing clear objectives, time frame and sequence of policies, performance benchmarks, and transparent systems to monitor the impact of policies and measure its sustainability. Stewart and Ayres cited in Aulich et al. (2001), comment that the most crucial aspect of the policy process includes ongoing consultation, monitoring, and evaluation. They further argue that the information generated in this way can be used to "fine-tune, restructure or even terminate the policy/program."
3. Efforts made by donor agencies/countries to support a particular policy, principally through technical

assistance, will not succeed if indigenous ownership and political will is absent. In addition, transplanting overseas models, even the New Zealand and Australia model, requires a match with the emulating countries needs, as differences in social, economic, and political variances can result in faltering or failure of the policy.

4. The institutional capacity must be strengthened; there needs to be good governance and demand for policy changes. Mobilization of the voices of the community through genuine democracy and involvement can stipulate successful implementation. This is supplemented by greater stakeholder participation. As stated by Stewart and Ayres cited in Aulich et al. (2001), "there is no greater cause of policy breakdown than failure to consult key interests."

5. The success not only depends on building a wide public consensus on the need for and importance of the policy, but also implying the need for a greater space for civil society and the private sector, focused on establishing viable modalities for policy change. All these actors are to coordinate and network with each other more through horizontal linkages which are both non-hierarchical and non-bureaucratic. Such cooperation can lead towards leveraging the financial, technological, and managerial strengths of the sectors involved to ensure feasibility of reforms. These sectors can also clarify and develop consensus on the policy issues, develop constituencies and coalitions for change and an understanding of policy requirements and complexity, plan and take appropriate and practical advocacy and implementation steps, and further review and monitor actions taken in support of their plans.

6. The importance of involving the ministry officials, or those who are to be affected by the policy change is critical. The chief factor is to encourage positive commitments. The policy dialogue process, which includes the participation of key government actors, serves to encourage officials to publicly commit to desirable policies and their implementation. This can help to generate commitment and ownership for reform implementation, and build a basis for accountability.

7. For any policy to be implemented among the other preconditions, requires proper communication, teamwork, and coordination.

8. Policy implementation must take a more integrated and holistic approach. The various components of the policy cycle must not be disjointed. A piecemeal, short-fix solutions approach should be avoided.

CONCLUSION

Policy making and its implementation is an area that requires careful analyses. Where policies were designed and separated from the main thrust of implementation in the cycle, major bottlenecks and deadlocks have resulted. Through empirical analysis and Fiji case studies, this research highlights why policy reform succeeds and fails. Though the Fiji cases could not adequately explore all the policy implementation preconditions (Figure 1) and administrative cultural norms (Figure 2) that were conceptually outlined at the beginning of the article, some major implementation challenges and cultural constraints have been identified. By analyzing good and bad examples the article examines the challenges of policy implementation in the South Pacific countries in general and Fiji in particular.

The research is a contribution towards the growing body of knowledge on "public policy discourse" and sheds light on the preconditions for successful policy implementation. The challenge areas include leadership, commitment, policy legitimization, resource accumulation, coordination, consultation, and capacity. The article concludes that while NPM approach in civil service/public sector reform brought breakthroughs in New Zealand and Australia, it failed somewhat in Fiji because of various administrative cultural influences including leadership and capacity constraints. This article has taken a modest approach towards identifying the institutional loopholes and envisioning a future in which certain requirements must set the foundation for success of policy implementation in public sector reforms in Fiji.

REFERENCES

Alesina, A. (1994). Political models of macroeconomic policy and fiscal reforms. In S. Haggard & S.B. Webb, S.B. (Eds.). *Voting for reform: Democracy, political liberalization and economic adjustment*. New York: Oxford University Press.

Ames, B. (1987). *Political survival*. Berkeley, CA: University of California Press.

Appana, S. (2003). New public management and public enterprise restructuring in Fiji. *Fijian Studies: A Journal of Contemporary Fiji, 1*(1), 51–73.

Appana, S. (2011). Public sector reforms and democracy: The case of Fiji. *Journal of Management Policy and Practice, 12*(5), 72–85.

Arrow, K. J. (1963). *Social choice and individual values*. New Haven, CT: Yale University Press.

Asian Development Bank. (2004). *Governance in the Pacific Focus for Action* 2005–2009. Manila: Asian Development Bank.

Aucoin, P. (1990). Administrative reform in public management: Paradigms, principles, paradoxes and pendulums. *Governance, 3*(2), 115–137.

Bale, M., & Dale, T. (1998). Public sector reform in New Zealand and its relevance to developing countries. *The World Bank research observe*. Washington, D.C.: The World Bank.

Bogdanor, V. (2005). *Joined-up government*. British Academy Occasional paper 5. Oxford: Oxford University Press.

Boston, J., & Eichbaum, C. (2005). *State Sector Reform and Renewal in New Zealand: Lessons for Governance*. Paper presented at the Conference on Repositioning of Public Governance: Global Experiences and Challenges. Taipei, 18–19 November.

Brinkerhoff, D.W., & Crosby, B.L. (2002). *Managing policy reform: Concepts and tools for decision makers in developing and transition countries*. Bloomfield, CT: Kumarian Press.

Carlin, T., & Guthrie, J. (2003). Accrual output based budgeting systems in Australia: The rhetoric-reality gap. *Public Management Review, 5*(2), 145–162.

Chand, P. & White, M. (2006). The influence of culture on judgements of accountants in Fiji, *Australian Accounting Review, 16*(3), 82–88.

Christensen, T., & Lægreid, P. (2001). New public management: the transformation of ideas and practice. Farnham, UK: Ashgate.

Christensen, T., & Lægreid, P. (2007). The whole-of-government approach to public sector reform. *Public Administration Review, 67*(6), 1059–1066.

Christensen, T., & Lægreid, P. (2009). *Democracy and administrative Q17 policy: Contrasting elements of NPM and post-NPM*. (Working Paper) Stein Rokkan Centre for Social Studies. Retrieved from http://hdl.handle.net/1956/5379

Considine, M., & Lewis, J. M. (2003). Bureaucracy, network, or enterprise? Comparing models of governance in Australia, Britain, the Netherlands, and New Zealand. *Public Administration Review, 63*(2), 131–140.

Doig, W., & Hargrove, E.C. (Eds.). (1990). *Leadership and innovation: Entrepreneurs in government*. Baltimore: Johns Hopkins University Press.

Duncan, I., & Bollard, A. (1992). *Corporatization and privatization: Lessons from New Zealand*. Auckland: Oxford University Press.

Duncan, R. (2007). A 'clean up campaign' for Fiji's economy. *Pacific Economic Bulletin*, Vol 22, No. 2, pp. 119–126.

Dwivedi, O. (1999). Administrative culture and values: Approaches. In O.P Dwivedi. and I.G James (Eds.), *From bureaucracy to public management: The administrative culture of the government of Canada*. Peterborough: Broadview Press.

Fiji Sun Fiji loses Foreign Friends (2006, December 12).

Fimreite, A. L., & Lægreid, P. (2005). *The regulatory state and the executing municipality: Consequences of public sector reform in Norway*. Paper presented at the 21th EGOS Colloquium in Berlin, June 30-July 2 2005.

Friedman, M. (1953). *Essays in positive economics*. Chicago: University of Chicago Press.

Gillespie, P., Girgis, M., & Mayer, P. (1996). The great evil: Anticipating political obstacles to development, *Public Administration and Development, 16*(5), 431–453.

Gregory, R. (2006). Theoretical faith and practical works: de-autonomizing and joining-up in the New Zealand state sector. In T. Christensen and P. Lægreid (Eds.), *Autonomy and regulation: Coping with agencies in the modern state* (pp. 137–161). London: Edward Elgar.

Grindle, M.S., & Thomas, J.W. (1991). *Public choices and policy change: The political economy of reforms in developing countries*. Baltimore: John Hopkins University Press.

Halligan, J. (2006). The reassertion of the centre in a first generation NPM system. In T. Christensen and P. Lægreid (Eds.), *Autonomy and regulation: Coping with agencies in the modern state* (pp.162–180). Cheltenham, UK: Edward Elgar.

Halligan, J., & Adams, J. (2004). Security, capacity and post-market reforms: Public management change in 2003. *Australian Journal of Public Administration, 63*(1), 85–93.

Hayek, F. A. (1978). *New studies in philosophy, politics, economics and the history of ideas*. Chicago: University of Chicago Press.

Hood, C. (1991). A public management for all seasons? *Public Administration, 69*(1), 3–19.

Hood, C. (1995). The New Public Management in the 1980s: Variations on a theme. *Accounting, Organizations and Society, 20*(2), 93–109.

Hook, S. (2007). *The economic performance of PI economies*: Paper presented at the 10th Pacific Islands Political Studies Association (PIPSA) Conference, Port Vila, Vanuatu. December 7–8, 2007.

Klingner, D. E. (2000). South of the border. *The American Review of Public Administration, 30*(4), 365.

Lal, B. L. (2007). This process of political readjustment: Aftermath of the 2006 Fiji coup, Discussion Paper, Australian National University, Australia. [Online]. Retrieved Feb. 6, 2008, from http://www.fijilive.com/archive/showpdf.php?pdf=2007/07/2006coup_aftermath.pdf

Ling, T. (2002). Delivering joined–up government in the UK: Dimensions, issues and problems. *Public Administration, 80*(4), 615–642.

Lodhia, S. K., & Burritt, R. L. (2004). Public sector accountability failure in an emerging economy: The case of the National Bank of Fiji. *International Journal of Public Sector Management, 17*(4), 345–359.

Management Advisory Committee. (2004). *Connecting government: Whole of government responses to Australia's priority challenges*. Canberra: Management Advisory Committee.

Marwa, S.M., & Zairi, M. (2009). In pursuit of performance-oriented civil service reforms (CSRs): A Kenyan perspective. *Managing Business Excellence, 13*(2), 34–43. Retrieved from: http://www.emeraldinsight.com/journals.htm/journals.htm?articleid=1793727&show=html

Mazmanian, D.A., & Sabatier, P.A. (1989). *Implementation and public policy*. Lanham, MD: University Press of America.

Ministry of Finance and National Planning. (2001). *Economic and fiscal update—Supplement to the 2002 budget address: Building confidence for sustained growth*. Suva: Government Printer.

Niskanen Jr, W., & Niskanen, W. A. (2007). *Bureaucracy and representative government*. New York: Aldine-Atherton.

Parker, L., & Gould, G. (1999). Changing public sector accountability: Critiquing new directions. *Accounting Forum, 23*(2), 109–135.

Pollitt, C. (2003). *The essential public manager*. Maidenhead: Open University Press.

Prasad, B., & Reddy, M. (2002). *Structural reforms, political instability and economic growth in Fiji: Sustainability in the long run*. Retrieved from http://www.fdc.org.au/files/prasad.pdf

Press Releases, Fiji Government: Awareness on Reforms to Target Divisions, February 17, 2006. Retrieved from http://www.fiji.gov.fj

Reddy, M., Prasad, B., Sharma, P., Vosikata, S., & Duncan, R. (2004). *Understanding reform in Fiji*: Papua, New Guinea: Institute of National Affairs.

Reddy, N. (1997). *The implications of public sector reforms on human resource management in the South Pacific: The case of Fiji*. Paper presented at the Conference on Human Resources and Future Generations in Islands and Small States, University of Malta, Valletta, Malta.

Richards, D., & Smith, M. (2006). The tension of political control and administrative autonomy: From NPM to a reconstituted Westminster model. In T. Christensen and P. Lægreid (Eds.), *Autonomy and regulation: Coping with agencies in the modern state*. Cheltenham: Edward Elgar.

Ryan, C., & Walsh, P. (2004). Collaboration of public sector agencies: Reporting and accountability challenges. *International Journal of Public Sector Management, 17*(7), 621–631.

Sabatier, P. A., & Mazmanian, D.A. (1981). The implementation of public policy: A framework of analysis. *Policy Studies Journal, 8*(4), 538–560.

Savoie, D. J. (1995). What is wrong with the new public management? *Canadian Public Administration, 38*(1), 112–121.

Schiavo-Campo, S. (1994). *Institutional change and the public sector in transitional economies*, World Bank Discussion Paper, No. 241, Washington, DC: World Bank.

Scott G. (1994). *Toward better governance - Public service reform in New Zealand (1984–94) and its relevance to Canada*. Presentation to A Symposium on Public Sector Reforms in New Zealand and their Relevance to Canada, Office of the Auditor General of Canada, Ottawa, November 29, 1994.

Sutherland, W. (2000). Global imperatives and economic reform in the Pacific Island states. *Development and Change, 31*(2), 459–480.

Thomas, P. G. (1998). The changing nature of accountability. In B. G. Peters and D. J. Savoie (Eds.), *Taking stock: Assessing public sector reforms*. Montreal: McGill-Queen's University Press.

Wikipedia Encyclopedia. [Online]. 2006 Fijian coup d'etat (2008). Retrieved Feb. 6, 2008, from http://en.wikipedia.org/wiki/2006_Fijian_coup_d'%C3%A9tat. [2008, February 6].

Administrative Culture and Incidence of Corruption in Bangladesh: A Search for the Potential Linkage

Sk. Tawfique M. Haque

Public Policy and Governance Program, North South University, Dhaka, Bangladesh

Sheikh Noor Mohammad

Ministry of Public Administration, Government of Bangladesh, Dhaka, Bangladesh

This article analyzes the possible link between administrative culture of Bangladesh and corruption. Hofstede's four cultural dimensions—power distance, uncertainty avoidance, individualism vs. collectivism and masculinity vs. femininity—have been used to search for the link between administrative culture and corruption and to examine the norms, values, and customs as visible in the Bangladeshi administrative culture. The history, evolution of administrative system and institutions of Bangladesh have therefore, been investigated to validate the assumption. There are mixed findings on the possible link of cultural dimensions embodied in Hofstede's model with corruption. Bangladesh's high level of uncertainty avoidance and relatively high collectivism largely account for breeding corruption embedded in administrative culture in the form of mechanistic adherence to hierarchy, centralization, abuse of discretionary power, nurturing tadbir and sycophancy. The other two dimensions, power distance and masculinity-femininity, could also be used to explain the pervasiveness of corruption in some cases.

INTRODUCTION

This article focuses on the interrelationship between the administrative culture and corruption in Bangladesh. It seeks to examine the perceived relationship between these two administrative and social phenomena. The dimensions of national culture suggested by Hofstede have been used as an analytical framework to explain the historical and cultural perspectives of corruption in Bangladesh. The major objective is to examine the potentiality of Hofstede's cultural dimensions to explain the incidence of corruption in Bangladesh. Corruption has become a root cause of economic, political, and institutional weaknesses and shortcomings in Bangladesh. This article will try to answer the general questions raised by many social scientists- does culture matter vis-a-vis corruption? How do characteristics of the existing administrative culture in Bangladesh contribute to the high level of corruption? Different historical accounts, relevant literature, and observation methods have been used to study the link between administrative culture and corruption.

Traditionally, Bangladesh was a part of British India until 1947. Thereafter, Pakistan ruled it until 1971. The administrative culture and administrative system of Bangladesh are therefore largely dominated by those of British India and Pakistan. The vice-regal tradition[1] that Bangladesh inherited from colonial states was classified by centralization, hierarchism, and nepotism. Thus corruption in the name of bribery,

---

[1] The authoritarian forms of administration or governance introduced by the British Raj in the Indian Sub-continent. Characterized by the preeminence of a hegemonic civil service, the bureaucracy had signs of systematic obstinacy against possible changes. The elitism and protectionism of the civil service demonstrated a negative attitude towards politicians, a generalist heritage, and a paternalistic mindset—all of which are the legacy of a vice-regal tradition. Being once a part of Indian Sub-continent, this vice-regal system of rule is still a predominating trait of the administrative system of Bangladesh.

tadbir,[2] flattery, patronage, abuse of discretion, graft, and embezzlement was deeply rooted in the administrative culture of this sub-continent. Large-scale corruption dominated public life. It has been observed that corruption prevailed on a larger scale in India during medieval times and the ones that followed (Padhay, 1986).

Corruption was also evident during the British rule in India. There is almost regular and systemic corruption in the political and administrative hierarchy. There was an underlying belief among officials of *making hay while the sun of British Raj shone*. With the passage of time corruption has become an integral part of administrative culture in Bangladesh. The norms, values, and symbols of the administrative culture of Bangladesh and its potential interrelations with corruption are the prime focus of this article.

CONCEPT OF CULTURE, ADMINISTRATIVE CULTURE, AND CORRUPTION

Culture is the way of life for an entire society that includes codes of manners, dress, language, religion, rituals, art and literature, norms of behavior, lifestyle, value systems, and traditions and beliefs. Hofstede (2010) defines culture as the collective programming of the mind that distinguishes one group of people from another. Most anthropologists and sociologists tend to agree that culture cannot be genetically transferred because humans are not born with a culture but rather born into a society that teaches us the collective ways of life we call culture (Robertson, 1981). Actually culture is the learned behavior that helps human beings adapt to an ever-changing environment.

Hofstede's (2010) classification of national culture is employed in this article as a point of departure for a more elaborative description and analysis of corruption in Bangladesh politics and administration. The sheer scale of his study—the size of the sample and geographical coverage—was very impressive. He carried out a survey of IBM employees in 76 countries (after last extensions of the study) and generated data. Bangladesh was included in the original survey. Hofstede's work has been widely used and criticized by the researchers.

His four-dimensional model of national culture involves: 1) Power distance, 2) Uncertainty avoidance, 3) Individualism vs. collectivism and 4) Masculinity vs. femininity. Fifth and sixth dimensions were added later: 5) Short-term orientation and Long-term orientation, and 6) Indulgence vs. Restraint. The last two dimensions are comparatively new and they deserve more attention and investigation. This article covers only the first four dimensions of national culture suggested by Hofstede to limit the article's purview.

Power distance is the degree of inequality among people, which the population of a country considers normal, or to the extent a society accepts the unequal distribution of power. This represents inequality that is defined from below, not from above; it suggests that a society's level of inequality is adjudged by its followers as much as its leaders. *Uncertainty avoidance* refers to the degree to which people in a country feel either comfortable or uncomfortable in unstructured situations. It reflects their propensity to take risks and the attitude towards change and innovation. *Individualism* indicates the degree to which a culture emphasizes personal initiative and achievement rather than collective concerns. *Collectivism* pertains to societies in which people from birth onwards are integrated into strong and cohesive in-groups (relatives, clan, organization), that through people's lifetimes continue to protect them in exchange for unquestionable loyalty. According to Hofstede, *masculinity* refers to a culture that emphasizes masculine norms like assertiveness, task orientation, ambition, and competition whereas feminine norms emphasizes soft values such as caring, nursing, and maintaining warm personal relationships. Feminine culture implies societies in which gender roles overlap (Jamil, 2007). According to Hofstede, power distance and uncertainty avoidance influence our perception about organization while individualism and masculinity affect our perception about people in organizations rather than about organizations themselves.

Administrative culture refers to dominant norms and values that shape and influence bureaucrats' interpersonal relationships, attitudes, and performance. Administrative culture is the product of not only people's perception about and orientation with their administrative system but also the entire gamut of traditional, societal, historical, and cultural values that influence as well as govern the bureaucracy's own behavior and its professional norms, i.e., rationality, impersonality, technology, and efficiency (Jain, 1990).

Corruption is public officials' behavior that deviates from accepted norms to serve private ends. From the perspective of administrative culture of Bangladesh offering, giving, soliciting, or acceptance of an inducement or reward, which may influence the action of any person holding public office, is corruption. Corruption is most commonly defined as the misuse or the abuse of public office for private gain (World Bank, 1997). According to Transparency International, corruption involves behavior on the part of officials in the public sector in which they improperly and unlawfully enrich themselves by the misuse of the power entrusted to them. Thus corruption means an act done with an intent to give some advantages inconsistent with one's official duty and the rights of others, which includes bribery also.

Kiltgaard (1996) has developed a model to explain the dynamics of corruption: C=M+D-A-S. Where C=Corruption; M=Monopoly; D=Discretion; A=Accountability, and S=Public sector salaries. In other words, the extent of corruption depends on the amount of monopoly power and

---

[2]A process of cajoling and personal lobbying which are important mechanisms in getting business done quickly in public offices.

discretionary power that officials exercise and the degree to which they are held accountable for their actions. The necessary conditions for corrupt practices are (1) existence of power or position of power or protection of powerful persons, (2) existence of opportunity to use such power deliberately for personal or parochial gain, and (3) absence of an accountability and watchdog agency (Ahmed, 2005).

Even a desultory look enables one to discover that none of the widely used definitions of corruption has tried to link it directly with administrative culture. This article tries to find out the causes of the lack of accountability and misuse of discretionary power as an outcome of the cultural dimension of administration in Bangladesh and the challenges faced by it. Hofetede's findings and conclusion about the national culture will be used in the article to explore the interrelationship between corruption and administrative culture in Bangladesh. But before analyzing the dimensions of corruption and its linkage with administrative culture, this article will present a brief history of the infiltration of corruption into the politico-administrative heritage, especially in the civil service of Bangladesh.

ADMINISTRATIVE CULTURE AND CORRUPTION, A HISTORICAL LINK

Corruption is a universal, complex phenomenon. It's rooted in the history of civilization and it is the primary cause of many administrative problems. The British East India Company, which effectively seized power in Bengal in 1757, perpetuated a highly corrupt system, paying its employees subsistence wages, thereby compelling them to resort to private business and extortion. Robert Clive[3] described the employees of the company as a set of men whose sense of honor and duty to their employers had been estranged by the larger pursuit of their own immediate advantages (Mahmood, 2010). This allowed a government official, particularly at the lower level of field administration, to treat his office as a legitimate tool of generating personal revenue in cash and kind. Citizens paid a relatively small amount of money for services rendered by public servants. Nobody complained unless the charge exceeded the normal rates (Kochanek, 1974). The institutionalized system of paying speed money to process documents, to move files, to clear customs, and to receive services continued in post-colonial Pakistan (Islam, 2004).

Corruption did not emerge suddenly with the creation of Bangladesh. Pre-independence Pakistan and prior to that pre-independence British India, where feudal culture was

strong, had a somewhat institutionalized system of corruption with high-level officials presenting or receiving gifts. During the Zamindari[4] system a similar institution existed in the Indian Subcontinent in the name of "Punnah" and carried over into British colonial rule

The Bangladesh Civil Service holds a lineage to the Civil Service of India during the British period and to the Civil Service of Pakistan during the Pakistan period. The culture of corruption in the name of exchanges of money/gift and privileges are deep-rooted in the inherited administrative culture of Bangladesh. Although, historically, corruption has been a part of politico-administrative heritage of Bengal, there is little denying the fact that after independence the tentacles of corruption have engulfed the entire society. The influence of corruption in the administrative culture of Bangladesh is so strong and sustained that most people felt constrained to accept it as *fait accompli*. In case of the corruption at the lower level of government it is widely believed that civil servants with insufficient salaries to meet the living expenses of their families are driven by necessity to engage in corrupt practices. Aside from encouraging corruption, low pay has other detrimental effects on the attitudes and performance of public employees (Myint, 2000). During the period 1947–71, the emoluments of a secretary to the government stood at Rupees 3000/= per month. This was equivalent to the price of approximately, 2,830 kgs of rice. Today the emoluments for officials of the level of secretaries stand at Taka 40,000, equal to the price of approximately 1,000 kgs of rice. The increased cost of living or inflation was always a driving force for corruption in the Bangladesh civil service.

Since independence, Bangladeshi leaders have often condemned the high incidence of corruption, but even since the return of democracy during the 1990s, successive governments have not been able to take effective action to address the systemic issues which allow corruption to flourish. The business community has put up with it; many would argue, it has benefited from it. It has unfortunately been the taxpayers and ordinary citizens, especially the poor, who have largely had to pay for it. The World Bank estimates that a significant portion of GDP growth is lost due to corruption each year. Per capita income could double if the government restrained corruption (TIB, 2009).

CORRUPTION AND POLITICS-ADMINISTRATION NEXUS

Corruption is largely responsible for the criminalization of politics. Buying political influence and buying votes from

---

[3]Major-General Robert Clive, (September 25, 1725–November 22, 1774), also known as Clive of India, was a British officer who established the military and political supremacy of the East India Company in Bengal. He is credited with securing India, and the wealth that followed, for the British crown. Together with Warren Hastings he was one of the key early figures in the creation of British India.

[4]A zamindar was an aristocrat, typically hereditary, who held enormous tracts of land and held control over his peasants, from whom the zamindars reserved the right to collect tax (often for military purposes). Over time, they took princely and royal titles such as Maharaja (Great King), Raja (King), Nawab (Lord), Chowdhury (Lord), and many others. Although Zamindars were considered to be equivalent to lords and barons, in some cases they were also seen as independent, sovereign princes.

the electorate are common manifestations of political corruption in many countries including Bangladesh. Because money is needed to be active in politics and to contest elections, financial needs and pressures make politicians easy prey in accepting payoffs unless he or she has enough financial resources to undertake such activities. It has been argued that loss of ideological focus in France and Italy was caused by the need to finance political activities, giving rise to "Businessman Politicians" (Meny & Siicle, 1996). This is also the case in Bangladesh.

Lewis (1996) argues that the considerable influx of foreign aid into Bangladesh provides fertile ground for the cultivation of corruption. The improper use of aid not only leads to local corruption but also to failure in achieving the goals of the development projects. Aid is used for purposes other than poverty alleviation. The rich therefore become richer, the poor become more dependent, more vulnerable, and more alone (Younis & Mostafa, 2000). The "Wheat Game"[5] in Bangladesh is an example of misuse of funds which has now become so deeply rooted in local management that it has not only corrupted many civil servants but also many elected officials (UNDP Report, 1993).

The most common forms of political and administrative corruption in Bangladesh are pecuniary bribes, abuse of authority, nepotism, favoritism, tadbir, fraud, patronage, theft, and deceit whereas in many cases corruptions are intertwined with their consequences. High power distance and inequality everywhere, proliferation of complex rules and regulations, obligation originating from moderately collectivist social structure and materialistic competition within the society provide the reasons and incentives for corrupt behavior. Bribery at the service delivery point is routine and commonplace. Maintaining or upgrading land records; clearing goods through customs; registering a police report (First Information Report [FIR]); securing a driving license; admission to public schools, universities, and hospitals; getting a plot for private building or setting up a factory; housing loan approval sanctioned; getting an electricity connection; and even collecting a copy of the order passed by the court could be obtained quickly through a bribe. Concealment of income, under valuation and evasion of taxes and duties, black-marketing, rigging of share prices, and money laundering are common phenomena in Bangladesh.

According to the Corruption Perception Index (CPI) of Transparency International (TI), Bangladesh ranked as the most corrupt country in the world from 2001 to 2005. However, the figure indicates a slight improvement since 2006, particularly in score (See Table 1). CPI score relates to perceptions of the degree of corruption as perceived by business persons and risk analysts and range between 10 (highly clean) and 0 (highly corrupt).

TABLE 1
Corruption in Bangladesh: Transparency International Ranking, 2001–2011

Year	Score	Rank from Bottom	Rank from Top	No. of countries included
2001	0.4	91	1	91
2002	1.2	102	1	102
2003	1.3	133	1	133
2004	1.5	145	1	145
2005	1.7	158	1	158
2006	2.0	161	3	163
2007	2.0	173	7	179
2008	2.1	171	10	180
2009	2.4	139	13	180
2010	2.4	134	12	178
2011	2.7	120	13	182

Source: Compiled from the *TI Corruption Perception Index, 2011.*

Political parties are identified as the most corrupt institution around the world and in Bangladesh, the Police are perceived to be the most corrupt institution—according to 8 people in every 10 in Bangladesh (ACC, 2008). The public administration has been chosen as the second most corrupt institution (7 people in every 10) followed by the judiciary (4 people in every 10). Experience of petty bribery with different service providers is widespread. In a group of 10 persons, 8 persons had to bribe the police, 7 had to bribe the judiciary, and 5 had to bribe the land administration (TIB, 2010).

It is a paradox that a democratic government governed the country from 2001 to 2006. The non-party caretaker government's arrival in state power since the last part of 2006 and its massive anti-corruption drive ushered in immense hope in the people. According to the National Household Survey on Corruption 2007 by Transparency International Bangladesh (TIB), despite the caretaker government's anti-corruption drives, corruption in education, health, land administration, local government, and the utility service sectors increased in the first half of 2007. A report of UNDP, "Corruption and Good Governance" (1997), found that if bureaucratic corruption and inefficiency were to be reduced in Bangladesh, its investment would shoot up by more than five percentage points and its yearly GDP rate would rise by over half a percentage point.

Corruption in Bangladesh undermines people's trust in the political system and its leadership, comprises the quality of programs, skews priorities, reduces efficiency, erodes the rule of law, hampers economic growth and effort for poverty reduction, undermines accountability, and reduces transparency. Corruption in the police and the judiciary, especially, leads to gross injustice and violation of human rights in Bangladesh (TIB, 2010).

The corruption history in Bangladesh has some commonalities with other countries; it has some unique characteristics also. The colonial legacy of the British and Pakistani period, criminalization of politics, influx of foreign aid, and the culture of tadbir are some of the unique contextual

---

[5]A program through which government provides wheat for distribution to people in need is used by Upazila (sub-district) Project Implementation Officers (PIO) to bribe visiting superiors.

characteristics of the corruption pattern of Bangladesh. As already stated, this article attempts to analyze the current and historical contexts of Bangladesh with Hofstede's four-dimensional framework of national culture. These four dimensions of national culture are elaborately discussed in the next section to explore the relationship between administrative culture and corruption.

INDIVIDUALISM AND COLLECTIVISM IN THE BANGLADESHI ADMINISTRATIVE CULTURE

According to Hofstede, Individualism refers to a loosely knit social framework in a society in which people are expected to look after themselves and their immediate families rather than being members of cohesive in-groups like family, kinship. According to Hofstede, collectivist societies can be characterized through unquestioning allegiances to the (extended) family that, in turn, lead to the building of dense networks of kinship. The workplace in highly individualistic cultures is largely contractual and work is controlled and organized with reference to individuals and assumed economic rationality and self-interest. In collectivist societies, the employment relationship is morally/immorally based and management of groups is salient, with personal relationships prevailing over tasks. Trust is the essential requirement for cooperation in collectivist societies. In collectivist countries like Indonesia, Taiwan, and Bangladesh it is important for the organization to establish linkages between private and work life (Islam, 2004). Table 2 illustrates the differences between individualism and collectivism.

TABLE 2
Characteristics of Individualism and Collectivism

Individualism	Collectivism
• Focus on the individual	• Focus on the group
• Responsibility for themselves and immediate family	• Responsibility for family and extended family
• Management mobility	• Employee commitment
• Private and work life separate	• Work and private lives intermixed
• Pleasure from individual achievement	• Pleasure from group achievement

FIGURE 1   Individualism-Collectivism Index.

Individualism _____ Collectivism

91	20	6
UNITED STATES	BANGLADESH	GUATEMALA

Bangladesh scored very low in individualism and comparatively very high on collectivism in Hofstede's study.

Figure 1 shows that out of 76 countries compared by Hofstede, Bangladesh ranked 58–63 with a score of 20 on individualism whereas the United States ranked the most individualistic society with a score of 91 and Guatemala the least with a score of 6 (Hofstede, 2010).

In Bangladesh, individualism in the sense of western society does not exist in rural areas. In rural areas samaj[6] tradition is prevalent and determines roles, the role expectations of group members, and how one should relate to other roles. For a long period of time, the close-knit village community life influences the interpersonal relationship. Samaj is usually a hierarchic system based on a person's social position, caste, status, educational background, seniority, and gender. Usually, no one in rural areas goes against the social norms. If anyone dared to go against the verdict of the samaj, he or she has to be ostracized from that society.

Manno kara (obedience) and shradha (deference)[7] to seniors is an important norm and value in a hierarchic society like Bangladesh. This hierarchical relationship by strong group norms encourages conservatism. The principle of hierarchy in interpersonal relationships has for hundreds of years been accepted as necessary and morally right in rural Bangladesh (Jamil, 2007). This hierarchical structure is so strong that it has penetrated the bureaucracy and political system of Bangladesh.

Literature provides ample evidence that in collectivistic societies, there is a higher vulnerability to illegal transactions in cooperation with friends and relatives or through other types of personal networks (Lipset & Lenz, 1999). Lipset and Lenz (1999) find that countries with familistic cultures have higher levels of corruption. The hierarchical and kinship-based social structure of Bangladesh has given rise to the culture of tadbir which is usually associated with corruption. Tadbir is a pathological peculiarity of Bangladeshi administrative culture. Tadbir is a kind of lobbying to manage a decision taken or to be taken by an authority through over-ruling, breaking or bending existing rules, norms, and practices (Jamil, 2007). Tadbir is a process that paves the way for corruption because it flouts the authority of standard administrative norms, values, and rules.

It has been observed that for cancellation of odd transfer order even if it is made in the public interest, for getting lucrative placement, to be enlisted on the fit list of promotion, for obtaining nomination for foreign training, personal lobbying or tadbir with senior officials or even tadbir or showing loyalty with political leaders has turned out to be a common phenomenon in administrative culture of Bangladesh. At times, the civil servants who entertain tadbir are considered tactful, manageable, and professional officers by senior bureaucrats as well as political bureaucrats. These tadbir-friendly officers are often expected to fulfill the extra-official desire of senior bureaucrats and ministers. Again, if a civil servant decides to turn down tadbir, he or she is likely to be despised by friends, relatives, and even

---

[6]Literally "samaj" means society. It reflects the dominant cultural and societal norms and values accepted and agreed upon by a majority of citizens.

[7]A strong patron-client relationship and hierarchic norms and values supported by religious belief are deeply perpetuated in the social order of Bangladeshi society.

colleagues and is considered self-centered, tactless, unprofessional, and impractical and, therefore, not desirable to their respective ministries by the senior bureaucrats and ministers. The situation is common in field administration also (Siddiqui, 1996). Tadbir is so rampant in the civil service that OSDs[8] are not given any posting without it. Officials wait for tadbir to take action in files; sometimes they move only with tadbir or else files are declared missing (Anisuzzaman, 1985).

To get business done in the public offices of Bangladesh, the usual practice is to locate a person who is close to the decision makers or is an influential actor in the decision-making process. In this process, kinship, regional affinity, familial and matrimonial ties are often exercised to gain access to the decision maker. At times a person who receives a favor from employing tadbir, returns the favor to the person who has favored him or her. Such reciprocity is common in the administrative culture of Bangladesh.

The culture of tadbir in Bangladesh Public Administration is a direct result of a hierarchical and collectivist society which promotes the patron-client relationship within the society. Generalized collectivism may be beneficial for society as we may observe in Japan but its narrow manifestations are a detriment to the redistribution of resources in society. The collectivist nature of Bangladesh society has created an environment within the public offices where work and public life are mixed together.

UNCERTAINTY AVOIDANCE AND THE PUBLIC SERVICE

Uncertainty Avoidance indicates the degree to which a culture programs its members to feel either comfortable or uncomfortable in unstructured situations. It is the cultural tendency to feel uncomfortable with uncertainty and risk in everyday life. Uncertainty avoidance societies have more formal laws and informal rules controlling the rights and duties of employers and employees. Where power distances are large, the exercise of discretionary power by superiors replaces to some extent the need for internal rules.

Hofstede has found a high degree of correlation between a rigid, autocratic way of political governing and a high level of uncertainty avoidance at the societal level, and, conversely, between a loose, democratic way of governing and lower level of uncertainty avoidance in society. Table 3 illustrates the major characteristics of low and high uncertainty avoidance. It is suggested that high uncertainty avoidance societies tend to avoid any kind of reforms that change their secure and well-known environments, in which

TABLE 3
Characteristics of High and Low Uncertainty Avoidance
(Islam, 2004)

Low uncertainty avoidance	High uncertainty avoidance
• Few rules	• More formal rules
• Leader is facilitator	• Leader is the expert
• Open-ended learning	• Structured learning
• Innovation and achievement are important	• Precision and security are important
• High labor turnover	• Low labor turnover
• Less resistance to change	• More resistance to change

FIGURE 2   Uncertainty Avoidance (UA) Index.

corrupt relations between bribe-taker and bribe-payer have been well established (Shleifer & Vishnu, 1993).

Bangladesh ranks fairly high on Hofstede's Uncertainty Avoidance Index (UAI) with a rank of 47–49 and a score of 60 out of 76 countries (Figure 2). The highest scoring country is Greece with a score of 112 whereas Singapore is ranked as the lowest Uncertainty Avoidance country with a score of 8 (Hofstede, 2010). Bangladesh's highly hierarchical pattern of administration blended with centralized power is used as the prime means to reduce uncertainty. Every office is burdened with a good number of rules, regulations, and procedures that lead to unnecessary delay in decision making and in the delivery of services. Many of the rules are found vague and repetitive, and are selectively enforced and twisted, conveniently, to favor relatives and friends.

The degree of the society's tolerance of bribery and corruption in administration varies across countries. In many countries, corruption is not regarded as a malfeasance, but as a culturally accepted form of gift giving and gift-taking (Ackerman, 1999). In environments characterized by highly uncertain outcomes of formal institutions, genesis of corruption often goes back to informal institutions and social conventions. In this context, administrative activities in many transforming cultures are shaped by "codes of conduct" based on the principle, "if others behave illegally, so can I" (Tonoyan & Strohmeyer, 2004). If an individual adheres to the law while he or she could profit more by engaging in illegal transactions, then he or she behaves irrationally. This leads to the belief that the end justifies the means even if the means include the use of illegal channels since "who is fair is not smart."

In the name of the excessive rules and procedures, officers at times deliberately indulge in delay in processing files, which is a popular hint to the service-seeking citizens to offer a kick-back, a common practice in most of the government offices Bangladesh. In welfare-oriented offices people's

---

[8]Officers on Special Duty (OSD) refers to the officers posted under the ministry of Public Administration and usually keep waiting for a placement. Sometimes OSD also includes officers who are likely to face disciplinary actions or being sent to either local or overseas training.

welfare should be considered first but the rule-bound official culture does not do so. As the common people of Bangladesh are not aware of the presence of the applicability of law/rules, they fall helpless prey to the officials' malpractices in many spheres of their life. That is why the attitude, norms, and behavior of the public officials are now in question. In only a few cases do some young officers have the intention to help people even if they are to go slightly beyond the existing rule or convention but ultimately they fail to do so because they fear being mistreated by their superiors. Again the superior's stand on strict compliance with the rules is seems to be correct in the sense that if he or overlooks their behavior, subordinates will possibly misuse the power or tend to favor someone, leading to another form of corruption.

To avoid uncertainty, every public organization in Bangladesh produces a host of rules, procedures, and by-laws, which ultimately aid the growth of corruption over the years. This situation is directly linked with Klitgaard's model of corruption (discussed earlier) which focuses on the discretionary power of administrative officers as one of the main sources of corruption. Ironically, the propensity to avoid uncertainty and collectivist orientation result in a paradoxical situation. As more and more rules are created to avoid uncertainty, more ingenious ways of circumventing the rules are found simultaneously (Islam, 2004). Rules are selectively enforced and twisted to favor the client illegally. Often when the rules are enforced, these are used deliberately to stall a decision to give time to the favorite clients or solicit a bribe. A popular saying in this regard is: "For friends everything, for enemies nothing and for the rest strict application of rules."

Bangladesh's moderately high level (60) of uncertainty avoidance in Hofstede's ranking can be attributed to its excessive rules, regulations, and licensing requirements, which impede the functioning of markets and encourage rent seeking. As compared to Bangladesh, Singapore has low uncertainty avoidance score (8), and has minimum number of laws, rules, regulations and administrative orders which encourage the business and economic activities. Singapore is also one of the least corrupt countries (with a score of 9.3 out of 10) in the world according to Corruption Perception Index (CPI) of Transparency International. In a high uncertainty avoidance country like Bangladesh administrators and politicians are granted large discretionary powers with respect to interpreting rules, are given a lot of freedom to decide on how rules are to be applied, are vested with powers to amend and alter the rules. This discretionary power when abused turns out to be a cause of corruption in Bangladesh.

POWER DISTANCE IN THE BANGLADESH ADMINISTRATIVE CULTURE

Power distance signifies the extent to which the less powerful members of institutions or organizations in a country expect

TABLE 4
Characteristics of Low and High Power Distance (Islam, 2004)

Low power distance	High power distance
• Superiors and subordinates considered equals	• Superiors and subordinates not considered equals
• Flatter organizations	• Taller organizations
• Decentralization	• Centralization
• Employees seek involvement	• Employees accept direction of hierarchy
• Prefer participative management	• Respect for authority and status
• Accept responsibility	• Accept discipline

104	80	11

Highest PDI _____Lowest PDI

MALAYASIA   BANGLADESH   AUSTRIA

FIGURE 3   Power Distance Index (PDI).

or accept that power is distributed unequally. It reflects the degree to which people are likely to respect hierarchy, status, and rank in organization. Dependence of the subordinates on bosses is limited in small power distance countries and there remains scope for consultation—i.e., both the superiors and subordinates are locked in an interdependent relationship. Subordinates can easily approach and contradict their bosses (Hofstede, 2010). A high power distance society accepts wide differences in power in organizations. Employees exhibit a great deal of respect for those in authority. In countries with large Power Distance Index (PDI) scores, subordinates feel dependent on their superiors and are afraid to express disagreement. Table 4 makes a comparison between low and high power distance.

Bangladesh ranks high on Hofstede's PDI with a rank of 12–14, scoring 80 among 76 countries (Figure 3). Austria has the lowest PDI, scoring 11, whereas Malaysia has the highest,104 (Hofstede, 2010). This indicates that Bangladeshis have a propensity to tolerate a high degree of inequality.

Corruption is facilitated in highly hierarchical and pyramidal societies with high power distance ranking. In large power distance countries, emotional distance between the superior and the subordinate is large. Subordinates fully comply with the orders issued by the authorities and they seldom contradict them. They do not learn to discuss their opinion with their superiors, and instead accept their superiors' point of view. That is why innovation or creativity of subordinates is simply ignored in large-scale power distance organizations. Persons living in a high power distance country would prefer centralization in organizational structures and a greater number of hierarchical levels. A low power distance orientation leads to employee demand for participative or democratic leadership. The people's voice is rightly evaluated in low PDI (Power Distance Index) culture.

Since independence, a series of experiments has been tried with the administrative culture of Bangladesh. To reconstruct the economy, industry, and the infrastructure, the first Awami League (AL) regime distributed large-scale patronage among the party leaders, workers, and supporters and put them all in high posts in the nationalized industries. The Constitution provided for nationalization of the industrial sector and the banking sector (Ali, 2004). Soon after independence, the rulers tended to centralize the power. There was a sense of deep insecurity across the land as chronic shortages of food and resources reached the level of a crisis and the government appeared to be completely overwhelmed by the situation. Against this backdrop, corruption not only took hold of the politico-administrative structure, but also became almost a way of life (Ahmed, 1983).

Administrative culture in Bangladesh is also undermined by the legacy of military rule. Bangladesh remained under military government or military-backed presidential rule from 1975–1991. Military rule eventually weakened the morale of civil servants and used them to concentrate power in the hands of the army and also absorbed military officers into the civil and foreign service on a quota system (Ali, 1994).

From 1991 to 2006 a democratic government ruled the country. In order to get timely promotion and lucrative posting against huge unplanned recruitment, some officers explicitly or implicitly began to show loyalty to the party in power during this period. This problem intensified in the period of successive governments and is gradually increasing. The loyalty of civil servant therefore, lies with their political ministers. The situation is so bad that if a secretary intends to act on rules at the implementation level, he or she will be either embarrassed by the government or marginalized by demotion because the government perceives (mostly wrongly) that this officer is not able to serve the interest of the party in power, since he or she is not loyal to the ruling party.

Thus, in many cases, civil servants feel constrained to pay loyalty to the political party to protect their job or to avoid undue harassment. Because of prevailing large scale of power distance and the sense of loyalty to the party in power civil servants fail to prove that they are accountable to the people (Younis & Mostafa, 2000). And they are not only loyal to party, but in many instances also loyal to their kith and kin.

The tolerance for high power distance has led to a culture of sycophancy throughout the administrative system of Bangladesh. Sycophancy induces corruption. Those who practice sycophancy in their profession get rewarded subsequently. Drewry and Butcher (1991) point out that it is not desirable to have a civil service made up of officials who will always say and mean "Yes, Minister." In the Bangladeshi context, the same view can possibly be held but the conduct varies from one government official to another.

This is one weakness of the Bangladesh Civil Service that the disposition of its members is not uniform and consistent. There are government officials who will really mean when they say "Yes, Minister." There are others who will say "Yes," Minister, and at the same time suggest that the issue needs examination in the light of laws, rules, and precedence. But the number belonging to the latter category would be few (Ali, 1994).

So the "Yes boss"-type relationship is always prevalent in subordinates who also expect the same behavior or gestures when they advance up the career ladder. In this way subordinates tend to use flattery as a tool to bridge the power distance with their superiors that is considered a legacy of the administrative culture of Bangladesh. In the Bangladesh administrative culture power distance is at such a high level that junior employees' ideas, efforts, and initiatives, even if constructive, are not usually entertained. There is a common norm—"juniors are to obey". In this traditional system the top officials or leaders do whatever they like and are therefore perceived as being autocratic. This large-scale power structure creates a high degree of inequality and rampant discrimination in the society, leading to favoritism and corruption.

Centralization of power, politicization of administration, and sycophancy as the key characteristics of culture of high power distance in Bangladesh administration have led to irregularities and malpractice in many cases. However, it is a challenging task to prove the prevalence of corruption in Bangladesh as the direct and only consequence of high power distance. Malaysia, with a high Power Distance Index (PDI) score (104) is doing better in terms of its place (28th position) in the Corruption Perception Index (CPI). In contrast, Bangladesh is doing worse in the CPI (13) with a high PDI (80) score. Both the countries have a high Power Distance Index, but the prevalence of corruption is different in the two countries. In fact, setting up a strong link between corruption and power distance is possible in some cases but not in all scenarios.

MASCULINITY-FEMININITY DIMENSION IN THE ADMINISTRATIVE SYSTEM OF BANGLADESH

According to Hofstede, masculinity is the extent to which a society values achievement, assertiveness, aggression, and competitiveness. To be precise, masculinity refers to the *material success* as opposed to femininity that concerns with the *quality of life* (Hofstede, 2010). Also, masculine societies place more emphasis on the segregation of gender roles, i.e., traditional roles for, and belief in inequality of women, as well as paternalism. In a masculine society, children grow up with an aspiration to career development whereas in feminine society children grow up towards modesty, solidarity and both men and women may and may not be ambitious

TABLE 5
Characteristics of Masculine and Feminine Societies (Islam, 2004)

Masculinity	Femininity
• Gender-based occupational segregation	• Less gender-based occupational segregation
• Assertiveness and material acquisition	• Relationships among people, concern for others, quality of life
• Belief in individual decisions, equity, and competition	• Belief in group decisions, equality, and solidarity
• Admire achievers	• Sympathy for the unfortunate
• Women nurture	• Men and women nurture
• Live to work	• Work to live

```
              5              55            110

Femininity _____Masculinity


       SWEDEN       BANGLADESH      SLOVAKIA
```

FIGURE 4   Masculinity-Femininity Index.

about career advancement. Table 5 identifies the differences between masculine and feminine societies.

Bangladesh ranks moderately high on masculinity according to Hofstede's Masculinity-Femininity Index (Figure 4). Its score in the Masculinity-Femininity Index is 55 as compared to Sweden. Sweden is considered the most feminine and Slovakia, the most masculine country out of 76 countries with scores of 5 and 110, respectively (Hofstede, 2010).

Husted (1999) and Getz and Volkema (2001) find a positive correlation between masculinity and corruption at the societal level. They argue that the stronger the societies' striving for material prosperity and wealth, the higher the probability of engaging in corruption. Dollar et al. (2001) and Swamy et al. (2001) show that corruption is less widespread in countries where women comprise a larger share of the labor force and members of parliamentary . The negative impact of gender on corruption remains robust even after adjusting for control variables such as the GDP per head. It is suggested that women are particularly effective in promoting honest governments because they have higher standards of ethical behavior, are more trustworthy, and appear to be more concerned with the common good or altruistic conduct. So it is often said that the stronger the striving for material prosperity, the higher the inclination to corruption.

The Bangladeshi culture is considered a moderate masculine culture as compared to some other Asian Muslim countries. The practice of "purdah[9]" is still responsible for the exclusion of women from the mainstream of

development process in this country. Gender differentiation of roles confines women to domestic activities, early marriage, and taking care of children. The UNDP's Human Development Report 2007–2008 puts Bangladesh 112 among 157 countries in its Gender Development Index and 81 of 93 countries in the Gender Empowerment Measure. According to the UNDP's Human Development Report 2011 Bangladesh is in 112 (value 0.550) position among 187 countries in its Gender Inequality Index. However, over the last 30 years, the legal status of women has improved in some sectors because emphasis has been given to ensuring gender equality and mainstreaming gender issues through various policies and strategies to ensure employment of women in various professions. Nongovernmental organization (NGO) activities have generated awareness of discrimination against women in recent years.

In Bangladesh women's representation in the Jatiyo Sangsad (Parliament) indicates that opportunities do exist for women in politics. From 1991 to until now (except two years of a caretaker government in 2007–08), both the leader of the Parliament and the leader of the opposition in Parliament were women. In 2013 the Parliament also elected a woman Speaker which makes a new history of having three major women leaders in the government (Prime minister, Speaker and Leader of Opposition). However, there were only four directly elected women members of the Parliament in 1991. The creation of a constitutional provision of 30 seats reserved for women increased that number to 34 and, by 2006, women accounted for 15 percent of MPs, up from 10 percent in 1991. Due to the provision for reserved seats for women in local government, especially at the Union Parishad level, the number of women's participation in local government bodies has increased significantly. In the ninth parliamentary election of 2008, 55 women candidates contested 60 election areas whereas the number was 38 in 2001 and 36 in 1996. It is a matter of achievement that 22 women candidates out of 55 were directly elected on December 29, 2008, in the National Parliament Election and of them six were appointed members of the Cabinet. The election of 45 MPs from reserved seats, compared to 30 in the eighth Parliament, is considered a breakthrough in women's empowerment and in the narrowing of the gender gap in the politics of Bangladesh.

In case of the civil service, the situation is no better than in politics. In the top-most position of the civil bureaucracy, out of 64 secretaries only 3 were women until 2011. In fact, only in the Ministry of Education, Ministry of Primary and Mass Education, Ministry of Women and Children Affairs, and the Ministry of Social Welfare, the number of women employees is significant in number. Other than these ministries women comprise under 15 percent of the workforce(Kabir, 2011).

Bias towards inequality in the distribution of power and privileges between genders increases the prospects of

---

[9]Purdah or pardeh (Persian meaning "curtain") is the practice of concealing women from men. This takes two forms: physical segregation of the sexes, and the requirement for women to cover their bodies and conceal their form. Purdah exists in various forms in the Muslim and Hindu faiths.

In some Muslim countries, the practice of veiling is very common and is seen as a fundamental part of Islam.

corruption. Women's participation at different levels of organizations to a large scale may help in increasing the transparency and accountability and making the service delivery system in Bangladesh more efficient. It is a common belief that female officers are committed to work and sensible in ensuring the quality of work. In the Bangladeshi administrative culture it has been observed that female officers command trust and they are more sincere about their responsibilities.

The characteristics of masculinity also influence the attitude and conduct of female officers. This is occasionally seen in the organizational culture of Bangladesh. Junior female officers usually become victims of masculine superiority but when they are promoted to senior posts, many of them ironically become authoritarian and create an unfriendly environment in the office. Hence, the tradition of the office and its internal environment thereby become jeopardized which indirectly encourages favoritism, nepotism, and corruption. Higher level of competition, materialistic attitudes, and demonstrations of wealth in Masculine societies (within both male and female) some cases make administrators resort to corruption to fulfill their illegal needs.

It is, however, challenging to establish a strong relationship between corruption and the cultural dimension of masculinity/femininity. There is not much empirical evidence to prove a relationship between these two variables in the case of Bangladesh. Women's participation in administration and politics has increased gradually in Bangladesh in the period between last two decades as has the prevalence of corruption. Though the recent Corruption Perception Index (CPI) of Transparency International shows that corruption is low in those countries that are predominantly feminine, like the Scandinavian countries. But it is difficult to explain why the intensity of corruption varies within different masculine societies. Japan has a highly masculine society with an index of 95 and Bangladesh has a moderately masculine society with a score is 55. In the case of the Corruption Perception Index (CPI) of Transparency International, Bangladesh's score is 2.7 out of 10 (highly corrupt) whereas Japan's score is 8 out of 10 (less corrupt).

CONCLUSION

Corruption is not the product of culture only. There are cultural attitudes and practices that lead people to become engaged in corruption. The existence of a patron-client relationship[10] reinforces corrupt practices in all spheres of

public dealing. In almost all political regimes in Bangladesh, corruption reigns over organizational culture. Only the nature and extent of corruption varies depending on the character of the regime, its key leader, and his or her power base. Corruption in the political arena has emboldened public servants to be unabashedly corrupt.

This article has sought to find the link between different cultural dimensions of Hofstede and corruption in the case of Bangladesh. There are mixed findings on the possible link between cultural dimensions and corruption. The collectivist orientation and high uncertainty avoidance nature of the Bangladesh public administration system are found to be two major contributors to pervasive corruption. Bangladeshi collectivist society can be characterized by examining the unquestioning allegiances to the family that, in turn, lead to the building of dense networks of kinship and nepotism. The tendency to favor one's in-group (family, friends, or peers) has a link to corruption. Saving the family honor and enhancing the family status take precedence over rational norms within the political and administrative structure of Bangladesh. Supporting the family member through thick and thin is a primordial obligation. Families often become the source of the motive for corruption at all levels of administration (Islam, 2004). Immediate and extended families of the political leaders and senior civil servants are involved in the tadbir game, rule-breaking, and shady wheeling and dealing.

The Bangladeshi administrative culture's association with high uncertainty avoidance leads to the creation of voluminous rules, regulations, and procedures. But the non-application or selective application of these rules and procedures leads not only to injustice and undue harassment but also to corruption, favoritism, and nepotism. Power is allowed to be concentrated at higher levels in administrative culture of Bangladesh and ample discretionary powers are assigned to senior officials. Discretionary power without adequate accountability is likely to induce high officials to misuse public power for private purposes.

Historically, Bangladesh inherited a high power distance society and administrative system. The unquestioning loyalty and positive attitude of the people of Bangladesh towards authority turn out to be correlated to centralization of the organizational decision making process. The high power distance index of Bangladesh's public bureaucracy also follows a tradition of sycophancy throughout the administration. The tolerance of inequality and power distance has jeopardized the development of transparency and institutional accountability in administration during the last 40 years of the nation's history. Although centralization of administration and the practice of sycophancy created some irregularities and mismanagement in the administration, the evidence to prove a strong link between prevalence of corruption and high power distance in the case of Bangladesh is not available always. Moreover, some other Asian countries with high power distance indices like

---

[10]Relatively a dominated portion of the society who had good terms with influential ruling masters takes over the patronage network. They become the patrons "buying off" the demands of potential clients from among the aspiring intermediate classes and using this political, administrative, and economic power to bargain for resource allocation to their particular faction or getting the work done for them.

Malaysia and Singapore have better Corruption Perception Index (CPI) ratings than Bangladesh.

The traditional and conservative values towards women's role in the family and in political, economic, educational, and administrative institutions in Bangladesh have created a masculine culture within the organizations. More specifically, positive attitude towards unequal distribution of power and privileges between genders in terms of roles, acquisitiveness, status, and aggressiveness are the core characteristics of a masculine administrative system. It is widely believed that the female workforce as a whole demonstrates a higher standard of ethical behavior, commands trust, and are more responsive to public needs than their male colleagues. Still it is difficult to present enough facts and figures to justify this conventional wisdom. Women's participation in politics and administration of Bangladesh has increased slowly but steadily in the last two decades. At the same time the materialistic attitude of society as well as the intensity and volume of corruption in Bangladesh have also accelerated. It would be a challenging task for future researchers to establish a strong link between corruption and masculinity with empirical evidence.

Hofstede's four dimensions of national culture have some potential to analyze and explain the corrupt practices of developing countries like Bangladesh. His original study was conducted on private sector (IBM officials) and some of his critics raise questions regarding its applicability in public sector studies. Even after considering the built-in limitations of this model this article found some interesting observations. Hofstede's cultural dimension of Individualism-Collectivism and Uncertainty Avoidance are directly relevant to analyzing corruption in the Bangladesh public service. The other two dimensions, Power Distance and Masculinity-Femininity, could be used effectively to explain the pervasiveness of corruption in some cases. Empirical research in future might open up the avenues or prospects of the applicability of Hofstede's cultural dimensions in corruption study.

REFERENCES

Ackerman, R. S. (1999). *Corruption and government: Causes, consequences, and reform.* Cambridge: Cambridge University Press.

Ahmed, M. (1983). *Bangladesh: Era of Sheikh Mujibur Rahman.* Dhaka: The University Press Ltd.

Ahmed, M. (2005). *Governance, structural adjustment and the state of corruption in Bangladesh.* A paper prepared for Transparency International, Bangladesh, p. 2.

Ali, A.M.M.S. (2004). *Bangladesh civil service: A political administrative perspective.* Dhaka: The University Press Limited.

Ali, S.M. (1994). *Civil-military relations in the soft state: The case of Bangladesh.* Bath, UK: Bath European Network of Bangladesh Studies Occasional Paper.

Anisuzzaman, M. (1985). Administrative culture in Bangladesh: The public-bureaucrat phenomenon. In Khan, M.M., & Hossain, S.A. (Eds.) *Bangladesh studies: Politics, administration, rural development and foreign policy* (pp.18–29). Dhaka: Centre for Administrative Studies, University of Dhaka.

Anti Corruption Commission (ACC) (2008). *Annual report of Anti Corruption Commission, Bangladesh, 2007–2008.* Dhaka: ACC. p. 43.

Dollar, D., Fisman, R., & Gatti, R. (2001). Are women really the fairer sex? Corruption and women in government. *Journal of Economic Behavior and Organization,* 46(4), 421–469.

Drewry, G., & Butcher, T. (1991). *The civil service today.* New Jersey, USA: Blackwell Publications.

Getz, K.A., & Volkema, R. J. (2001). Culture, perceived corruption, and economics. A model of predictors and outcomes. *Business and Society,* 40(1), 7–30.

Hofstede, G., Hofstede, G.J., & Minkov, M. (2010). *Culture and organizations: Software of the mind intercultural cooperation and its importance for survival.* London: McGraw Hill.

Husted, B.W. (1999). Wealth, culture and corruption. *Journal of International Business Studies,* 30(2), 339–360.

Islam, N. (2004). Sifarish, sychophants, power and collectivism: Administrative culture of Pakistan. *International Review of Administrative Sciences,* V70(2), 326.

Jain, R.B. (1990). The role of bureaucracy in policy development and implementation in India. *International Social Science Journal,* 123, 31–47.

Jamil, I. (2007). *Administrative culture in Bangladesh.* Dhaka: A.H. Development Publishing House.

Kabir, S. L. (2011). The status of women employees in the government sectors of India, Pakistan and Bangladesh: Do they get the right share? In I. Jamil (Ed.) *Understanding governance and public policy in Bangladesh* (pp. 111–132). Dhaka: North South University.

Kiltgaard, R. (1996). *Controlling corruption.* Berkeley, CA: University of California Press.

Kochanek, S.A. (1974). *Business and politics in India.* Berkeley, CA: University of California Press.

Lewis, D.J. (1996). Corruption in Bangladesh: Discourse, judgments and moralities. *UK: Bath Centre for Development Studies Occasional Paper,* p. 5.

Lipset, S.M., & Lenz, G.S. (1999). *Corruption, culture, and markets.* Fairfax, VA: George Mason University.

Meny, Y., & Siicle, F.D. (1996). Corruption: change, crisis and shifting value. *International Social Science Journal,* 149, 309–320.

Myint, U. (2000). Corruption: Causes, consequences and cures. *Asia-Pacific Development Journal,* 7(2), 33–57.

Padhay, K. S. (1986). *Corruption in politics: A case study.* Delhi: B.R. Publishing Corporation.

Robertson, I. (1981). *Sociology.* New York: Worth.

Shleifer, A., & Vishny, R. (1993). Corruption. *Quarterly Journal of Economics,* 108 (3), 559–617.

Siddiqui, K. (1996). *Towards good governance in Bangladesh: Fifty unpleasant essays.* Dhaka: The University Press Limited.

Tonoyan, V., & Strohmeyer, R. (2004). Corruption and entrepreneurship: How formal and informal institutions shape small firm's behavior. A cross-national comparison between East and West Europe. *Paper presented at the 8.te Interdiszilinare Jahreskonferrnz zur Grundungsforschung,* Stuttgart, p. 6.

Transparency International Bangladesh (TIB). (2010). *Global Corruption report.* Dhaka: TIB.

Transparency International (TI). (2008). *Corruption Perception Index (CPI) report 2008.* Dhaka: TIB.

UN Development Program (UNDP). (1993). *Report on Public Administration Sector Study.* Dhaka: UNDP.

UNDP. (1997). *Corruption and good governance.* Dhaka: UNDP.

World Bank. (1997). *Helping countries combat corruption: The role of the World Bank.* Poverty Reduction and Economic Management Network. Washington, D.C.: World Bank.

Younis, T.A., & Mostafa, I.M.D. (2000). *Accountability in public management and administration in Bangladesh.* London: Ashgate Publishing Limited.

Index

For Product Safety Concerns and Information please contact our EU
representative GPSR@taylorandfrancis.com
Taylor & Francis Verlag GmbH, Kaufingerstraße 24, 80331 München, Germany